Heaven
Is A Place On Earth

CHEVONNE MCGREGOR

PARTRIDGE

ISBN: Hardcover   978-1-5437-6963-0
             Softcover   978-1-5437-6965-4
             eBook   978-1-5437-6964-7

All Scripture quotations are taken from the Holy Bible, New Living Translation

Print information available on the last page.

To order additional copies of this book, contact
Toll Free +65 3165 7531 (Singapore)
Toll Free +60 3 3099 4412 (Malaysia)
orders.singapore@partridgepublishing.com

www.partridgepublishing.com/singapore

Opening Scripture Readings:

Genesis 3:24

Psalm 51:10

Galatians 4:6

Revelation 21:1-2

CONTENTS

DEDICATION

This book is especially dedicated to,

Our Lord Jesus,
for His forgiveness,
for countless of blessings received;
for the outpouring and infilling of the Holy Spirit in 2002;
for reconciling me to Abba, Father, in 2002;
for rescuing me from darkness in 2006,
For his discipline during my healing,
for my healing and deliverance … 2008~2009,
for reaffirming that I belong to Him,
and for constantly reassuring me that he will never leave
me, that I am a child of God.

I have written this book in honour of my Lord, my God,
my King, my Redeemer and Saviour.
"I love You, I adore You, I appreciate You."

To my readers,

'May the Holy Spirit touch your hearts and anoint you with
wisdom, power, peace and love as it did unto me when I
answered His call in the year 2000 to return to His church
and help to rebuild His Kingdom for His return.'

Lastly, in the loving memory of my late father, who passed
on in March 2012. I thank God for the gift of you. He blessed
me with the best earthly Father I could ever wish for.

"Rest in the Lord, papa."

ACKNOWLEDGEMENTS

The Christians behind beliefnet.com for giving me the opportunity to taste a bit of every faith and bringing me back to Christ Jesus 'The Way, The Truth and The Life' through 'The Sayings of Jesus' and 'God's Daily Promises' by Left Behind Prophecies. You are God's miracle to me. Thank you for sharing His word and works with so many...

Fellow Christians from 'Jesus Saves Mission' for their search and rescue efforts and fellowship.

God's Missionaries on the web: e-Responders.com, Jesus Central.com for spreading the gospel of our Lord Jesus and equipping the saints.

Bro. Josef Chow, Glen & Michelle Andrews, Anne, Rosemary, Emma, Monica, Aunt Judy, Annette, Faith, Mr & Mrs Chong and members of the 'Fettes Park Baptist Church' worship team, for their help in ministering to me during my healing and deliverance from 2008 till 2009 and for their continued support and encouragement rendered to me to write this book.

Ps. Sara of 'Tabernacle of Worship' for bringing me to the 'Word of God' sevenfold. God makes no mistakes!

Andrew Danker, for his continuous support, encouragement and prayers.

Fr. Marshall Fernandez of 'Church of the Immaculate Conception', for being so patient with me during my time in the 'wilderness' and for his loving kindness.

The 'Alpha' team from 'Church of the Holy Spirit' for their patience, loving kindness and healing presence of the Holy Spirit. Thank you and God bless and keep you always~

The missionaries who lend their voices and spread God's grace and messages of peace and love through the beautiful music they make by bringing God's 'Word' to live in our hearts, minds and souls. There are so many of you out there...

Pastor Yoselana and Sandra Devi for your patience and guidance in ministering to me and helping me to be an overcomer of fear.

Paul Wilbur Ministries for all your anointed songs of worship.

Julius and Martha Suuibi of Exploits Worship Centre; Pat Francis Ministries - Chayil Family: for equipping me to be a soldier for Christ, for lifting me up so that I DO NOT GIVE UP and that I continue to intercede for others.

Derek Prince Ministries; David Wilkerson; Charles Stanley; Agora Group; Pastor William Lau and Lucille Lau of The Elijah Challenge: I'm truly blessed by your teachings and sermons. Thank you for equipping the saints with sound biblical teachings of 'The Great Commission'. I understand now. I have a clearer picture of my calling.

One Twenty Ministries: Rev. Pastor Pat Owyang and Bro Anthony for your wonderful teachings about 'Financial Wisdom' from the parables of Jesus (talents and minas). Rev Pastor Pat Owyang, your prophecies over my life are spot on.

My appreciation and thanks to my editors, Helenn Wevers and Razak Musa, and also to Fr Marshall and Pastor Asher

Ang for their kind words and summaries. I couldn't have done it without you!

May God continue to bless us all with His strength to carry the call and follow through what He has started in us. May He continue to bless you with knowledge, wisdom and meekness. God has heard our cries for more workers for the 'Time of Harvest' and He has answered our call. Amen.

~ 'I love you all. Thank you' ~

INTRODUCTION

Dear Friends,

Have you ever wondered what heaven would be like? My journey through life has taken me to many places; some very dark moments and some very light moments; some life changing events that have prompted me to write this book. These life changing events have had a great and positive impact on my life and I wish to share it with you so that your lives may be enriched and blessed too.

I am often reminded that we are all part of God's mysterious plan. We do not choose to become Christian. Rather, it is by God's divine mercy and grace to reveal Christ, His Only Son, to us. It is God who chooses us. We are all part of His wonderful plan. It is not a coincidence that some of us are born again or raised as Christians from birth, or become Christians later in our lives.

(Scripture Readings: Ephesians 1:4; John 15:16)

It has been twelve years now since I was first diagnosed with the dreadful disease 'schizophrenia' in August 2009. In this book, I will try my very best to explain in detail, the events which led to me being diagnosed with this 'disease'. Now I know my Lord will never leave me and I know for sure that I have a place in His Kingdom as the Holy Spirit has revealed to me of its existence and I have experienced it in my heart. We need only to obey and do the will of our Father in heaven. I press on towards that goal and hope and pray for God's grace and guidance to persevere and endure with love and patience even under persecution.

Be thankful always and at every moment in your life, give thanks and praise to God. With these, I leave you with a scripture taken from

(Scripture Reading: Ephesians 3:18)

For It Is the Number of a Man

I had been attached with an airline, based at the Penang International Airport since the beginning of November 1995.

In May 1999, I committed a grave sin. I had broken one of the Ten Commandments and my sin and guilt led me to isolate myself from my workmates and my family. No one at my home and at my workplace knew what I was going through.

Sometime before the millennium...

In my moment of weakness, the evil one came to tempt me while I was alone at work one day. It was my duty at the Golden Keris Lounge and I was busy replenishing drinks at the bar...

These are the accounts of what happened...

"Come in, GKL."

"Go ahead, *Departure*."

"We're ready for boarding now. You may send your passengers down now."

"Right away, *Departure*. Thank you."

"Attention, Ladies and Gentlemen! Flight GK195 is now ready for boarding. You may proceed to gate number 9. Thank you."

As soon as all the passengers had left the lounge, I hurriedly locked the front glass doors and switched off the air-conditioning as it was too cold and musty. I had to clean up the lounge and replenish the food and drinks for the next flight.

While I was checking the drinks at the bar, I had the eeriest feeling that I was being watched. There had been occasions when I had seen a dark shadow near the bar area where a huge potted plant sat even though I was alone in the lounge.

On this occasion however, I felt something very cold and chilly moving close behind me and I had goose bumps all over my body. The hairs on my neck stood on every end and 'it' stopped on my right side. At once, I looked up at the mirrors of the bar to check if there was anyone beside me. I saw no reflection but felt a cold sinister presence standing next to me. A dark, black mist started to form and there, standing before me was a 'handsome middle-aged man' dressed very modern, all in black from head to toe. He looked like an 'Indian or Pakistani' national. He was fair skinned and had thick black hair with slight curls and wore a thick dark moustache. Startled, I quickly moved away from the bar taking a few steps backwards as I summoned the courage to command the apparition to go away.

"Get lost! Leave me alone!" I commanded, in my anger and disgust towards 'it'.

As soon as I made that command, the mysterious black figure took a few steps backwards, sat down in the blue armchair next to the bar, then gave me a most disturbing grin as though saying, "I've got you now".

Then, as mysteriously as 'it' had appeared, 'it' vanished into thin air. It was eerie, almost as though 'it' knew I had been stained. I could not have spoken out in courage to rebuke it if Jesus was not with me. I was led to tears by my sin and guilt.

I immediately knew why 'it' had appeared before me. "Oh, no!" I cried. **"Oh, God! What have I done?"** I sobbed miserably as I crouched on a sofa. Tears welled from my eyes. "Please forgive me. Will you ever forgive me? I am so sorry."

That same night, I cried out to Jesus and pleaded for His mercy and grace. I poured out everything to Jesus, from my sin to my problems at work. The room was suddenly filled with pink clouds. That night I slept so peacefully. I awoke the next morning thinking of the poem 'Footprints'. I felt my spirit lifted and was amazed because over the next three days that followed, there was no conflict at work. No disturbances, only perfect peace. I also experienced the pink clouds in the office. I felt as though I was 'floating' on these pink clouds. It was the most tranquil moment I had ever experienced.

From then on, I started to have stirrings in my heart which I could not understand back then. I felt I had to make some changes to include God in my daily life. I was aware that I had not been keeping the Sabbath day. So instead of focusing mainly in my work, I focused more on God by keeping the Sabbath Day of rest for a start. I started rejecting overtime and I felt 'lighter' whenever I travelled home by bus after a half day's work.

As my work required me to do a lot of overtime even after rejecting most of them, I finally made the decision to leave the airline industry. I realized how I had neglected my family members especially my eldest brother, Jonathan. The stress from the flight delays and rerouted flights in the late 90's and start of the millennium made me ponder on whether these were the causes of Jonathan's mental breakdown. Back in 1997, he had suffered from a nervous breakdown whilst working at the Singapore Airport and had to be treated by a doctor at the Penang General Hospital upon his return home to Penang. His doctor placed him on medication and he was diagnosed as suffering from schizophrenia.

Jonathan pleaded with me for help upon his return from Singapore in 1997. I could see that he was struggling; that something was bothering him but I could not understand what he was going through back then and I was too preoccupied with my work to help him.

I finally handed in my resignation in September 2000 even though I had no clear direction or plan on what to do next. The stirrings in my heart were just too great.

I prayed the following prayer sometime between December 1999 and January 2000 and wrote it down in my diary:

'Lord Jesus, I need You.
Thank you for dying on the cross for my sins.
I open the door of my life and receive You
as my Saviour and Lord.
Thank You for forgiving my sins and giving me eternal life.
Take control of the throne of my life.
Make me the kind of person You want me to be.   Amen.'

I also took the following 'messages' down in my diary when I came across them on a 'notice board'. They served as a guide and I started to follow them faithfully...

- ❖ **G** - Go to God in prayer daily (John 15:7)

- ❖ **R** - Read God's Word daily (Acts 17:11)
  begin with the Gospel of John

- ❖ **O** - Obey God moment by moment
  (John 14:21)

- ❖ **W** - Witness for Christ by your life and words.
  (Matthew 4:19; John 15:8)

- ❖ **T** - Trust God for every detail of your life.
  'Cast all your anxiety on Him because He cares
  for you. (1 Peter 5:7)

- ❖ **H** - Holy Spirit : Allow Him to control and empower
  your daily life and witness.
  (Acts 1:8; Galatians 5:16,17)

The Breakup ... Soul Searching

Early 2000...

Even before I resigned from the airline, my relationship with my boyfriend, Matthew had soured. We had already started to drift apart after our trip to Brisbane, Australia and he had become very cold towards me upon returning from our holiday in New Zealand. So, to escape from my crazy world, I took an eight day holiday to the beautiful island of Langkawi. I told Matthew that I needed some time alone.

Being adventurous and at the same time wanting to be pampered, I pre-booked accommodation at three different hotels. One near the airport, one near a 'port' and one in the heart of the city. Carrying only RM800 with me, I contacted Lynnette, a friend whom I had not met since our school days. She was studying at a university in Langkawi at that time. What a coincidence! Her campus was just next to the hotel I had booked near the airport.

I remember staring at the sparkling blue sea when I was in the taxi on my way to the hotel. All my troubles and worries disappeared the moment I reached the hotel. My spirit was lifted the moment I stepped into the hotel lounge. I especially loved the 'Great Eagle' décor in the middle of their spacious and comfortable lounge, just opposite the reception area.

'What a relief! At least there is a place to hang out to drown my sorrows,' I thought to myself, turning to the lounge and bar after checking-in at the reception area.

There were two tour counters at the reception area so I took their brochures and made comparisons on the tours they offered and also the prices. Then, I walked straight to my room to unpack my luggage. My heart leapt with joy when I entered my really spacious room. It gave me great comfort to just rest under the soft white covers of their super king-sized beds.

After going through the brochures, I called Lynnette to ask her to join me on some tours. She had to request for permission from her campus director to leave the premises so that she could spend a few nights with me. I had to bear in mind that she had a full schedule of classes to attend during the day but I was really excited about meeting up with her again.

Returning to the reception area, I booked a few tours from both operators. Lynnette came over to stay with me the next night. I suggested that we dine at the hotel restaurant as I had seen their promotion banner for seafood steamboat outside the restaurant. We gasped for breath when the waiter served us the food portion. We both enjoyed the sweet and salty taste of the steamboat soup. I can also remember the crazy photographs we took then of Lynnette holding up her 'crab'. We had a smashing time sharing conversation as Lynnette told me about her future plans. Although I was happy for her, I was also not all there. I told her about my relationship with Matthew. I really wished that someone could understand what I was going through at that time. When the bill came, I was shocked that it only cost RM20 as stated on the banner.

We talked and had some drinks at the lounge area till late. Liquor used to be really cheap then. My favourite is still 'Bailey's Irish Cream'. You do not get drunk on Bailey's! I cannot remember how many glasses I had. I kept returning every day for Bailey's till I checked-out of that hotel.

Lynnette only joined me for a day at the crocodile farm, 'Book Village' and our then Prime Minister's Gallery. It was an enjoyable time. I especially loved the landscaping at the 'Book Village' and the beautiful exotic gifts at the gallery. The 'Book Village' could do with more books and better ones. There were only two rooms of books when we were there.

I felt really sorry for 'Bujang Kawi', one of the oldest crocodiles at the farm because he was born with no teeth. We got to watch the handlers feeding the crocodiles during 'feeding time' and also the crocodile show. I really did not feel at ease when the handler tried to put his head in a crocodiles jaw. Luckily he could tell that the crocodile was not in the right 'mood' for a show, so he called off that stunt. Although it was mostly still and quiet, I could sense a lot of aggression from that large beast. It was the largest crocodile at the farm... 'I wonder if it is there still?'

I really do not understand why so few people go to the 'Galleria Perdana'. It showcases the gifts sent from rulers and delegates from all over the world to our former Prime Minister, Tun Dr. Mahathir Mohamad. The gifts were not only interesting, some were really beautiful. I felt inspired to learn some history of friendship and the relationships between nations through these gifts.

One other place that I loved visiting most on Langkawi Island was the 'Underwater World'. I still prefer our aquarium to the one on Singapore's Sentosa Island. The aquariums on Langkawi were bigger, more spacious and well organised. They were labelled properly according to the different species of marine life and each compartment was spacious enough to house each species. The walkway for visitors was wide enough so I did not feel cramped inside the dark alleys even with so many tourists at the time of my visit.

At some parts, the aquariums were dark and we were not allowed to take photographs at these parts. I understand that it is to protect the marine life because the deep part of the ocean is very dark. But I could not resist it so I stole some shots especially of the big fish. I remember taking shots of the red piranhas, groupers and the really huge crustaceans. I also loved the various species of tortoises and terrapins as well as the sea horses.

As I approached the outdoor section of the park, I noticed that the fish that were kept in the aquariums along the walkway were smaller ones of various colours. The tiny fish in these aquariums are so colourful. They range from bright orange, yellow and red to blue and green. Directly opposite these aquariums was a small pool with two otters in the outdoor section. I guess these two cute otters were kept there to entertain the visitors. I wished I could just hold them in my hands…they looked so cute swimming in the pool.

I walked outside to catch some sunlight and also to enjoy the fresh air. The outdoor section was beautifully landscaped with trees and a small man-made waterfall. The colours of the yellow and blue parrots as well as the red ones also added colour to this beautiful scenery. It captured the beauty of nature. I was simply in awe and wonder that I also made it a point to visit this park whenever I was on Langkawi.

Lynnette came over to the hotel on some days but could not stay. For a few days I walked her back to her campus because the area got quiet in the evenings and the road was dimly lit at certain parts.

One bright sunny day, she brought me over to her campus to introduce me to her campus director. It was a privilege to get a tour around the campus. Lynnette brought me to her 'cabin' to show me where she stayed and introduced me to one of her room-mates. Although the structure of the cabins looked lovely, I was wondering how any student could concentrate in their revision while cramped up together in one cabin. They had to share work stations and I am one who needs space. It is a good thing these universities and colleges had libraries.

Since Lynnette had a busy study schedule, I joined other tour groups on river boat rides. I remember a guide on one of those tours who was an expert in his field. His name was Bilal. He thoroughly explained to me and the other British tourists in our boat about how the locals caught fish using the 'bubu' and even showed us the 'catch'. During his tour, we were taken to the 'Charcoal Village' where some Thai immigrants worked. The place where they 'baked' the mangrove trees to make charcoal was small and shaped like a dome. I did not want to go near it because it was hot and too smoky. I took some photographs of the children and wives of the workers. The kids looked so cute with their rosy chubby cheeks. They had tan skin like mine.

It was already late afternoon when we got back as our guide had spent so much time sharing his knowledge with us. After taking the British tourists back to their hotel, he rushed me to his village where he lived. He asked me to wait with his wife and children while he rushed off to work. I sat down in his home listening to his wife nagging about him leaving her alone to look after all their children. In and about their home, I saw children running and crying and

Bilal's wife was carrying a young toddler in her arms as she ranted on. She was petite and looked like she needed much rest. I think they had about nine children. They were also small in size like her. She obviously needed some extra help. I listened and watched but due to my tiredness and because I could not communicate effectively in our local language 'Bahasa Malaysia', I remained quiet. I could only acknowledge her to show her that I understood her plight.

When Bilal returned, I thanked his wife for her kind hospitality. Although I sympathised with her, I did not have all the answers or time to help her. I saw that Bilal was a very busy man running all his tours to support his family.

On the way back to the hotel, we stopped at a popular stop for tourists to buy some locally made 'traditional medicine oil' for aches and pains or insect bites.

On a different tour the next day, I was taken on a boat ride to the mangroves and open sea, near the islands. I remember how the guide threw some 'feed' into the waters for the eagles and how beautiful the eagles looked as their magnificent wings spread out when they swooped close near our boat to grab the feed. Our local eagles have white heads. Some have brownish feathers while most have reddish brown ones. I had not expected to see that many eagles in the mangroves and I was in amazement and wonder at their beauty. It was simply awesome. There were just so many of them and I felt really lucky to be able to watch them from close up. This experience has always remained in my heart and mind. I always recommend this tour to my friends and family.

I had joined several other tourists to the mangroves. We were taken to the 'Lake of the Pregnant Maiden' after the mangrove tour. I watched a European child jump into the waters. He looked like he was having so much fun. We were joined by several other tourists from Hong Kong, Taiwan and China among many locals. The waters looked so inviting; they were like emeralds glowing in the sea. But as I approached the end of the deck, I suddenly had a very eerie feeling. I decided not to swim there despite the wonderful legend and folk tales about this place.

Another experience that I truly enjoyed was the 'Pulau Payar' trip. We were warned to be careful about sea urchins and given some safety instructions. As I could not swim, I held on to the sides of the platform and floated next to it. Wearing goggles, I pressed my face into the sea. I could see so many tiny fish swimming around. There were a few of the same species but still I was in wonder seeing them swimming in circles; in formation; in schools. They were beautiful and colourful. You could watch them swimming in groups. Some tiny ones of the same pattern and species swam in large groups while the bigger ones were 'bolder'. They were all over the place. I later found out that these bigger ones were sharks.

While on the 'glass boat' taking us to the shore, I engaged in conversation with some tourists from Japan. We could also watch the fish swimming beneath the boat through a thick transparent glass which separated us from the fish. At the shore, I saw some baby sharks swimming around. The tiny black sharks would swim up near the shore around us. We could see them clearly because the waters were so clean.

By the time we got back from Pulau Payar, it was already late evening. I was seated in the middle of the bus. I remember the driver dropping off all the other tourists and I was the last one on that tour bus. I may have fallen asleep for I only realised I was all alone when the driver suddenly drove to a remote area. It was already getting dark. I remained calm telling myself nothing would happen to me. I was also very tired after the day's trip. The driver stopped the bus and told me he may have to change vehicle or refuel. He got down to meet someone and they talked for awhile. I looked around. It looked like a place to repair buses. After about maybe fifteen minutes, he came back. Without saying a word, he drove me back to the hotel. Thank heavens nothing happened to me then. Luckily, in such situations, I am usually calm… focusing and trusting that all people are good and nothing 'bad' would happen to me. I never realised that God had always been watching over me. I had been in these types of situations so many times, but God never allowed anyone to 'touch' me.

I have always trusted that people are good. Many of my friends and also my family members said I was gullible and naïve but I digress. Sometimes it may be my own curiosity that gets me into trouble.

I informed Lynnette that I would be changing hotels and asked her to contact me when she was back in Penang. After touring most of Langkawi Island, I moved to Awana Porto Malai. This hotel is located right at the end of a cape on the island. I was immediately taken up by the grand view of the sparkling deep blue sea upon entering the lounge and reception area. At first, I could not wait to check out the room and enjoy the pleasant view. I had to take a very long walk to my room which was right at the other end of the hotel and had to climb up two flights of stairs.

'How inconvenient!' I thought to myself.

The bed was comfortable and the colour scheme was very different from other hotels. However, I was not happy with the view from my room. The strange structure above my window blocked my view of the open sea. I found myself peering over at the chalets on the other side of the bay instead. Feeling down again, I spent one whole afternoon strolling along the promenade. The dining area was overlooking the sea so I could just sit there and enjoy the splendid view and the warm but gentle breeze. Small yachts would berth next to the hotel.

I was still feeling down and my face probably showed it. I had wanted to catch a movie at their in-house movie theatre but when I checked, I was informed no movies were showing either that day or the next. It began drizzling that evening and the air turned cool. Soon it became windy and started to rain. As I walked back to my room, I found that the lights in the walkway on the ground floor were not working properly, the roof was leaking and rain water was dripping onto the pavement. Even the fountain was not in working condition. I was feeling even more depressed that I had to be confined in my room. I decided then that I would take a taxi down-town the next day to do some shopping.

The next morning, I found myself in a crowded dining area for our 'western breakfast' buffet. They were mostly men and women who were there probably for a convention or meeting. They were smartly dressed in working attire. I cleaned my plate and went upstairs to change. I spent that afternoon in town, shopping for chocolates, clothing, souvenirs and gifts for my family and friends. It drizzled again that evening after I returned from a few hours of shopping. After having breakfast the next day, I walked around the hotel again. This time, I bought some items from the gift shop. It poured throughout every evening during my stay at this hotel.

> **11 January 2015:**
>
> **As I am writing these memories down, I am smiling because now I know why God sent the rain. God knew I was in pain. He knew of my sorrow. He sent angels to minister to me when I cried. I have learnt that there will always be leaking roofs and broken fountains and fused lights. I am smiling now because I know God is bigger than my problems. There is nothing God cannot fix. God can mend a broken heart. I have learnt to place my trust in Him. For nothing is impossible for God.**

I spent the last night of my holiday on Langkawi at GC hotel. It was located in the heart of town where people did most of their shopping. It was also near the jetty. I was upset when I was told that the hotel had not received confirmation of my payment from the bank. However, after giving them my personal details, they allowed me to stay.

I rested well at this place. The very next morning, I observed a tall, tan man swimming at the poolside as I walked to a table to have my breakfast. As I sat down, a waiter came up to me and said, "The gentleman over there sends his greetings to you." He smiled as he continued... I cannot remember if he said whether the man was the 'Raja Muda of Perak or Kedah' but he claimed to be a member of royalty. The waiter gave a wide grin as he said that. I took a quick glance behind me and the tall, tan guy who was swimming earlier was seated at a table not too far from me. He gave me a weird smile but I quickly turned my back on him in disgust and ignored him. I did not believe what the waiter had said and I did not want to be bothered. Finishing my last day of shopping, I stayed in my hotel room till I checked-out from the hotel.

I took the evening ferry back to Penang Island and arrived at the Penang jetty about eight in the evening. It took about three hours by ferry from Langkawi Island to Penang Island. As I disembarked from the ferry and walked along the pier, I felt pain and sorrow again. I wished my 'holiday' would not end and that I could stay away for just a little while longer. I made a 'promise' to 'escape' to Langkawi Island every six months for a break if I could.

My father was waiting for me outside. He had always been a reliable and responsible father. He must have known something was not right with my relationship with Matthew. But he never said anything. Somehow his tender eyes just spoke a lot about what he felt; it spoke a lot about himself. He was a devoted and caring father. He was always there for me.

Back at work, I was very quiet and kept to myself most of the time. The burden that was within me had not lifted since my return from Langkawi Island. I was refreshed but something else was bothering me. I spoke to my father about resigning from my workplace. He was a little apprehensive and asked me to think carefully about it. He knew I loved my job very much even though I complained a lot about my problems at work with my colleagues. He advised me that there were problems in every workplace but all his advice fell on deaf ears. I could only hear myself speaking then. My mother and sisters encouraged me to leave my job to work with 'professionals'. They said that many people were getting much higher pay than I was, working in the airlines. It was true. Even factory operators were getting higher pay than us and with less overtime.

September 2000...

I felt really lost and unloved and it became quite obvious to me that Matthew was no longer interested in me after we both resigned from GK airlines on the same day. Whether he ever loved me or not, I do not know. The first thing I did after handing in my resignation was to go back to church on Sundays and to look for another job while also taking up part time courses at a local college. My father was very pleased with me for returning to church and continuing my studies at his place of work. He worked as a librarian at the college. I soon took up a part time job working in a 'time-share' company. The job however, did not last very long...

As an administrator cum vacation counsellor, I was trained in tele-marketing and taught how to use the computer to update data. There were also a lot of paperwork to be done after each sale. I was usually the earliest to arrive at the office to open up for business. Matthew was not happy about me working with this company. He called me less and we saw less of each other. At first, I thought that it may have been his new job in the freight forwarding industry that kept him busy. Soon, his cold treatment became too annoying and I realised that he did not love me any more. Feeling rejected, I told him I wanted to end our relationship. At first, he remained quiet. Deep within me, I was really feeling hurt and dejected. I was angry with him but tried not to show it. At first, he did not say anything. It seemed as though he was avoiding confrontation. However, he did not realise that his cold treatment was making me more miserable.

We were invited to have hi-tea with his new friends from the freight forwarding industry at a popular German restaurant one hot sunny afternoon. He introduced me to his lady boss and some of his colleagues. After a short meeting, we excused ourselves as Matthew had some work to attend to. So we bade his friends farewell and left the restaurant. As we were walking along the side-walk towards his car, I suddenly dropped to the ground and landed hard on my knees. I must have missed a step on the side-walk. I was about to laugh about it but instead of helping me up, Matthew scolded me for being clumsy. He must have felt embarrassed to be with me. I was deeply shocked and hurt by his words and actions. Yes, all this played in my mind and I could not accept his proud and arrogant character.

Finally, when we were at a shopping mall one day, I lashed out at him and walked off. After that day, I again told him I wanted to end our relationship. When we met up, he drove me straight to his home, parked the car in his front porch and told me to wait in his car. I was not sure what he was going to do but he came out with my belongings in a tiny plastic bag. My heart just sank like an anchor thrown into the deep blue sea. I may have cried a little but that experience made me guard my heart even more.

Back at my new workplace, my colleagues and I spent late nights having supper and getting to know each other. All was good until they started visiting night clubs and discotheques. The guys who were fresh from college and universities spoke openly about their 'adventures' in bed with their course mates and even mature women. When I joined them at these clubs, I stood back just observing them. While one of my colleagues pretended to be drunk so that women would offer to take him home...I asked them to throw a bucket of ice over his head as a remedy. I did not like what I saw in these clubs. Men were ogling at women pole dancing and modelling on bar counters as though they were sex objects. I was deeply disheartened by what I saw. Gone were the days when you could just sit back and enjoy real music from live bands. And instead of hard liquor, you could enjoy a good cup of coffee, tea, milk or ice cream. Whatever happened to roller-skating rinks and ice-cream parlours? I am not talking about brands here but places where great relationships are formed and relished with good family values; godly values!

It had been raining heavily the night before when I arrived at my workplace one morning. As I unlocked the front glass doors, I noticed a lot of cigarette stubs on the ground near the door and the front of the reception area. I did not suspect anything at first as I locked the doors behind me. When I walked in, I saw heavy, muddy footprints on the floor and the drawers of my manager's desk strewn on the floor of his office. Feeling frightened that our office had been broken into and that the culprit might still be in the premises, I quickly went outside to call my branch manager. He contacted the police and came over to the office immediately. With a worried look on his face, he rushed into his office and found that someone had been through his things. He was very relieved that he had kept the previous days cash sales in a safe place.

Together, we went upstairs to inspect the place and found that the culprit had broken into the premises through the rooftop of one of the rooms. The room was filled with rainwater. The items in the room were destroyed. Thankfully, no one was around when it happened.

My branch manager hurriedly went downstairs to inspect the premises again before reporting the break-in to our employer. As he spoke with her privately over his mobile, I walked over to where I had seen the cigarette butts. I noticed that they were of the same brand one of our colleagues often smokes. He was the only one who smoked Dunhill and I was told that he had approached our manager to borrow some money just a day earlier. Not only that, there were clear dirty finger prints on the door handles.

By then, most of my colleagues had already arrived and were wondering what had happened. The place was abuzz about the break-in when two policemen came to inspect the premises and speak with our branch manager. I was standing outside when our dear colleague, Paddy, walked in through the front gate. I noticed him taking out his handkerchief from his side trousers' pocket to slowly wipe the metal handles of the glass doors. Angeline and I stood watching him wipe the fingerprints off the handles. He had a worried look on his face as he stared at the two policemen and our branch manager but he was very calm. Two days later, everything was back to normal in our office as though nothing had ever happened. It was back to work as usual.

After just three months working at the time-share company, my employer advised me to complete my studies first as it would take up more of my time and effort.

I was still feeling emotional after my break-up with Matthew. I knew I had to pick myself up again and find a good job. I attended a few interviews and was glad when I finally found one that seemed to suit my requirements. Still, the thought of how Matthew left me with emptiness in my heart hurt like a deep cut within me. After breaking-up with him, I did not have any contact with our friends from the airlines. I wanted a fresh start; a new beginning. I wanted to leave all the hurts behind.

One night, when I could not contain my emotions any longer, I poured out all my hurt and sufferings to God. I cried about the bullying I had to endure at my previous workplace. It hurt me that those who I trusted and were closest to me were the ones who betrayed me. I was not quite sure if I was more upset with a friend who started rumours about me and constantly stabbed me in the back or the people who accepted those lies and ostracised me.

For the first time in my life, I felt so alone in this big world. There I was surrounded by 'friends' at shopping malls, movie theatres and discotheques but somehow all these people around me and the material things of this world did not make me feel good about myself. A sudden feeling of loneliness crept up within me. It dawned on me how so many people who see themselves as extroverts and who always need people around them are actually very 'lonely'. It also dawned on me that just like these people, I was actually searching for love in all the wrong places.

"How awful it must be for those living on the streets. Those without family or true friends to confide in," I cried.

'Why?' I thought to myself.

"Lord, I have been through so many relationships and all I want is love. Why did he treat me this way? Why did he have to leave me when I needed him most," I poured out my heart to Jesus.

Lying on my bed in my room, I sobbed till the sheets were wet. Then I continued to 'talk to Jesus' about the type of man I wanted. Still sobbing, I told Jesus that I wanted a man like Joseph, who took Mary to be his wife knowing very well about her 'condition'. He had stood by her and gave her his love and protection. He was truly a godly man.

"Lord, I wish that I could meet a godly man who like Joseph is both strong and courageous. I wish that my 'husband' would forgive me despite knowing my past," I prayed with desire in my heart. "I cannot lie about my past. Neither do

I want to hide it from him. It would be wrong," I continued praying.

After praying this prayer, I felt a blanket covering me and I started to 'talk to Jesus' about love. I do not know who put these words on my lips but in a prayer-like manner, I begged Jesus to teach me about love. About His love.

I remember praying very simply, these words, "Teach me how to love. I want to know what love is."

As I am writing this I also remember one of my favourite songs by 'Foreigner', 'I Want To Know What Love Is'.

Most men want only to marry virgins but they go about defiling women. This is something I can and will never understand about men.

I fell asleep halfway while 'talking with Jesus'. That same night, I dreamt of 'Joseph'. I saw an image of a man with curly hair like how Catholic or Christian art would paint images of 'Joseph, the carpenter' and a true descendant of King David by blood.

Before I awoke at dawn, I had another dream. This time I saw a man's face like an actor in a movie I had watched not too long ago. His eyes were unusual. One was blue and another green. I also saw this actor in 'Legend of the Falls' starring Anthony Hopkins and Brad Pitt. I think his name is Aidan Quinn.

I was given spiritual insight about loneliness: 'being alone' and 'feeling lonely'. I pondered about it for awhile. The two bear different meanings. The latter was how I felt the previous night... such a scary feeling.

Some people say I am an extrovert but I know I am more of an introvert. Although I love being alone most of the time just like my father, especially when I need some moments of peace and quiet, I know I cannot shut myself off from this world. My father enjoyed the company of his friends. When he was home, he would keep himself busy with housework and gardening. I prefer to stay at home keeping myself busy reading and cleaning house or redecorating rather than shopping. It is just that the feeling of loneliness that enveloped me the previous night gave new meaning to the word 'lonely'. I may be the life and love of a party in a room filled with people but still feel 'lonely'. Part of me was feeling 'void'. Some people may always keep to themselves but they feel loved; they are brave, bold and confident.

While I was 'talking with Jesus' the previous night, I felt someone beside me as all these were 'revealed' to me. And as 'He' 'comforted' me, I still did not realise it was the person of the Holy Spirit, the 'Sweet Paraclete', the Advocate promised by Christ Jesus. I had been sobbing till the bed-sheet and pillows were covered with my tears but I felt warmth when I fell into a peaceful slumber.

An Answered Prayer ...
Happiness and Bliss

*I wrote this portion directly after the previous chapter on,

22 November 2014:-

I was listening to the CD album 'Moments For The Heart' – The Very Best Of Ray Boltz and was suddenly reminded of the time when I was asked to leave my family home in 2001 because my mum was upset that my father had to send me to work every day. My work place was quite a distance from where we lived. I was distraught. I did not want to be separated from my family but at the same time I was tired of having to catch two buses just to reach my work place. In a way, this may have been a blessing in disguise. Now I know that it is God who wanted me to leave all the people I love behind so that He could work in me.

I have been tested with fire and am still in the race till He returns. As the song 'Is There A Heaven For Me' by Ray Boltz was playing while I was writing this, I was reminded again of the time when I felt so alone in this world... I was brought to tears because I know that God was listening to my 'heart' and that He still loves me.

22 March 2001 - I reported for work on my first day at a factory along Kimba Bay, situated near the Penang International Airport. As it was a new factory starting up making speaker parts, every staff had to cover multiple tasks. As Sales and Purchase Assistant to the General Manager, I was assigned various duties in the Shipping and Purchasing department as well as the Sales department. Apart from these duties,

I had to assist our Storekeeper with the monthly stock-take of raw materials and finished goods.

I was a little nervous at first, having to work for a foreigner. Mr. Oshiro hailed from Japan and was only in his early thirties when he took up his position as General Manager for our factory in Penang. His English accent tickled me. On my first day at work, he personally introduced me to most of the staff in the various departments. The staff from the accounts department were assigned to guide me. I still remember them well for their pleasant attitude, hard work and guidance. The factory engineer introduced me to most of the operators and technicians.

After a few days at work, I was called downstairs to meet Daniel, a young technician. He had been on leave when I started work at the factory. His eyes sparkled when our eyes met and we were introduced. He was not that good looking but he had chiselled cheek bones and I noticed his head of hair.

I thought to myself, 'It is unusual for a Chinese guy to have natural curly hair'.

Actually I had never met a Chinese man with natural curly hair before. Most of them had straight black hair. At first glance, I was already asking myself if he could be 'the one', the man I had dreamt about.

My duties required me to work closely with all departments except the operators. This allowed me to get to know Daniel better. He was very shy. Everyone loved him and often teased him because he was such a 'good boy'. I also knew that some of our colleagues were trying to match-make us. His close friends had teased him in front of me and pestered him to ask me out.

One fine day, some of the staff made arrangements to celebrate a technician's leaving with a farewell party and they invited me. Daniel and I got the opportunity to share a little about ourselves.

Daniel and I worked well together. He would help me check the heavy copper wires during stock-take, whenever I needed his assistance.

Mr. Oshiro brought me to our customers' factories in the Northern region to introduce me to the people I would be corresponding with in the Sales and Purchasing departments as well as the Shipping departments.

As hard as I tried to focus entirely on my new job, the moment I reached home I would be so exhausted. My father continued to send me to work every morning and would try to pick me up after work in the evenings. I relish the times when we would have our family dinners at the Malay chicken rice restaurant nearby the factory.

Soon after, I was required to stay back after work to assist with the stock-take and daily records of raw materials and finished goods. I had no choice but to take the public transport home. The bus service during and after rush hour were not frequent so I sometimes had to wait till late evening. I would be so tired upon reaching home, sometimes even as late as eleven at night. Getting up as early as six thirty in the morning to get ready for work seemed like a big wall. My father knew I was tired. When my mother scolded me for making him late for work at times, I argued with her trying to make her understand that it was difficult for me to catch the second bus to my workplace on time. I was tired.

The last straw came when my mother shouted at me, "You're going to kill your father."

I immediately started looking for a room to rent near my workplace. A young couple were looking for a house-mate in Bukit Jambul Apartments and I responded to their advertisement. The apartment was next to a shopping mall so we made arrangements to meet on the ground floor of the mall. I waited at a fast food restaurant and was met by a young Indian man named Falak together with his Chinese girlfriend, Xiao-Xing. After introducing ourselves, they told me a little about the room in the apartment before allowing me to view it. There was a guard house next to the pedestrian walk at the front of the apartment and the only access to the units upstairs was by individual screen cards.

I moved into the third room which was furnished with a single bed and nothing else, shortly after we made a verbal agreement on the monthly payment. I was allowed to use Falak & Xiao-Xing's television set and DVD player in the living room. My parents and aunt and uncle who lived nearby came over for a visit and to view the apartment and its surroundings. What I loved about this apartment were the facilities within the apartment and its central location which had easy access to public transport, food and shops. I felt quite safe here because of the tight security and there were always people around. Unfortunately, I only got to use the sauna once or twice before the management closed it down for servicing.

Daniel would take me home after work whenever he could. One evening, we rode straight into town after work. He did not tell me where he was taking me. Just before we reached the heart of town, a middle-aged couple rode past us as Daniel slowed down. He told me that they were his parents. I was confused as Daniel did not stop and the lady pillion rider on the other bike did not have a cheerful look on her face. However, it did not get my hopes down. I was enjoying Daniel's company and friendship. When he took me home, I asked him again who the couple on the other bike was. He told me that his parents wanted to 'see' me. Still puzzled, I asked if I could meet them at his home. He gracefully replied that they were actually busy clearing out their old home to move into their new apartment. In time, he would introduce me to his immediate family members.

Daniel and I had common interests. We both loved toys and watching movies. He spoke a lot about his hobbies. He would come by to visit me during weekends at my rented apartment and we would talk and watch the movies he rented. He always left early to go back to have dinner with his family, so he never stayed after seven in the evening. I was very glad to have found this 'perfect gift' as he was a filial son. I told myself that I would never come between him and his mother as I would not want the same to happen to me. It would have been wrong. I remembered my prayer to God to teach me about love and to love. I felt the Holy Spirit had not only counselled me but was changing me because I never treated anyone which such deep respect and love before. Daniel could do no wrong in my sight and I treated him like a king. Whenever he left the apartment, he would make sure I locked the door and we would bid each other with a warm farewell. I would usually caress his curly hair gently with my fingers.

I was overjoyed when Daniel told me that his father was a carpenter. This confirmed that he was the one I had prayed for. My 'Joseph'! What a coincidence!

Not long after we started courting, our colleague Bik Zhin got married. She resigned leaving her accounting position vacant. It did not take my General Manager long to find a replacement. Interviews were held quite often to hire technicians and operators as well. Our new accountant was very knowledgeable and did not require much training.

Although many staff had left, Daniel kept in touch with them. Soon they formed a group to play badminton and I was invited to join them. We rented badminton courts and played only during the weekends. I was not very good at first but the others coached me to form. I built up more stamina playing this game. My father was pleased when he heard that I was playing badminton with my new found friends and colleagues. He probably thought I needed the exercise too.

Usually, Daniel and I would walk around town to cool off after our game. We would either join his friends window shopping or visiting parks before going home. My parents were very happy when I introduced them to Daniel. I had spoken about him very often. He was rather shy with them especially with my mum.

Daniel would always make it a point to take me to church on Sunday evenings. I tried to persuade him to attend mass with me as the more I prayed, the more joyful I was. I felt thoroughly blessed by God and wanted Daniel to share the experience of God's love. We were both doing very well at work, our relationship was growing stronger and there was perfect peace within our families.

The Holy Spirit

Almost a year into working at the factory, I was approached to work for a forwarder as their Customer Services come Sales Coordinator. They were setting up a new branch office near the airport. I jumped the chance to secure this job for better prospects and stability. Daniel, however, remained working at the factory.

At first and under the guidance of our Sales Executive and Senior Sales Executive, I was told to look through the old files to learn how to prepare quotations. They also took me to visit their existing customers. I received a lot of help from the other staff of the air freight, sea freight and accounts departments. Upon my Branch Manager's advice, I started using the internet to look for sales leads and to make calls to secure appointments for our sales team. In addition, they also got a book with the list of factories printed by the Penang Development Corporation near our office.

In June 2002, while searching for leads for our sales team online, I stumbled upon a very interesting website 'beliefnet. com'. I think it must have been the links from the 'Chicken Soup for the Soul' stories which led to this website or vice versa. Anyway, I subscribed to some of their newsletters such as 'Chicken Soup', 'God's Daily Promises', 'The Sayings of Jesus', 'Daily Muslim Wisdom', 'Daily Buddhist Wisdom', 'Angelic Wisdom' and various prayers of different faiths.

Every day I would open my email to read God's promise for me for that particular day. I was astounded as each time I read His promise, it was as though I was living it. It became real. Whatever emotions I was going through at that moment and the rewards I was getting were all written in the scripture verses I read daily. I also found some comfort in reading the 'Daily Muslim Verses' as they were quite similar to biblical verses. I could actually find peace within myself then. If I did not understand or if I did not find any peace reading any of the materials I subscribed to, I would either delete or discard them or rewrite them according to 'my faith' which is in Christ Jesus. As my colleagues were 'Muslims', I decided to fast along with them during their holy fasting month of Ramadhan.

I found great comfort and support in discussing religion with Fadil, our Accounts Manager. We spoke a lot about the end times. Fadil printed out holy verses from his Quran on the end times for me to read. The verses stated that during the end times, the 'Sun' would descend nearer to earth and as all people were gathered in a 'field', tongues of fire would descend upon their heads.

'This is definitely the work of the Holy Spirit,' I thought to myself. It is indeed similar to our Christian faith and most Christians already have gifts of the Holy Spirit when they received the baptism of the Holy Spirit.

However, I kept my thoughts to myself then, as I was not ready to preach to Muslims about Christianity especially since it is against the law in my country to do so.

There was a different theme each week and each theme would have various scriptures with messages from God's Daily Promises to claim for each day of the week.

I only managed to print some out from June 30 till December 24, 2002 before I left for Langkawi in January 2005. After pasting them into calendar form in 2010 and reading them again, I realised that they were from 'Left Behind Prophecies' or 'Left Behind.com'. I had tried to search for their newsletter again through beliefnet.com while I was working as a parish clerk for my church, but they had been removed...

The promises which I had claimed from June 30 till December 24, 2002 which I pasted like a 'calendar' are as follows:

{June 30 ~ July 5}
Theme: **Obeying God brings great joy**
Scripture verses: James 1:2
                    2 Corinthians 12:8-10
                    Daniel 12:3
                    Matthew 6:19-21
                    Matthew 25:21
                    Galatians 5:22

At the beginning of each week, there would be an explanation along with each promise of the week for the believer to fully understand God's compassion and love for us.

{July 6 ~ July 12}
Theme: **God is slow to get angry with us**
Scripture verses: Psalm 103:8
                    Proverbs 15:1
                    John 2:13-17
                    Matthew 5:21-26
                    Proverbs 11:29
                    Romans 1:18
                    2 Chronicles 12:12

{July 13 ~ July 19}
Theme: **God takes care of us**
Scripture verses: Psalm 23:6
Genesis 2:15
Deuteronomy 1:31
John 2:16
James 1:27

For some reason I do not have a printout for July 17 & 18 of 2002.

{July 20 ~ July 24}
Theme: Overcoming discouragement brings great blessings
Scripture verses: Galatians 6:9
1 Peter 5:8-9

My heart was filled with joy each time I reflected on these scriptures. I felt a strong, holy presence with me. I had also been subscribing to the 'Chicken Soup for the Soul.' Reading their articles helped in my spiritual growth. One such article that I read was a true account titled 'How We Open Our Hearts to God' written by Coretta Scott King and another one on 'Forgiveness'.

One night while I was saying my prayers before I went to bed, I heard a voice telling me that God loves me and that by His grace, I had been forgiven. Then, the voice told me to forgive 'Melissa'.

'Melissa? But how come? Why?' I thought.

Melissa was my ex-colleague from Golden Keris Airlines. We had been best friends but our friendship had soured. Both of us formed our own cliques at work and the situation only got worse for both of us.

I felt awkward but before I could think of anything else, the voice whispered again in a soft, gentle manner,

"God loves Melissa, too."

I felt a deep cut in my heart when I heard that. I knew I had to obey. It is God's will. All the materials I had been reading on forgiveness was God's way for preparing me for this moment. I prayed that God would forgive us and that the Holy Spirit would give me the strength and that God would give me the grace to forgive Melissa. I had made my choice to forgive her. It was not forced upon me but I immediately understood God's will and obeyed. The audible voice was very gentle and loving.

I prayed for both of us to receive God's blessings. I was blessed with a raise in my pay-check and given more duties at my workplace.

One morning, I had arrived an hour early for work. Haliza my colleague from the air freight department, walked in next. I greeted her warmly but she gave me a grunt and didn't even look at me. Before I could react, a voice gently breathed in my right ear, 'It's her husband,' and I clearly understood immediately that she had a quarrel with her husband. Instead of being judgemental as I usually would be, I was not angry and felt sorry for her. I realised then, that the Holy Spirit was a 'person' walking alongside me. An advocate sent by God to counsel, help and encourage me as well as to help me to pray for others.

Throughout my youth, I had acquired knowledge and wisdom from books and listening to people, collecting quotes on wisdom by wise and famous people. So I thought I had wisdom. However, when I started reading bible verses from my email subscriptions, I realised how little I knew as the Holy Spirit began to reveal many truths to me about who

God is. God's wisdom far surpassed all of what the world had taught me. Nothing can compare to Him. No one is greater than Him. As the Holy Spirit counseled me, I was being transformed slowly and gently. For once I understood what confidence meant. I experienced it when the Holy Spirit revealed to me that I was God's child.

I remember Fr. Ignatius Huan's sermon in 2002 when he was serving at the College General, a training college for seminarians. He would sometimes celebrate mass at my parish. I was 'awakened' by his sermons and the Lord's holy presence during the masses as I actually felt the Lord speaking directly to me when the gospels were being read and when my ears were 'opened' to hear and take heed of the messages in Fr. Ignatius Huan's sermons. In one of his sermons, he mentioned that 'In every good person, there is a little evil in him and in every evil person, there is a little good in him'. We are to find Christ' light or goodness in each person we meet. These words have remained in me and have assisted me whenever I need to share the gospel of Christ with others.

We should be like God for God is love. We love others as God first loved us and as God is light we should always seek God's light and goodness in others.

I often shared about Christ' love with Daniel and his family members and on one occasion, his mother brought up the subject about 'forgiveness'. She told me that this was the one thing she could never do and believed it was impossible to do. Someone had hurt her badly and did not want to change her habit of hurting others. I wanted to share more on forgiveness with Daniel's mother but something kept me from speaking.

At weekends, Daniel would bring me to church for the evening mass. He would wait outside while I attended mass. His mother forbade him to ever change his religion. She told me once how she caned her youngest brother, Jacob, for converting to Christianity. Jacob left the family home and she had never heard from him again. According to Daniel's mother, Christians came to take Jacob away from their family home.

'Could this be the reason why she hated the religion so much?' I thought.

I am regretting this now as in 2017, I learnt that Daniel's mother was taken ill and had to be admitted into the General Hospital for heart complications. I only prayed for her to be healed and comforted. Could I have done more?

2003…

Not long after, Daniel's mother requested that I move to a rented flat closer to their home. She quickly found me a flat to rent in Lip Sin Garden, so I moved out from Falak and Xiao-Xing's rented apartment. We still kept in touch after that.

Daniel spent his evenings in my flat after work. We would watch a movie before he went home. One of the movies we rented and watched together was 'The Clash of the Titans' starring Harry Hamlin. Watching this movie reminded me of my early childhood days. I shared these memories with Daniel; memories of the time my father would gather the family, all packed in his old red Renault and drive us to the Rex theatre in town to watch 'The Ten Commandments' starring Charlton Heston as Moses and other movies such as 'The Blackhole' and 'Star Wars'. I enjoyed the special effects and cinematography of Ray Harryhausen's 'Clash of the

Titans' as compared to our present day 'Science fiction' movies. The creatures were more realistic and the actors were passionate about their 'work'. What I mean here is the actors of the 50's and 60's really put their hearts and soul into the characters they played. It was as though they were living the parts they played. I remember having to sit on my mum's lap during the movie and at one part during 'The Blackhole', I fell asleep.

It was so good that Daniel had possession of all these old movies. That night, during my quiet time with Abba Father, I was given 'spiritual insight' by the Holy Spirit. He guided me through Genesis 6. Then I remembered how I used to love reading those heavy green hardcover series of 'Greek Mythology' which sat in a row in a corner shelf of the library where I was schooled during my childhood days. I started going to the library during my 'free periods' upon the suggestion and advise of my new school headmistress, Ms Ang and upon the kindness of my school librarian, Sister Nicole. I had always thought of her as a very strict and fierce lioness. She was always firm. In her English language class, she would make us stand row by row while we were drilled during her grammar lessons. However, I saw a different side of her when Ms Ang took me to see her at the library. She treated every child equally. I always rushed to the little corner behind where Sister Nicole sat in the library to read a chapter of these stories of Greek heroes during my free periods in 1987. There were some parts which carried terrifying pictures of monsters, so I skipped them.

As the Holy Spirit revealed to me who these heroes actually were, I began to understand why I started to lose interest in Greek Mythology when I attended high school. Maybe this is also the reason why I stopped believing in fairy tales and why I am not drawn to myths and legends. I may read for leisure or knowledge but I do not obsess over them as I did during my childhood days.

(Scripture Reading: Genesis 6:1-4)

History is history. But what happens when people start turning history into myths and legends and vice versa? Would memories of our kings and queens, Prime Minister and governments officials one day fade away? I believe that this is the reason why we ought to keep typed or handwritten records of our genealogy and historical documents which of course is encouraged and proven in the Old Testament and also the New Testament. In the Old Testament, we have knowledge of these records in 1 Kings, 2 Kings, 1 Chronicles, 2 Chronicles, Ezra and Esther. While in the New Testament we have the sole purpose of the written word, the bible.

(Scripture Reading: John 20:30-31)

> **Christ Jesus is the reason why I am still here today and recording my testimony of His healing presence and life-giving power in his holy name and for His glory. As I am writing my testimony, I am also recording memories of all whom I love and hold dearly. Jesus continues to humble me and I will surrender myself to Him. May He shape my character and body into perfection according to His will. May I always submit to His will and obey His laws and decrees to love, to serve and to live as He lives. Our Saviour has won victory over death and Hades (the graves).**

As my faith in God grew deeper, I found myself starting to praise Him for being a good Father. I would call Him, 'Abba, Father' in my prayers. One weekend, I awoke thanking Abba, Father, for my hands, fingers, toes, feet, eyes, ears, nose and every part of my body I could think of. I felt the presence of the Holy Spirit moving actively around me as I continued to thank God for creating me and giving me fresh air to breathe and a life to live. I was led by the Holy Spirit to look at myself in the mirror. Something I had not done in ages (since I was little). I stared into my eyes and started to thank God for my eyes to see and ears to hear. I realised then that my life had value in the sight of God, Abba, Father. I was his little girl, His creation.

My eating habits also changed. I never liked fish and vegetables growing up. I had a sweet tooth. Always indulging in cakes and ice cream. Somehow, after fasting with my colleagues, I ate a lot of fish and vegetables. I even stopped eating my favourite food...pork! Before the start of the fast, I even boasted to my colleagues that I could never stop eating pork and that it was delicious. All that had changed. My desire for certain meat just died.

I continued to share God's love with Daniel and his sister, Anastasia. Anna, for short. His parents often invited me over to their home at weekends. Daniel's mother wanted me to come over his place every evening for dinner. Daniel and I spent a lot of time discussing our favourite characters from the Hong Kong movie 'Wind and Cloud.' The movie is an adaption of the Hong Kong comics of the same title. I would watch the series together with them almost every evening.

While Daniel's parents were watching their favourite Chinese series in the living room one evening, Daniel brought me into his room to show me his collection of miniature swords, toy figurines, books and comics based on the comics of the same name, 'Wind and Cloud'. His huge showcase took up half his room. His toy figurines were nicely placed, each in its own plastic case. No one else was allowed to see or touch his precious collection. I understood why Daniel didn't want his little nephews entering his room now. But

Daniel was generous enough to give some of his collection away as gifts. He had imported some directly from Hong Kong through catalogues. I enjoyed listening to Daniel talk about his collection. At least he had an interesting hobby.

In turn, I showed him my collection of Beanie Babies and soft toys. My first Beanie Babies came from China. I bought them when I visited Beijing while I was working in Golden Keris Airlines, in 1997. All of my Beanie Babies have birth dates and a poem written about them.

On some occasions, I would follow Daniel and his family to Kulim, a neighbouring state, to their second home to collect their monthly rental. Daniel's family owned two shops there. This is where his father made his furniture out of rattan. On two occasions, we travelled to Ipoh to visit their relatives, his father's cousins. I was invited for Daniel's cousin's wedding there. It was my first time to Ipoh and I was brought to a famous Buddhist temple. I do not recall its name but it was a beautiful place. The temple was built in a huge limestone cave and at the back of the cave that was well lit, there was a big lily pond in the middle. I remember seeing gigantic dragon fish in the ponds outside the entrance of this temple.

We were almost three years into our relationship when Daniel's parents brought up the subject of marriage. For the Chinese the main event was the wedding banquet. Daniel's mother told me she would give us twelve tables. I was overjoyed when Daniel and his family talked about our marriage. I was glad I wasn't going to be an 'old maid.' Daniel and I agreed to set the date on my 28th birthday, come end of December. I conveyed the good news to my parents who shared my joy.

Back at work, things were starting to change. Catherine, our General Manager at the main branch in Kuala Lumpur wanted more sales revenue from our Penang office. She decided to hire only Chinese sales executives since my colleagues were all Malay. I was tasked to contact the applicants and set the appointments for the interviews. Our Penang Branch Manager, Yahya finally hired a young Chinese boy with a strong sales record from his previous company, a courier company. Yahya was also the one who hired me into this company. I gave him the respect he deserved as he was a very good boss. He was a good leader who listened to his staff.

Shortly after Shane, our new Sales Executive was hired, Adil, from my department was promoted to Assistant Sales Manager. Yahya and Adil directed me to guide Shane and asked me to take Shane to all the companies we had visited in the past. Some had become our customers while some were still pending. As I did not drive at that time, I had to go with Shane in his car. At first, I took him to all the small factories surrounding our industrial area in Bayan Baru and Bayan Lepas to familiarise him with our quotations and procedures. Later, Yahya gave us some leads that were located on the mainland. There were times we came back late to the office because of our late appointments and the rush hour traffic on the bridge. I could tell from Daniel's looks that he was jealous of Shane but I did not say anything since he didn't bring it up. However, I gave him my assurance that it was all work and that I would not cheat on him. I thought this would ease his mind.

It was around this time too, when I got a house-mate to rent the vacant room at my rented flat. Manar was a sweet young Malay girl. Fair skinned with dark eyes and eye brows, and short black hair. She was the accountant of one of my clients. I had gotten this account before Shane joined us.

I shared my experiences about God with Manar and she was quick to listen. We could talk for hours and soon we became good friends. She would go back to her village in a neighbouring state in the north every weekend.

I often thought about religion. I wondered why there was no peace when religion taught people to do good and to become better people. I also wondered why Christians were so against Catholics praying to Mother Mary. Many Catholics I know prayed to Mother Mary to intercede for them. I wasn't used to praying to Mother Mary but I sincerely want Christians and Catholics to be as One in Christ.

During my prayer time one day, I asked Abba Father to reveal Mother Mary to me. He did answer my prayers but not in the way I quite expected. He transformed my nature into a more mature Christian. I became gentler in nature, loving towards my colleagues, friends and especially my family. I was also more patient. So patient that I waited lovingly for four hours for Daniel at a coffee shop once. He had been delayed because he had guests in his home and couldn't give me the time he could pick me up. Instead of letting my thoughts run wild and cursing him, I took this time to pray for him and his family.

Temptations and the Devil

Back at work, Shane began showing his 'nutty' side. He would be serious and hard-working at times, and crazy and difficult the next. He joked all the time and made me laugh. Everyone in the office could hear us.

Shane wasn't ashamed to show his true emotions. He started showing interest in me and expressed his anger towards me for going out with Daniel. I told him that nothing could come between me and Daniel and that I was devoted to him. I love Daniel unconditionally. Maybe Shane was angry because I told him that I took him more like a 'son'. It was a coincidence that his mother's name was the same as mine and I had been sharing with him too, about my encounters with God. I told him that I had fasted along with our Muslim colleagues the year before and wanted to try it again this year. However, this time round, it was quite difficult for me. I didn't understand why and thought maybe it was due to stress. Yahya had given Shane a warning about his sales. He had worked with us for three months but still hadn't brought in any sales.

One day, however, Shane's car broke down on the mainland because it was overheated. We had to wait for the car to cool down before we could head home across the bridge. I contacted Daniel immediately so he would not worry. By the time we got back to the office, it was late. Daniel was extremely angry. He hated Shane and felt I was getting too close to him. He started to demand for sex and although I gave in, I didn't enjoy the times we were together because it started to feel like lust.

I had been menstruating twice a month for a period of maybe three to four months or more and once I awoke to find a tiny part of my bed wet with water even though I had slept soundly throughout the night and that wet area was away from the air conditioner. Also I remembered where I had arranged my toy 'Beanie Babies' and the 'Chameleon' was always 'moved'. I did ask Daniel if he had moved the 'Chameleon', but he neither admitted nor denied moving that toy. All these puzzled me and I was worried that someone had been entering my room without my permission when I was out.

Daniel and his parents brought me to their home come workshop in Kulim to view their 'wedding gift' to us. His father had made us a rattan bed with his own hands. It wasn't ready yet. I was a little embarrassed about the gift especially when Daniel reminded me that we would be sleeping on it on our wedding night.

Back at my apartment one evening, I noticed a change in Daniel. We had just finished watching a DVD. I walked over to my cupboard to fold my clothes leaving Daniel lying on my bed. Something made me turn back to face him. I saw a 'mirage' moving like a 'worm' in front of his lips. I was horrified.

I did not know what it was but I was thinking to myself then, 'No wonder he keeps on pestering me to have sex all the time. Our love seems to have lost its original 'spark' and he no longer loves or trusts me.'

Most men who are insecure would use sex as a means to 'control' their partners. I understood this fully well as I had been in these kind of relationships before. But I also knew that the change in his behaviour had something to do with his new colleague from Ipoh. I could not say or do anything at that time as Daniel would not listen to me.

Things started to get crazy at work! Shane would scold me for no apparent reason and accuse me of coming between his 'girlfriend' and him. Our colleagues thought he had gone mad. He even made me cry once.

At work one morning, Adil, our Assistant Sales Manager told me that I was losing focus and was becoming too playful. He explained that I had been very disciplined when I first joined the company.

"What has happened to you?" he asked.

I smiled to try to hide my embarrassment. I accepted his discipline and tried to buck up.

> **The following includes excerpts from my writings in my 'examination pad' of dreams and visions which I shared with Fr. Murray and his companions (dated 2nd December 2009).**

Between April and October 2003...

Some time during the seventh or eighth Chinese calendar month, I had a very strange dream. This dream is told through the eyes of a young lady. She is dressed in a pair of beige pants, matched with a beige collared short sleeved blouse. Her smooth, unblemished face is framed with soft, short black curls.

This dream begins with the young lady pulling up in her car and parking near the front entrance of a wild-life park. She enters the park through the front entrance and walks along some tall fences and through some empty cages. She calls out to the care-taker of the premises. He hears her and takes a peek through the window panes from inside his living-quarters but she does not see him. She calls out to him again and is greeted warmly by a smiling middle-aged man. Tears roll down their cheeks as they hug each other. The man invites her to stay for lunch. She obliges.

She sits on a stool made out of a tree trunk in the backyard while he goes in to prepare lunch. They start a conversation about the woman's late husband. The man and the woman's late husband used to work together on some scientific experiment. They were very close before the latter died. They had kept their work a secret.

After her husband's sudden death, she went away for many years before returning. Her husband had developed some kind of rare skin disease and illness just before he died. She starts probing about the experiments the two were conducting. There is complete silence. No reply comes from the man. He comes out with the meal he has prepared and hands her a plate. He sits next to her and begins eating, avoiding conversation. She eats the food and finds it has a weird taste.

"What's in this?" she asks, pointing into her dish.

Before she receives any reply from the man, she sees a clutch of headless black feathered chickens scurrying about in the backyard. The feet of the chickens were all covered with sores. The lady looks down and stares at the food on her plate. The man turns to her, then slowly pulls off his wig. His head is covered with sores and the skin on his head is peeling. Reeling in shock, the lady drops the plate in her hands to the ground.

I awoke in cold sweat but went back to bed as it was still dark (about four in the morning). As soon as I went back to bed, I had another dream. The dream is set on Calvary or Golgotha as it is also known...

'I am watching a hill burning from a distance. I see three crosses on the hill. When the fire burns out, I walk towards the crosses. There is a body hanging on the cross in the middle but it is badly burnt. As I approach the cross, the body suddenly drops to the ground. The figure looms towards me. I am terrified. Still burning and with his face peeling off, the burnt man comes right at my face. He points back at the cross and he screams at me, "God, put me up there!"'

I immediately woke up from the dream in cold sweat. This dream is the most terrifying dream I have ever had.

> I did not tell anyone of these visions but only recorded them down on pieces of paper in 2009 and journalled the miracles I encountered in real life from 2008 during my healing and deliverance. In 2010, I showed my journal to one of my friends and also my then parish priest. My parish priest told me that my dreams were about me and told me to pray about them. He told me that I was the best person to interpret these dreams and that he could not do so for me.

The first dream or rather 'nightmare' I had, caused me to pray for drug trafficking victims. I followed closely on the stories especially about the drug cartels in Mexico. I read in the newspapers about the many graves which were unearthed and the bodies found headless.

During this time, I tried to fast with my Muslim colleagues again but for some reason, I could not.

'Was I resisting the Holy Spirit's counsel? Had I become haughty? Did I think of myself as better than others?'

I wanted to know and understand why I could not pray and fast as before. It should have bothered me but as the season of fasting passed, I thought less of it. I kept myself busy with work. I had so much fun with Shane, I didn't realise I was spending more time talking with him than to Daniel.

Work went on as usual and on one special occasion I had arranged for Shane and his 'girlfriend' to meet Daniel and some of my friends from New Zealand who were in town visiting for the first time. We had dinner at a Chinese Restaurant in Gurney Drive. It was good catching up with Glen and Pippa from New Zealand. But it was a mistake bringing Daniel and Shane together. It felt terribly awkward after the dinner. After we bade farewell to our guests from New Zealand, Shane left peacefully with his 'girlfriend'. Daniel had brought his friend (colleague) from Ipoh. He stuck to him all night and ignored me completely. I tried to strike up conversation with Daniel and his friend but both completely ignored me. They both spoke in Cantonese, a Chinese dialect which I did not understand. This really made me upset. Why was Daniel giving me the cold shoulder?

Days passed on to weeks and suddenly there was no more talk about marriage and our wedding. I really felt a change in Daniel and it made me upset. I was even more distraught to learn that Shane was let off from work. I tried to contact him but he refused to answer my calls. I started to stay back at the office until late every day. I no longer had the enthusiasm to work. I also tried to avoid Daniel. I was a total mess! I was confused! With so many disappointments going on, I decided to stop seeing Daniel for awhile. I remember telling him that I needed some time to be alone. Daniel stopped coming by my place and his calls were less frequent. I guessed he was also busy at work because he had told me that he was working more overtime then.

One late night, I hitch-hiked a white vehicle back. I asked the driver, a kind Indian man, if he always picked up strangers and he told me that he was used to helping people, especially ladies like me. He dropped me off safely at my rented flat.

I met the stranger again when I finished late from work. This time, he asked if we could go for a drink. He took me to a pub. After drinking a glass of wine, I asked to be taken home. I wanted to get back quickly so I hurried to his car. Once in the car, I started crying like a baby. The stranger asked me why I was crying and I uttered these words, "I love him."

The kind stranger then drove me safely back to my apartment. Up till now, I still do not know if I was crying over Daniel or Shane. I was so mixed up then. I also do not know who this stranger was. He was very kind to me. I am just thankful to God that he took me home safely and did not take advantage of me.

October 2003...

I walked into my parish church grounds to attend mass early one evening and was greeted by some parishioners outside the entrance of our church building. They were volunteers of the 'Daughters of St Paul' who were around that weekend to spread the gospel of Christ through media. I browsed through their mini book stall and this little booklet caught my eye. 'Come Be My Light'. I immediately grabbed this small little booklet because I loved 'Mother Theresa'. Her fragile face graced the cover of this little blue booklet. I was inspired by her works. What caught my attention was not the publisher or the occasion of the 'Beatification of Mother Theresa' but the contents. Her calling from God through the intercessions of our Lord Jesus Christ to serve

His people was the one thing that touched me. I wanted to emulate her. She was just like the women mentioned in the Holy Bible who were obedient to God's call.

Using the booklet, I meditated on the prayer 'Radiating Christ'. I found that it brought healing to my soul. My perspective of others changed and I was able to reach out and offer encouragement to those around me.

Strengthening myself with the words written by Cardinal John Henry Newman of this prayer to 'Radiate Christ', I interceded for my family members to receive God's divine blessings. My brothers and sisters secured good jobs, had better prospects or offers and my eldest sister was receiving promotions at her workplace.

Although I was happy that my prayers for their successes in their careers were answered, my heart was still seeking God's peace and the fullness of His joy over my life and theirs. I wanted so badly, especially for Jonathan to be healed and delivered. My father brought Jonathan to visit me at my apartment in Lip Sin Garden on two occasions. On every occasion we met, I would be distressed after parting with them as I wanted so badly for Jonathan to be delivered from the hands of his 'enemies' and healed. My family was constantly in my thoughts and prayers.

You probably know the feeling when a soldier goes off to war and their loved ones bid them farewell and a safe journey; fiercely anticipating and praying for their safe return to their homeland but at the same time knowing that the horrors of the war might steal the soldier away...that the soldier may never return home. Well, this was the burden I felt in my heart and how I poured out to Jesus when I was praying for Jonathan's safe return 'home' to Christianity since God started His work in me at the beginning of the millennium.

Spiritual warfare is very much like the sport 'boxing'; when you fall, you quickly pick yourself up and fight. You do not give up. Never give up!

Manar, my flatmate was engaged to be married in December 2003. I hardly had a chance to speak with her as she was busy preparing for the 'big day'. I gave her a gift and 'ang pow' (red packet) for her wedding. I was very happy for her but sad at the same time because she had to leave. I was lucky as she asked her younger sister, Jarnila who had recently graduated, to live with me. Manar moved out and went to live with her husband in December. Jarnila had just moved into my flat when the flat owner told us he wanted the flat back. He gave us two months to move out. Both of us searched together around the Bayan Baru and Lip Sin District for a place to rent. We finally found an apartment at University Village.

Early 2004...

Not long after we had settled into our newly rented apartment at University Village, I decided to stop seeing Daniel for good as we were beginning to grow apart. I was worried that he had turned into a 'green eyed monster' and I found it hard to just talk to him. He did not listen to me and he did not even look at me when we talked and he was angry most of the time we were together. Often times he would sulk and not say a word. Furthermore, the date of our 'wedding' was drawing nearer and now there was no more talk about that day. Regretfully I told Daniel I needed some time to think.

It was tiring having to move again from Lip Sin to University Village and I was too tired to unpack my things in this new place. My room was messy but I remained determined not to let my emotions get the better of me. The only clean and tidy area in my room was my study table where I placed a beautiful vase on a piece of table cloth and decorated it with lovely bright plastic flowers. This table was placed at the window and I would sit and pray there so I could see the sunshine. I continued to seek the Lord daily.

While I was staying at that apartment, I again had a dream. This time I saw the devil stabbing an angel and trying to cut off his wings. Both were struggling on the ground and 'my angel' seemed desperate for help. In the dream, I watched in horror and started shouting for Jesus. After about a time, a man appeared who looked like an image of the 'Jesus' we have in Catholic books and materials. My heart was not settled and I started shouting the name 'Jesus! Jesus!' over and over again until a very bright light appeared. The dream of the struggling angel was immediately replaced with this awesome splendour of God's light. It was so bright. My anxiety was gone and I knew I was in the presence of God. At first I stood up trying to get a glimpse of his face. In my heart I was saying, 'Abba Father, you know who I am. I would do anything for you. You are the one who says I am your child and have taken away my sins.' In an instant, I was brought to my knees and humbly bowed low. I could not hold my head up but I could see all this light around me emanating from Him. I felt like a soldier of Christ. I was ready to 'die' for Him.

Then He spoke in a deep, commanding but gentle voice,

"Why have you called? What do you want?"

Without hesitation, I asked, "Will I go to heaven?"

The dream ended then. Just like that. And like before I awoke in cold sweat. Trembling because I did not get an answer from God, my master, King of all kings and Lord of all lords. Again, I was reminded of being a God-fearing

Christian. I knew at once that if I had any sin within me, I would disintegrate in His Holy presence. He is God. There is no other. At the same time, I was greatly troubled because I did not get an answer from Him...

As I am writing this down, I am also questioning myself... "Who am I to question a great God? Have I finished what He has called me to do? The question that remains is still whether I am worthy of His Kingdom. Perhaps it was God who placed the question in my heart in the very first place as I had been interceding on this message for my family, friends and extended families since early 2014. Another thing that troubles me when this vision is brought to mind is that I did not and have not earnestly prayed for my angels. I started asking the Lord of Heavens Armies to bless my angels with power, strength and fully equip them for their battles against the evil rulers and principalities of this world only in 2014. May our angels always remain faithful in serving our good God.

I implore to the Lord and seek Him who is humble and meek for His divine help and wisdom of His Holy Spirit. 'Help us O God, in these times of trials and tribulation'.

In 2013, I told this dream to one of my Catholic friends and she asked me, "Why are you asking the Lord whether you can go to heaven or not? You were in His Holy Presence weren't you?" And with that I burst out laughing at my silliness. This same friend is the one who researched the meaning of my confirmation name "Chevonne". She told me that it means "God's grace."

How wonderful that God would use my friend to send these kind and loving messages to me. Isn't God just wonderful?

Back in 2004...

Every time I felt the presence of God, I would bow down on my knees and pray as the rays of sunlight shone through my open window.

I reserved one quiet and peaceful night to watch my DVD on 'Jesus of Nazareth' starring Robert Powell as 'Jesus' and Olivia Hussey as 'Mary'. I sat through the whole movie that night and at the end of the movie I was brought to tears. I was sobbing upon seeing Jesus crucified for 'my sins' and my heart was crying out to him for mercy... I felt so sorry for my sins and to see Him die on the cross for me. My face was wet with tears but then I heard the most comforting words whispered into my ear.

'He is alive! He lives!'

I immediately stopped crying. My face was clean and dry again as the Holy Spirit gently wiped away my tears. I felt tremendous joy and comfort with these words. I felt so much love and was overwhelmed with the joy of the Holy Spirit. I found myself smiling at this realisation that my God is a Living God and that He loves me. He has always been faithful; Omnipresent; Omniscient; Omnipotent One.

I went to bed early one night and on this occasion, I dreamt that I was caught up in the sky by God's spirit. In this dream I was soaring in the sky. I could not see who was carrying me but I could hear a voice telling me about this beautiful place He was about to take me to. I was in awesome wonder at the beauty and majesty of this garden we were hovering over. It was covered with mighty trees and colourful flowers. I could see birds and animals but I could not hear any sound. The gardens spread across miles and miles of land. We were still caught up in the air.

Then, it was time to go home. I resisted and kept persuading the Holy Spirit to let me enter the garden. My heart was full of desire to enter this beautiful garden. I kept on begging to see and enter this place but the more I begged, the less I saw. In the end, I saw only darkness and all was quiet again. I could not enter this place I was given knowledge of but I remember how my heart burned with desire to enter this magnificent place. 'Where is this place?' I thought to myself.

1st October 2008

I started reading the book of Genesis. It dawned on me that the garden could be 'The Garden of Eden'. It is real. The garden really exists. It is not just a story. It is real! I read until the part God banished Adam and Eve from the garden and only then did I understand why I was not allowed to enter the garden.

Also, Revelation 21 mentions about 'The New Jerusalem'. The Holy City. God is building a new place on earth for us disciples.

(Scripture Reading: Genesis 3:22-24; Revelation 21)

April 2020

Since 2018, I have been ministered to by a pastor and his wife from Surabaya, Indonesia. Their church is also praying for my family. They advised me to have a proper water baptism. I have had to postpone my plans to go to Surabaya for my baptism because of the Covid-19 situation that began to spread in Malaysia, in March 2020.

(Scripture Reading: John 3:3)

Over the next couple of days, I received the counsel of the Holy Spirit again. This time the Holy Spirit told me that the Kingdom of God is within me. He told me not to wait to go to heaven but to make 'heaven' a place on earth.

'Wow! This is great news,' I thought. My heart was so full of joy knowing that the Kingdom of God was within me. But I could not comprehend it then. God's kingdom meant healing the sick, delivering the oppressed and demonised and spreading the gospel of peace which is Christ Jesus. Jesus is the Prince of Peace. **(Scripture Reading: Isaiah 9:6)**. Furthermore, signs and wonders are supposed to follow those who believe. **(Scripture Reading: Romans 15:19; 2 Corinthians 12:12; Hebrews 2:4; Acts 2:43; Acts 5:12; John 14:12)**

Things were very different after Shane was let off from work and the management started looking for new executives and a new Branch Manager at my workplace. Yahya was also asked to move to our headquarters in Kuala Lumpur. First, our General Manager from Kuala Lumpur came down to hire our new Sales Manager, Reuben. Then they hired Eric, a local boy of mixed parentage, as Shane's replacement. His father was Chinese and his mother was a Eurasian, like me. Things were getting weird because our new Sales Executive showed me his mother's identity card. Her first name was also similar to mine and Shane's mother.

I returned home one evening and talked to my father about my name. I was curious as to why I did not have a middle name like my other brothers and sisters. He explained to me that he and my mother thought I would have been born a boy since they already had Shannon and Joan, my two elder sisters. And then came Jonathan. My parents dreamt that having another boy would be a perfect addition to the family. So they were prepared to name me 'Julian Mark'. However, my birth caught them by surprise so they had to think up of a name for me. I was told that my middle name would have been 'Mary' but somehow it was left out in the birth records. I had always loved and trusted my father, so I was quite glad he told me this. After researching on my first name, I found out that it actually means 'youthful one'. Ever since I knew the meaning of my name, I have used it in my prayers, asking God to bless myself and my family members with youthfulness and strength.

---

13 April 2015

My prayers to Abba Father, were answered. My father was admitted to hospital when he almost suffered from a stroke in his early sixties. Actually he had been admitted twice before. Using some prayers I downloaded from beliefnet. com, I prayed to God to restore his health to youthfulness and to add ten more years to his life. I am grateful, thankful to God for answering my prayer. I just wished I had told my father that I loved him before his death in 2012. His death was too sudden and came unexpectedly, exactly ten years from when I prayed for him. He had run his race and endured to the end. So you see, Jesus has already paid for our ransom and we are all living on 'borrowed time'. Some like my father are lucky to have gone 'home'. I am praying that I will get there...my new home 'The Kingdom of Our Lord & of His Christ'.

I was not close to Eric, our New Sales Executive. I found him very noisy and boastful but still cooperated with him in getting sales leads and quotations done. I didn't want history to repeat itself. Our new Sales Manager, Reuben got along well with Eric.

Things were not going so well for me at my workplace. Reuben was very arrogant and he was a womaniser. He made it seem as though I was interested in him. Prayer kept me going and I still continued to subscribe to 'God's Loving Promises' on beliefnet.com. However, my heart was no longer at my workplace. I missed Shane's jokes. He was like a jester in our office. Days dragged on to months and still no change. I was feeling miserable but tried my best to focus on my work.

Reuben introduced me to his friend, Taufek from one of the airline cargo freight forwarders. Taufek had invited me out for lunch one day on the pretext of giving me airline cargo rates for our company. However, he drove me to his friend's house and asked me to go in and sit for awhile.

"Let's go inside," he persuaded.

Sensing something amiss, I resisted. "I want to go back to the office," I retorted.

"But I need it," he replied angrily.

"I want to go back. Just take me back," I answered firmly as I folded my arms. I was disgusted with his behaviour. I was angry with Reuben too for introducing me to this man. I knew he was behind this. Taufek drove me back after his friend got suspicious. I went in and told Eric what had happened. I was furious. That was it. I had enough. I was up to my neck and I just wanted to quit.

Back in the office, I checked my emails and opened one of my subscriptions from beliefnet.com. I closed it as I did not have the 'mood' to read scripture. I took out my anger on God for what had happened that afternoon. For three days I did not want to open my email subscriptions. I was full of self pity over what had happened. I blamed it on society. The world being a men's world. Still angry, I questioned God,

'Why did you make me a woman?'

Finally on the third evening when I was calmer, I decided to open the email I had closed three days earlier. **The scripture cut me right in the heart. God's response to me was in Romans 9:20.**

You can't imagine how guilty I felt for offending my good, good Father, my Creator God. I repented immediately. I told God that I was sorry for condemning my sexuality. He had made me perfect in his sight. Who was I, the clay, to question God, the potter? Don't anyone of you ever question your sexuality. God has made you perfect in His image. God foreknew what I had been going through. He knew just how I would respond and react. It was no coincidence that, that scripture was kept for such a time and 'revealed' to me at such a time.

Reuben persuaded me to get a car and I did. It took me three months to get my driving license. At first, I thought I could cope but the hefty sum I had to fork out for the car's monthly instalment was too much of a burden. On top of that, I got into several accidents and had to fork out more money for the repairs.

The incident with Taufek, however, did not change my mind about looking for another job. I was resolved to get out of this industry. I missed working under Yahya. Reuben spoke of firing the 'staff' to hire more Chinese workers. To me he was a racist. I could not stand working under him. I should have prayed to God for direction but I was too upset about the things happening around me in the office. I could not focus properly and often times rely on my own understanding and my own strength to do things. Everything had to go 'my way'. I didn't stop and think for a moment to pray for God's guidance and leading. I had made up my mind to leave this industry.

I worked for another three months while searching the advertisements in the local papers for job vacancies. During this time, I got to know Jarnila better. She was very different from Manar, her elder sister. One night, Jarnila came back to the apartment and told me she was pregnant. She told me she wanted to abort the baby but I told her not to. She had tried working at a hotel but it did not work out. I wanted to help her but did not know how. I could only advise her. I told her to wait for my help. I called my cousin up and he prayed for us. The next night, I found out she had already gone to abort the baby. I was too late.

To better understand Jarnila, I had to understand where she came from, where she had been and talk with her more, without judging her. Manar and her sister, Jarnila had become my friends. She brought me to bike races and places with open air music that had bands like the ones in 'Hard Rock Café'. We shared our problems about our search for new jobs. I was sure she would do just fine with her education background in events management.

I went for an interview with a travel agency in Penang and got the job. Only, the posting was in Langkawi, Kedah, a neighbouring state in the northern district. This new posting would mean leaving my family and friends behind to begin a new life. But I was desperate. I didn't realise that I was actually running away from my responsibilities as a daughter, sister and friend. I was to report at my new office on 3rd January 2005. Jarnila and I moved out of University Place to start our new lives.

On 26th December 2004, there was a great tsunami that hit many nations throughout the world and which claimed many lives. Survivors told of the 'foaming' sea when oceans drew back and there were two gigantic waves just moments apart that rose high and hit shores hard, pulling back fishermen's boats, ships, cars and people, and anything in its' path.

My family and I were resting in our home in Tanjong Bungah on that fateful day, unaware of what just hit our little island of Penang. We heard sirens passing by, up and down repeatedly. It was only in the evening when we saw the news on television that we realised what was going on. We learnt that the sirens were actually ambulances ferrying people to the hospitals and that many had died. There was a calm atmosphere in my family household and neighbourhood, as it was a day after Christmas. We had just celebrated the day of the Lord Jesus and we usually stayed in or visited our relatives on 'Boxing Day', the day after Christmas.

(Scripture Reading: Psalm 46:1-3)

I had no sense of fear planning my three hour journey by ferry from Penang Island to Langkawi Island for my new appointment. I was to report to work on 3rd January 2005. Over the next few days, everyone was talking about the 'tsunami'. This was new in Malaysia. Before then, we had always thought that our country was protected from natural disasters. No one in my family household were worried of another possible tsunami hitting our island. God had calmed all of our fears.

(Scripture Reading: Psalm 91:4)

First Flight to Langkawi
... The Red Moon

Langkawi Island...

There is just something mysterious about this island that draws people to it. This island had been my place of escape whenever I faced problems and needed to release stress. I set off from Penang Island to escape to this beautiful island of Langkawi on 2nd January 2005. While most passengers were still asleep, I watched the mist covering the islands from afar as our ferry approached the Langkawi jetty. The skies were bright blue and the sea was sparkling like crystals and their colour like sapphire. It felt as though the islands were calling out to me. It was hard to imagine that a tsunami just hit days ago. We arrived at the Langkawi jetty at about 11:30am.

Aunty Shuang-Li, my mother's college mate, was waiting for me in her car outside the jetty. I was to stay with her until I found a place of my own in Langkawi. It was most gracious of her to open up her home to me. Her husband had passed on years ago and now she lived alone. Her three grown up children had left the island in search of greener pastures. She took me for lunch before we headed to her home in Cameron Ville.

When we arrived at her home, she showed me my room. It was very neat and tidy, and had a cosy feel to it. It was simple with two single beds at each corner of the room and a very large mirror on the floor leaning against two book shelves. I carried the heavy mirror and placed it atop the shelves. Aunty Shuang-Li came in to check if I had settled in already and offered to drive me to check the whereabouts of my new workplace so that I would not have to rush the next day.

It was a day after New Year's Day so most shops were closed. The roads were very quiet as she drove us to look for my workplace. It was on the other side of the island and she showed me the path to my workplace through Malut Hill. It took us about half an hour to reach the place. I loved the location. It had a quiet and peaceful surrounding.

Aunty Shuang-Li advised me that there were no buses to take me to work. Only taxis and it would be too costly. I told her that I would bring my car over to Langkawi from my home in Penang. She then offered to take me to work and pick me up after work over the next few days. She was ever so helpful and accommodating. She even cooked our meals. Sometimes, we went out. I helped with the cleaning and washing up.

Within the first week, she sat me down at the dining area and looked me straight in the eye. She told me that most people who came to Langkawi usually were people 'escaping' from the world. They were usually people who had problems with their relationships, be it with their family or friends. I opened up to her and told her that I was almost married to a loving man. I confided in her about my relationship with Daniel. Aunty Shuang-Li was a good listener. I could talk to her about almost anything. Sometimes she would give me advise. We both loved to share about our faith. Aunty Shuang-Li was a Buddhist.

Over the next weekend, Aunty Shuang-Li and I headed to Penang. She had made arrangements for her friend to pick us up at Kuala Kedah. Aunty Shuang-Li wanted to show me where to send my car, which office to pay for my car and get the proper documents when collecting my car in Langkawi. She preferred to travel via Kuala Kedah as the ferry service from Langkawi to Kuala Kedah was more frequent. There was a ferry service every one and a half hours till 6:30 in the evening.

The ferry ride from Langkawi to Kuala Kedah took about one and a half hours. When we arrived there, Aunty Shuang-Li's friend was already waiting for us. We got into her car and they showed me where United Shipping's office was. Along the journey to Penang by road, Aunty Shuang-Li gave me directions and showed me important signages so that I could remember how to get from Penang Island to Kuala Kedah. Aunty Shuang-Li was a big help as she had been accustomed to travelling in and out of Langkawi via Kuala Kedah and Kuala Perlis by ferry. She had friends and family living in the northern region.

I was excited to be back in Penang but even more excited about my 'new beginning' in Langkawi. Back home, I gave my parents assurance that everything was going well for me in Langkawi and that Aunty Shuang-Li had been of a great help to me. She dropped in to visit my mum for a while before her friend came to pick her up.

When I was alone with my father, I enquired about Jonathan's condition. I was devastated to learn that he had attacked Roger and broke His nose. My father didn't want to elaborate as he thought it might worry me. I was grieved by what had happened in my absence. My father gave me the assurance that everything was under control. I could tell that my father was actually hurting inside to see his 'favourite' son suffering this way.

"Why him? He was the good one," my father confided in me once.

That afternoon, I got to packing my belongings in my car. My books, CDs, clothing and soft toys all cramped up at the back seat of my car and car boot.

That night, Pistachio, my favourite pet cat slipped into the living room through the small opening of the front door and plonked his soft cuddly body next to my head. He slept on my pillow as he usually did when I was around. How I missed Little Pistachio. My little Pistachio! His sweet perfumed body was clean and warm. Pistachio was my most loyal companion. He was always there for me. Too bad I could not take him to Langkawi with me.

The next day, I drove myself all the way to Kuala Kedah and parked my car in front of United Shipping's office. I paid them about RM200.00 for the proper documents and to send my car over to Langkawi. The journey from Penang to Kuala Kedah took about two hours nonstop. I was very calm although this was all new to me. God had given me courage and His peace. I was also thankful that Aunty Shuang-Li had given me very clear directions to Kuala Kedah. Everything had gone smoothly and I boarded the ferry to return to Langkawi. Aunty Shuang Li made her own arrangements to return to Langkawi with her friends. My car would only arrive the next day, on Monday, in Langkawi.

In Langkawi the next day, Aunty Shuang-Li drove me to work and picked me up after work. She took me to the customs area in Tanjung Lembong, along Malut Hill to collect my car. Luckily I did not have to pay for anything upon collection of my car.

I was fortunate that my mother had arranged for me to stay with Aunty Shuang-Li. She gave me a lot of encouragement and taught me to be more independent. Actually, I was a little like her. I enjoyed my independence since moving out of my family home. Aunty Shuang-Li and I kept the weekends free to walk and exercise in the park close to her home, very early in the mornings. Apart from religion, Aunty Shuang-Li had a wide knowledge of health and politics. She was a politician herself, having been the head of the women's group in a party for many years. Now she was retiring to make way for new blood.

My colleagues at the Travel Agency were amazing too. Sandy, our Administrative Assistant became my close friend. We are now friends on Facebook. My job entailed me to travel from hotel to hotel to sell tours. In the first month, I made only RM6000. In the second month, I did better bringing back more than RM10,000. In the third month however, my sales dropped again to less than RM10,000.

At about 7:00 one evening, Aunty Shuang-Li called me while I was still in my office. She asked me to buy a packet of noodles so that she could cook vegetarian noodles for us the next day. It started to drizzle and I could feel the heat rising from the roads. I only closed my office at about 8:30pm and hurried back. I usually took the road through Malut Hill to go back to Aunty Shuang Li's home since there were less cars on this road.

As I drove past a Thai restaurant, I saw 'smoke' rising from the road ahead of me. I looked closely and saw that they formed 'skeletons'.

'I must be too tired. There are no such things as ghosts,' I thought to myself. 'My imagination must be running wild,' I thought again.

I did not stop but drove past the restaurant. Ahead of me was a blue car. As we drove nearer the shipping yard before Tanjung Lembong, I saw the biggest and bloodiest moon ever. It was the size of a living room and it was starring right at me. The blue car turned around the bend and disappeared in sight. Another car, a red one drove past me on the opposite direction. With both cars out of sight, the road was quiet again. But I didn't like the feeling I had then. It was quiet. It was eerie.

Suddenly, there was a strange white glimmer, a silver white beam right across the road about 50 metres ahead of me. I tried to avoid it by driving to the side of the road but my car went bump over it. I looked into my rear view mirror but saw nothing. It wasn't there anymore. I wasn't going to stop there. I held on to the cross of my rosary hanging on the rear view mirror and said a prayer to Abba Father, praying that I did not hurt anything, and whatever it was, it was not hurt. I was going at moderate speed and still there were no cars around that night, apart from the blue and red ones that I saw.

Before I got back to Aunty Shuang-Li's house, I stopped at a shop. I remembered the noodles. Luckily, the shop was still open. I paid the Chinese lady who served me and rushed back. I told Aunty Shuang-Li what I saw at Malut Hill. She looked worried but said nothing. She was the one who gave me the rosary that was hung at my car rear view mirror.

'Thank God I'm still alive! Was it an anaconda or python? It was shimmering. Maybe it was because of the reflection from the blood moon, the reddest I have ever seen.'

'What was it? How could it move so fast?'

All these thoughts razed through my mind. However, Aunty Shuang-Li and I did not talk about it anymore. We were tired and she had waited up for me. Both of us went to bed early as usual.

I did some research and learnt that the date the red moon appeared that year was 28th March 2005.

(Scripture Reading: Revelation 6:12)

The next day, I told my colleagues what had happened to me. They were all very afraid. Mazatul, another Tour Representative, offered to escort me back with her husband in their car. So that evening, they drove ahead of me slowly leading me through Malut Hill. They were caring enough to make sure I got back home safely. When we reached the Langkawi Hospital junction, we went our separate ways.

Three months was up and my probation period was over. My manager let me off on grounds that my sales did not meet my target. He showed me a clause that mentioned that the company could terminate my employment without a reason. This came to me as a surprise. I wasn't given any notice at all. Calmly, I bid farewell to all my colleagues and thanked Aunty Shuang-Li for all her help rendered to me and for being so accommodating.

Aunty Shuang-Li was surprised too that they let me go. I wanted to stay on in Langkawi to try other jobs but Aunty Shuang-Li advised me to get a job in Penang and to return home. She reasoned that the prospects would be better in Penang than in Langkawi. Before I returned to Penang, she gave me two Buddhist 'Dharma' books to read.

I had to make the necessary arrangements to send my car back to Penang via Kuala Kedah. Fortunately, I managed to clear customs without having to pay a cent in taxes when I left Langkawi with all my belongings in the car.

Third Encounter with Evil

I was back home again on Penang Island and this time I was jobless. My parents wondered why I was let off and I could only tell them of the 'Clause'. My sales were probably not good enough, but I was determined to get a job even if it meant I had to do sales.

I lost no time in contacting Daniel and Anastasia. I had not seen or heard from them for three months. I visited them at their home in Lip Sip Garden and took Daniel out for a ride in my car. We talked and parted as friends.

A week later, Anastasia called me to tell me that there was a vacancy at a printing company. She asked me to try for it and told me that they could pay well. I wasn't sure about the position but was determined to get a job fast. I called them up to arrange for an interview and was granted one. Within the next few days, I received good news that I had gotten the job as Sales Executive for their printing company in Georgetown.

Although I was only there for the three months of my probation, I was glad that I could pay my monthly car instalments and have some extra cash. My boss was very honest with me when he told me I was not suited for outdoor sales and that if he had other positions in that company that suited me I was welcome to try out. Unfortunately all positions were recently filled up. That fact didn't disturb me at all and we parted on good terms.

My father understood my situation and lost no time in contacting his friend at a college where he was working at that time, to find out if there were any suitable jobs for me. His friend was a dean of one of the colleges situated at my father's workplace. My father had already been working as their college librarian since he retired from teaching in the late 90's.

I was in luck. I received a call from Mr Tung, Dean of Dalton-Sowers, to attend an interview. At the interview, I learnt that one of their employees had just left to get married leaving her position vacant. I was to promote the Diploma and Degree Programmes to working adults and perform administrative duties whilst offering students counselling and support. I was excited about starting my new job when they hired me. I didn't want to let my father down. Furthermore, this was the kind of job I had been looking for.

I remembered my days in Black Cat Logistics when the Holy Spirit had counselled me about serving my employer as though I was serving God. So I gave my best at every opportunity. The college also gave me a chance to upgrade my skills by allowing me to enrol in their Executive Diploma in Business Management Programme. I was overjoyed. I took my job and studies seriously. I was very thankful and grateful to Mr Tung and my colleagues for the opportunity and support.

My colleagues and I coordinated well to give our best service and support to our students of Business and Human Resource Programmes. On top of that, we also offered other short courses and Certificate Courses. Our most popular Certificate course was on Early Childhood Education. I loved my job. I loved the students and I loved my colleagues.

Five months had passed very quickly. I had already sat for one of my examinations and it was during this time that one of our oldest students, Ganesh, an Indian man who was in his 70's started paying us extra visits to get help on his course in Human Resources. All seemed well, at first. But then, later, he began to become aggressive towards the students. Mr Tung had a word with him and we all tried our best to be as patient with him as we could. I was in-charge of coordinating his course programme so I had more communication with him and his classmates.

One day, while I was on duty during one of the Executive Diploma in Human Resources classes, I had to see their lecturer about their examination or class schedule. I entered the classroom full of students and was speaking with the lecturer when all of a sudden, Ganesh shouted in a raging voice,

"She is lying! She is lying!... You are breaking my heart!" he continued, ripping off his shirt to bare his chest.

There was a slight commotion in the classroom as the students whispered to one another. I was terrified. I was shocked. That incident was enough to draw me back to the time at the freight forwarding company. He reminded me of Taufek. Thankfully no one was harmed that day.

After that incident, Mr Tung gave Ganesh a stern warning. However, that did not stop Ganesh. He would stop by our office on a regular basis. I reasoned it was due to his assignments.

Then one day, he said to me, "I used to be a priest you know."

I did not want to listen to his nonsense so I just nodded my head pretending to hear him. I excused myself and went back to my work.

With the constant harassment from Ganesh, I made up my mind to resign from this job. Without giving much thought and again without seeking divine intervention, I submitted my resignation. I didn't even finish my diploma. I did not want to run in with Ganesh again.

I felt I had had enough working with people. I wanted a change and a new environment so I started looking out for job advertisements in our local newspaper.

I took some time to read the Dharma books from Aunty Shuang-Li and found that some of their ideas contradicted with bible scripture. So after finishing both books, I placed them on a bookshelf in a temple near my home. Having travelled miles and miles to and from Kuala Kedah with my belongings cramped in my car, I also realised that I didn't need some of my belongings. I decided to give away some old clothing and three bags full of soft toys. I drove to a nearby collection centre and left my clothing and toys there. I was finally letting go of some items which previously seemed hard to part with but I kept my Beanie Babies hoping to one day pass them on to my children.

In my search for peace one day, I drove to my old high school because I knew they had a chapel there. But when I got there, I found that the chapel was locked. I walked to the primary school area where the basketball courts were and entered the empty classrooms. It must have been a weekend or some holiday season as there were no students around at that time. Inside one of the classrooms I was shocked to find my eldest brother's full name written on the wall with what looked like blood stains. I had only heard of stories of the British soldiers being tortured in these classrooms during the Japanese occupation and that many had left their marks there by writing their names on the walls. I wasn't afraid but knew it was time to leave.

It was a fine day. After leaving my old high school, I then drove into The Blue Light Sisters in Machang Stone Valley because I remembered that they also had a chapel there. When I got there, I walked right up to the front of the chapel and knelt down, in front of the huge crucifix. I burst into tears and sobbed uncontrollably. All of a sudden, I heard soprano voices, angelic voices in the chapel. It was time for mass and the nuns had entered the chapel singing the entrance hymn. People started walking in to attend mass. I got up from my knees and sat where I was, afraid to move and not wanting anybody to see me. My face was all wet covered in tears. The mass or service lasted for only half an hour and the nuns went off. I got up to leave but was approached by the most senior nun who was visiting from France. She said that most girls like me were welcome there. She introduced me to a Superior there who asked me to stay with them over the weekends. During the next few weekends, I stayed together with the other young girls who were 'called' to become nuns. Only thing was, I was not ready to become one.

We all stayed in one large hall and slept on mattresses on the floor. It was really comfortable and I enjoyed my time there. We were all 'volunteers' to look after the elderly inmates of this home. We were to feed them, bathe them, wash and dry the dishes after the afternoon meals.

The nuns would get up at 5:00am every morning without fail. They would start their morning prayers in a cold room as early as 6:00am and we would pray in that cold air-conditioned room for an hour. After that, we could have our breakfast in the dining area for volunteers before we started feeding and bathing the elderly. After lunch, the nuns sometimes had indoor games in the games room. If they did not have mass in the chapel in the afternoons or evenings, we, the volunteers could go back earlier.

I remember how I suffered from sinusitis then and finished off two boxes of tissue each time we prayed in that air-conditioned room in the mornings. It wasn't that I wasn't a morning person. I found the air-conditioning too cold. On one occasion, I actually saw a demon with ram's horns been enthroned in the room while they prayed. When I closed my eyes to concentrate on praying, I saw the 'gold star' that the priests usually carried during benediction and had an eerie feeling about it. This was not good. My sinus was getting worse.

I shared what I saw with Marion, our Superior, and she told me not to share this with others and to keep it secret. She in turn told me that she saw a python coiling around me while she was praying next to me in that cold room.

'Was this the reason why I suffered from sinusitis?' I wondered.

Back home one evening, after I had returned from 'The Blue Light Sisters,' I found that my parents had gone out and that my mother had left some food in the kitchen for me. I sat down to have my dinner and as I was finishing, Jonathan entered the dining area.

"Have you eaten?" I asked. "There's some food left," I added.

He stood at the other end of our oblong dining table facing me sideways. I noticed his eyes were rolling and knew immediately to avoid him as he was not all himself.

"Who do you think you are?" he burst out angrily, unexpectedly. His voice raised. "You're a woman, you know! Bow at my feet!" he commanded.

Shocked! I stared at him while he continued in a gruff voice (not his own).

"I am Je... Je..., I am the First Son!"

Frightened, as this was the first time Jonathan had manifested, I quickly cleared my plate and walked straight to the sink. Jonathan followed me to the sink. I knew he was manifesting and that it was not his voice. I hurriedly washed up my plate, fork and spoon and noticed a knife in front of me. I turned to look at Jonathan and tried my best to keep calm. I left my plate and utensils to dry on the rack where the knife was and turned to leave the dining room but Jonathan blocked my way. He stood in front of me staring at my forehead.

'Why is he staring at my forehead,' I kept wondering.

Without warning, he smacked my forehead with the back of his palm. I could feel the force and there was a loud thud, but I didn't feel any pain at all. I didn't budge. As soon as his hand touched my forehead, he started shaking and hissing like a snake as though he had touched 'fire'.

'It must be the Holy Spirit's holy fire,' I thought.

Tears started to roll down my face. How my heart ached for my brother, Jonathan!

Jonathan walked away from me and sat down at the dining table. Again, sideways so that our eyes did not meet. Still in tears, I asked him to let me help him.

"John, please let me help you," I pleaded.

I shuddered as there was an evil grin on his face. He was still sitting sideways.

I quickly left the dining room wondering if I had said the right thing.

'How can I help him? What happened to him in Singapore?' I asked myself.

It had been eight years now since he returned from Singapore but he has refused to tell anyone what truly happened there. I waited upstairs in the living room for my parents to come home. Jonathan came upstairs and plonked himself in an armchair. He still looked angry and 'possessed' but tired. He always had this tired look on his face when his skin would turn yellowish green.

Our parents came home late that evening and when I had the chance, I told my father what happened. My father gave a heavy sigh.

Jonathan was now working in a hotel in Georgetown, in the Front Office Department. In fact, he had been working in the hotel industry ever since he returned from Singapore. We rarely had a chance to talk now. Things were different. He was different. Whenever I tried to strike up conversation with him, I would not get a reply from him. His mind would be wondering. He seemed to be in a world of his own. There were times when my parents were called to meet with his superiors at his workplace due to his unpredictable behaviour.

That night, I knew it was not him when he manifested but I could not discern the spirit then. The devil is a liar and had wanted to deceive me by claiming to be Jesus but he just could not say it out. He just couldn't because the name of Jesus is powerful. And I know that the devil hates Jesus and wants to replace him. I noticed too that Jonathan's pupils were dilated revealing only the whites of his eyes. I was fortunate that evening, that the Holy Spirit was with me and that the Spirit of God had protected me from any harm or danger.

Both my elder sisters, Shannon and Joan, had moved to the big city, Kuala Lumpur for work. They were both doing well in their workplaces and getting more exposure and opportunities in that big city. Shannon was still attached to Westpac Digital and was transferred from their Ipoh branch to KL only recently.

Joan, worked as a personnel assistant to a manager while juggling her career as a freelance multimedia designer and artist. She had sold many of her art pieces already.

On my fourth weekend with the nuns, Mother Superior from Sri Lanka asked me to wait for her in her office. She wanted to have a word with me. I waited patiently for her for what seemed like an hour. When she finally came in and I was alone with her, I could not help telling Mother Superior about my family problems. She hastily advised me that 'The Blue Light Sisters' was not the place for me. My heart was crushed. I didn't even get a chance to say goodbye to the other girls. Mother Superior quickly walked me out to my car. I didn't know what to do then but I knew I had to move on.

'Who do I turn to for help?' I cried desperately.

Jonathan needs to be treated but I myself did not believe in medication because the patients looked like zombies. I believed more in natural healing and spiritual healing. I could not help him in any other way except through prayer because I could not understand what he was going through.

Even Little Pistachio was acting strange. I was awoken at 3:00am one night because I couldn't breathe. It was Little Pistachio suffocating me. He had covered my mouth and nose with his little, snow white, furry body. I knew my angels had awoken me as the room was filled with pink clouds like before, during my time in the airline. Yes, I awoke to find Jasper, my other Bengal cat and Little Pistachio's younger sibling, staring at Little Pistachio.

'Are our pets angels? Hmm! Just a thought!'

I was still looking out for jobs when I bumped into an old friend, from my school days. We talked and I told him about my situation. Eu Jin invited me over to his office on the first floor of the building we were in. His office was filled with computer equipment and accessories. He then asked me if I wanted to help him out as his assistant, looking after his office while he was out. His regular assistant, a university student had to take time off to prepare for her coming exams. I agreed to help him while looking out for a permanent job. So the next day, I arrived at his office full of hope and inspiration.

Eu Jin was a successful businessman but never let success get to his head. He was very humble. He showed me the rest of his products and explained to me about his business ventures. He was also into smart home systems, education, printing and graphic designing as well as web-page designing and internet marketing services. He provided solutions for his clients.

We didn't have many walk-in customers; just students wanting to purchase computer accessories or computer games. So I had to go out to promote his products. I concentrated on getting traffic for his websites. I did this by approaching shop owners in shopping malls to advertise their businesses in Eu Jin's web site.

While working with Eu Jin at Ivory Tower, I made friends with some of our regular 'visitors'. One of them was Mark from the United Kingdom who used our office to promote his online travel agency. Another regular visitor was Saravanan, a local Indian guy who just happened to walk by one day.

I noticed that Saravanan was reading a similar book as Aunty Shuang-Li's son in Langkawi. I had seen the book in her son's shelf before. It had the picture of the human body on its' cover. I asked Saravanan what the book was about. He explained that it was about 'meditation' and 'out of body' experiences. I immediately told him that I didn't believe in it but he went on to tell me that he had a 'master' in 'Faith Movers' who could guide him during his meditation and 'out of body' experience.

"Faith Movers? I thought it was a Christian organisation" I uttered.

"Yes, it is," he replied, "Our master guides us through the process of out-of-body experiences and if you do what is evil, he is able to 'cut off' your line so you have to stop! He will travel with you and is able to know what you do," he explained further.

"Cut your line?" I asked. "What if you don't come back and your soul remains in limbo?"

I shrugged at the thought of it.

Saravanan went on to tell me that he was a Hindu who was seeking healing at Faith Movers and that the pastor attending to him was gifted in healing and deliverance. He then invited me to go there with him. He asked me to pick him up at 7:30pm on a Wednesday night when they had healing sessions.

Wednesday night came, and I drove up to the spot where I was to pick Saravanan up. I saw him waiting at a dark area carrying a motorbike helmet in his arm. I immediately chickened out and thought about my safety first since he looked suspicious carrying the helmet. I drove up to him, wound down the window of my front passenger seat and spoke aloud, telling him I had to cancel our plan, giving him some lousy excuse that I was needed back home. Then I drove off as fast as I could.

Saravanan still came over to our office to visit but we spoke less about Faith Movers. Thankfully, he was not angry about that night.

One evening, I got back home just in time for dinner. As I was approaching the front gate of my family home, I saw an owl fly from our fruit tree in the front yard, over the roof of our house. I suddenly had a grave feeling that something bad had happened.

I walked into the house and my parents broke the news that Little Pistachio had died. They had found its' lifeless body in the drain outside our home. My heart sank upon receiving the bad news. I cannot remember if I cried over my Little Pistachio or not but I was deeply saddened by its' death. I had lost my only companion.

Knowing that I always stayed back late in the office, Eu Jin told me about our neighbours who were robbed over the past few months. One was almost raped. So he advised me not to stay back too late in the office.

Over the next few days, things were relatively quiet in the office. Eu Jin had just paid me my salary and had locked up his office, leaving me all alone once again. It was lunch hour and usually it would be quite busy at the restaurants and shops downstairs. I decided to stay in to brush up my product knowledge on smart-home-systems and internet and mobile phone lines. As I was going through the files, a tall, tanned, Malay man stood at the doorway as though looking for something to purchase. Then he walked right up to me at the back of the office.

"Is your boss in?" he asked in Malay, still looking up at the computers and printers.

"No. But he should be back shortly." I replied.

"Do you sell computers?" he asked.

"Yes, we do," I answered, pointing to the computers and printers.

He then placed a rusty machete on the table in front of me and walked over to the side of the table. I stared at the dirty rusty machete wondering what the hell he wanted me to do with it.

Then he walked over to me and asked for my bag. Only then did I realise that this was a robbery.

'Why did he walk away leaving the machete in front of me?' I thought.

At first, I thought he wanted it cleaned. Ha! Ha! What a dumb thought. I calmly gave him my bag and he went off not to be seen again.

'What a weird robber?" I thought. He coolly took his own sweet time trying to get me worked up but I guess I was too tired because I was menstruating. At least my calm demeanour kept me from harm. I probably would have been injured or worse; I could have died trying to fight him off. He was probably high on drugs as I noticed his eye balls were rolling exposing only the whites in his eyes when he was looking up at the printers.

The next day, I related the incident to Eu Jin. Eu Jin pitied me and offered to take me to lunch. He reasoned that the robber could have been asking if we had CCTV's to avoid identification. We had just taken our seats at a café downstairs when a boy snatched my bag off my lap and ran towards his friend waiting on a scrambler nearby. They sped off before anyone could think of doing anything. What tough luck! Robbed two days in a row. Many students were targets of snatch thefts there. Eu Jin was as shocked as I was. It happened so fast and the thieves looked just like students themselves.

A few days later, I closed the office early to go home. I got into my car and placed my handbag on the passenger seat. I saw a Malay man on a scrambler looking at my direction. I quickly locked my car doors and sure enough he rode up next to my window and looked in. He stared hard at me. The robbers had marked me. I took down his plate number and handed it to the security guards of the student hostel next to our office building. They had just started patrolling the area in a royal blue jeep to guard the safety of the university students there. The security guards told me that students' bikes were also stolen from their campus in broad daylight! It was getting dangerous because I was marked by the robbers.

I had stayed back late one night in the office with the shutters closed, so I would be safe inside. I was getting desperate about my job search; depressed about the robberies and praying hard to find a solution for Jonathan's condition. I closed up and left my office at half past eleven that night.

My mind was clouded with worry and anxiety as I was driving back. Without warning, my car stalled at the side of the road. And of all places, the Western Road cemetery!

"God! What now? Why are all these happening to me?" I questioned.

I looked at my watch. My car was stuck in front of the cemetery and it was exactly twelve midnight. I was getting the jitters. I needed to call for help but I didn't have my mobile phone. It was also stolen during the robbery. I had to get a new one. I recalled making the police report and hearing the policeman telling someone that they had about forty break-ins a day. I had to pay a fee to get a new ATM card and was compounded for the replacement of my identity card.

The only thought I had when I was stuck at the cemetery was to call my father, my dear beloved father. But I had to get to a pay-phone. I decided to leave my car at the cemetery. After all, it was not going anywhere.

I walked all the way through Western Road and Brown Road to get to the patrol station to make a phone call to my father. My father awoke from his sleep and a little while later, he met me at the petrol station. We bought some petrol and he took me back to the cemetery to get my car. My father had saved the day. Thank God for my father. He drove back home and I drove back in my car after him.

After that night, I was sure I had to call it quits working with Eu Jin. My situation hadn't improved and I was dead broke. I had to use all my savings to pay my car instalments.

April 2006...

Again, I thought of a change of environment. I wanted to get out of Penang and go back to Langkawi to work. It was a coincidence that there was a job posting in Langkawi at Lang Animal Shelter. I applied for the position of Animal Helper and was called for an interview in mid-April. At the interview in Langkawi, I remember telling the owner, Nadine, that I preferred cats to dogs but she assured me that I would do just fine.

When I got back to Penang, I immediately told my father that I had gotten the job. My father trusted that I knew what I was doing. He believed in me. I lost no time in packing my belongings. I had about a week before I started work at Lang Animal Shelter.

I remember walking downstairs to the dining room and finding our family photo on the floor. Broken glass from the photo frame sprawled on the ground.

'It must have been the wind,' I thought, picking the frame up and clearing the pieces of glass from the floor. I placed the frame on the bookshelf and arranged the photo in place. It was our family photo.

Jonathan appeared from the kitchen and stood in front of me. I looked into his eyes and saw that this time, they were darkened, all black. He was manifesting again. I thought I saw him grow into a bigger man. His hair thick, dark and curly. His face more hardened and angular like a square. Then he spoke in a gruff voice, "Who put this photo here?"

"I did. Jonathan, it is our family photo!" I retorted. "Did you break it?" I asked.

He walked off without an answer.

Second Flight to Langkawi ... Runaway

May 2, 2006,

I reported for work with my new employer at Lang Animal Shelter in Langkawi. I did not know what to expect but I was full of enthusiasm to face any challenges that would come my way.

Nadine, my new employer, was owner of resorts in Langkawi and Kuala Lumpur. She loved caring for dogs especially strays and opened this shelter to take in unwanted dogs and cats.

I couldn't meet up with Aunty Shuang-Li as I was busy most of the time. I stayed at the staff quarters within our working premises and would rest on my days off. At times, I would shop for toiletries from nearby stores. I didn't go out much.

I remember Nadine 'introducing' me to the dogs. She had to allow me to familiarise myself with the dogs or rather, let the dogs get used to my scent and presence. Grant and Lady were the first ones to greet me. Some dogs, Rusty, Charlotte and Pippa were temperamental and could bite, but luckily these dogs were all chained up or kept in their enclosures.

The more friendly ones were let free to run within their enclosed areas in the bungalow and around the surrounding compounds outside the bungalow. Most of the dogs were quite shy and were not used to humans yet. They were not friendly with strangers because they were strays.

Poppy and Barney had to get around on wheels because their hind legs were paralysed. They were unlucky to have been involved in accidents but lucky enough to have met Nadine. She showered them with tender love and care. Although both dogs still had the use of their fore legs, they could not move around easily. They had to drag their bodies through the rough surfaces on the ground. Nadine and her partners had 'rescued' these dogs and had them fitted with 'wheels' to enable these dogs to be more mobile.

Nadine's bungalow was home to seventy dogs. They were all kept within the compound of the bungalow. And because Nadine ran a resort, other than Lang Animal Shelter, we, the Animal Helpers, had to ensure that the dogs were not noisy or else the noise might put off some guests. My duties included feeding and caring for the dogs, cleaning them and cleaning after them. Sweeping, mopping and some light gardening. There were also some hundred cats to be fed. The cats were caged across the bungalow. They were released every morning and would return to their cages every evening during feeding time.

The dogs and cats had their own personalities. Some were shy and playful, while others were moody and grouchy. I still prefer cats because the are cleaner. Their coats of fur smell like perfume. Somehow, I did not have the same compassion for the dogs and cats like Nadine did. I loved cats and dogs but I didn't know how to nurse them. I would avoid them if they had any illness because I was afraid that what they had might be contagious.

I felt bad when my own pet cat, Tess died. Her stomach had developed sores and she smelt so bad, I didn't dare go near her. We should have taken her to the vet earlier but regretfully, we weren't aware of the sores till it was too late. Sadly, she died after two months of 'suffering'. She had been our companion for almost twenty years, during which, she had borne litters of kittens in our home. Our family home was always filled with cats. Some we kept, others we had to give away at the local market. Thankfully, those cats would always find good homes.

I was aware of my lack of compassion during my time in the airlines. So one of the gifts I prayed for was for the gift of compassion. I realised that I had grown cold. I was grateful to the Lord to be able to put this gift to good use when I was caring for the elderly at 'The Blue Light Sisters'. An elderly Eurasian lady had told the nuns there that I was pleasant and gentle. This made me aware of the presence of the Holy Spirit and His work in my life. I desired God's presence more and more. The sad thing was, I was usually too preoccupied and tired from work to pray while I was attached to Lang Animal Shelter. I did not have inner peace because I forsook my prayer life. I got lazy.

While I was feeding the dogs one afternoon, I almost stepped on a long greyish black snake. It was about two metres long and it slithered at the gate entrance between the two enclosures. I had to walk back to a table to leave the dogs' food bowls there. I thought of getting a bamboo to kill the snake but I didn't have the guts to. Hastily, I called Hahn-Ne, my colleague and fellow Animal Helper, because she had the experience of 'dealing' with snakes. She came by as fast as she could. Grabbed the bamboo and started hitting the snake until it was dead. Then she threw it out at the garbage. Nadine learnt about the snake and told us it was probably a non-venomous snake. It definitely wasn't a cobra.

At 3:00pm one fine day, while I was on duty in the bungalow I noticed that Grant and Darlie were looking hard at something on the ground and that the birds above them were chirping frantically. I had just released Darlie while Rocky remained chained at the bench. Upon checking, I found Grant, our friendly companion standing over a shiny black cobra. The cobra seemed to be afraid of the dogs as it had its' head buried in the ground. I did not know what to do. Then I heard a voice tell me, "Go get the bamboo!"

I listened to the voice and rushed to get the nearest bamboo. In my heart I was wondering whose voice that was. It was only the dogs and myself. Boy! Was the bamboo heavy! It was almost comical. I returned to the scene but the snake was gone.

Nadine came by shortly after to ask what the noise was about and I told her about the cobra. She made me check under all the empty barrels at the poolside to make sure the cobra hadn't slithered underneath them. Luckily I did not find any cobras. I would not have known what to do if I had found one.

I was beginning to have the jitters about bumping into snakes. The more I thought about it, the more angry I was. I did not have the guts to kill a snake. I started asking myself if I was ready to work with people again, if I could trust them.

While I was at Lang Animal Shelter, I had a strangest dream. I dreamt that I hit a black snake until its' stomach burst open. The snake died but out of its' stomach came...not one but two, three...seven or maybe more, tiny little black snakes. All of the same kind. I stopped counting and awoke immediately from the dream. The snake was 'pregnant'! Whatever could this dream mean?

The next morning, I related my dream to Hahn-Ne. She bluntly told me that snakes lay eggs. They don't give birth. 'Oh, yeah!' I thought. But the 'one' in my dream did give birth…to about seven or more other little snakes. I was beginning to regret calling Hahn-Ne to kill that 'harmless' snake. I wondered if my dream had anything biblical about it, but I did not inquire from the Lord about it.

Plans were underway to move the dogs to a nearby sanctuary on a hill. It was only a matter of months before the completion of the new sanctuary for the dogs. At about this time, I was asking myself if I should take my father's advice to return to Penang to look for work again. I had reassured him that I was fine in Langkawi. I didn't want to leave Langkawi as I loved this place and was drawn to it.

On one of my days off, I had to pick one of my colleagues up from the jetty. Over there, I saw that there were many vacancies at the stores. I enquired within Chen Optical Store regarding their vacancy for a Shop Assistant. Mr Chen was urgently looking to recruit someone for his store selling branded sports and casual attire, as well as Oakley sunglasses. We exchanged numbers and I promised to get in touch with him soon. I didn't think much of it as I wasn't sure of my future plans yet. I wasn't ready to leave my present job at Lang Animal Shelter.

Back at work, I remember how I loved taking Diamond out for walks. She was old and weak but she was a good dog. Once, I stumbled and fell onto the ground letting go of my grip on her leash. I had expected her to run off but she turned and looked at me and waited for me. I had prayed hard for her to be strengthened and to recover from her illness and could see the results. She was getting stronger by the day and was soon off the drips. My colleagues and I usually took her by the lane next to the paddy fields so she could ease herself. Nadine had made me aware of the spectacular views of the horizon here, especially during the sunsets.

There was a black Persian cat that loved playing on top of Hahn-Ne's hut, making her dogs bark wildly. Hahn-Ne called her Onyx. The three dogs kept in Hahn-Ne's compound were Leo, Rex and Lucky. I started taking Onyx back to my staff quarters. I tried to hide her from my housemate, Oo, at first but she soon found out as Onyx did not like the idea of been locked up in the room. She loved to play. And Oo was not too pleased about the banging on the door.

Still, I tried to make Onyx stay with me but one night, she kept banging on the door to be let out. I let her out about 3:00am that morning and went back to sleep. I only found out the reason Onyx was behaving so strangely the next morning when I went to work. I had reported to work earlier than usual but felt that my back was all wet when I got in. So I went to use the bathroom to clean myself. I found that my back was covered with blood and as I sprayed my back with water, a leech fell off. I panicked upon seeing the leech and without thinking, I poured clorox on the leech and hosed it down the drain.

After a few weeks, while trying out some swimming suits at a store, I noticed that the 'triangular' mark on my back had disappeared. I had knocked the lower back of my spine against the corner edge of a cupboard years before and there had been a mark on my back since then. Well, until now. 'Oh! Why did I pour Clorox on the leech?'

It had helped clear the blood clot off my back.

Then late one evening, while I was resting in my quarters, Hahn-Ne came knocking at my door. She asked me to find Nadine at the compound next to her hut. Nadine had sent for me because there was a cobra in that compound. When I got there, I saw two kitchen staff armed with bamboo sticks ready to strike a king cobra. Nadine called me over and asked me to stand in front of the cobra to distract it. The cobra was poised to strike but luckily our kitchen staff acted swiftly. They both struck the head and body of the cobra but did not kill it. I believe they released the snake into the open fields behind the resort. Thank God nobody was bitten by that cobra. Thank God none of the dogs were harmed either.

On another occasion, I had just started my shift one evening and it came to Pippa's turn to go for a walk. As I reached out to put a leash on Pippa's collar, she sank her tooth right into my right palm without any warning. It felt like a nail had pierced right through my right palm. I stood there holding my palm in one hand,wanting to scold Pippa but I backed off seeing that it was going to lunge forward and attack me. I also noticed that its eyes were circled with a shimmering blue light. I opened the door behind me slowly and got out of that room as fast as I could closing the door after me.

As always, I called Hahn-Ne to the rescue. She helped me wash the wound and applied some Betadine solution over the wound. It was too late to see a doctor as the clinic was already closed.

Nadine came by to check on how we were both doing. I could still carry out my duties watching the dogs so Nadine told Hahn-Ne to go back to her hut. They both left and Nadine headed back to the resort to entertain her guests. She probably had an important function that night.

As soon as Nadine left the bungalow, a fierce storm started brewing. There was loud crashing of thunder and fierce lightning. Strangely enough, all the dogs remained calm and quiet except for Pippa. I do not know how it managed to get out of its enclosure but it did. I found the door left ajar.

"Oh, no! This has never happened before!" I gasped.

Then I saw Poppy snarling at Pippa. Pippa had made its way halfway upstairs. It was terrified of the thunder and lightning and was trying to hide in Nadine's room upstairs. I had to call for help again. Nadine and Hahn-Ne came over and one of them carried Pippa back to its enclosure. Hahn-Ne sat with Pippa till the storm calmed and cleared.

The very next morning, Oo drove me to the nearest clinic which was close to the airport. My whole right arm was stiff. Dr Singh examined my wound and told me I was lucky it had missed my nerves. None of my nerves were damaged. The doctor gave me a jab in the arm and some medication for the pain.

Work went on as usual. Praise God, I was able to work with my hands and feet. No serious damage done. I didn't have to wait long for the wound to close and heal completely. But it left a scar on my hand.

Things started getting busy at Lang Animal Shelter when we had to move the dogs to their new sanctuary. Nadine's friends came in their jeeps to help ferry the dogs to their new home. They had to make several trips up the hill and back to the resort until almost all the dogs were transferred.

Oo and I were sent to the new sanctuary to care for the dogs. After two weeks Nadine sent for me. I had to return to the resort to look after the dogs that remained in the bungalow. When I was leaving the new sanctuary, I saw that they had hired new Animal Helpers to work there. Nadine wasn't sure whether to place Rex at the bungalow or at the new sanctuary. I could not get any sleep when I had to look after Rex for two nights. Rex was a good dog. He did not bite and he loved people. But I just could not handle him. I did not know how to keep him quiet at night.

Finally on 19th October 2006, I snapped. I was on duty at the bungalow and I started having thoughts that someone was trying to kill me. My fear came out as rage as the more I thought about my encounters with the cobras, the more convinced I was that someone was out to harm me. I went back to my room, packed my belongings and started kicking my bags. I was so mad. I went over to the resort to inform Nadine that I was leaving. It was about 9:00pm when I asked the receptionist to get me a taxi.

Then I called Mr Chen of Chen Optical Store and told him that I would work for him. I was in luck because he arranged to pick me up at Kuah town in front of his other branch in Karuna. I waited for about an hour before the taxi came. I only know that it was almost 12 midnight when my taxi arrived at Karuna. Mr Chen was there waiting for me. He let me stay in his staff hostel together with another Malay staff of his. Jana, my new colleague had gone back to her village so I had to stay alone that night.

7th June 2019

I often think of how Nadine and Lang Animal Shelter are doing. I trust that they are all well. Now that I am better, I would love to visit the shelter again. Perhaps in the near future.

Face to Face with the Devil

I worked with Chen Optical from 20th October 2006 till 15th December 2006. During this time, I was running around like a headless chicken. I had forgotten about the nightmare I had in 2004, about the experiment and the headless chickens. Until today, I do not know why I felt as though someone had wanted to kill me in the month of October 2006.

I was calm when I met Mr Chen at Karuna the night of 19th October 2006. I was tired but assured of my safety by Mr Chen's kind and considerate demeanour. I felt relieved. Mr Chen handed me the keys to the staff hostel and told me to report to work at his shop below the hostel at 8:30am, the next day. I went upstairs to my hostel. Had my shower. Then slept undisturbed till the next morning. I was too exhausted that night. The hostel was big and spacious with very little furniture. The kitchen was really clean and tidy. I was alone in that big space that night but I had a sense of assurance for my safety unlike how I felt that night at Lang Animal Shelter.

October 20, 2006,

I reported for work at Chen Optical. I was punctual and so was Jana, my hostel mate. Jim, our Supervisor arrived shortly after and we introduced ourselves. I told Jana that I would be living in the hostel with her.

Over the next few days, Jim and Jana taught me my duties. I was later transferred to Mr Chen's store at the Jetty

Point selling sports and casual apparel as well as Oakley sunglasses. Mr Chen allowed me to stay with his family in their home in Cameron Ville. I followed Mr & Mrs Chen to their workplace daily. I later found out that Mr Chen was Aunty Shuang-Li's cousin.

Feeling homesick one night, I called my father to see how the family was doing. In the background, I could hear my mother's voice... 'What does she want now?' I heard her utter in a harsh tone.

My heart wanted to cry out to my father, that I wanted to go home to Penang to be with them but my heart sank upon hearing my mother's words. I wasn't earning much and had to continue paying for my monthly car instalments. I couldn't go home empty handed now.

'I have to work my way up again,' so I thought to myself then.

I decided then and there to look for another job. I felt I wasn't doing well at the store. I was also getting restless because I was starting to have strange conflicting thoughts that were harmful. It was all so confusing and I could not find peace within myself.

One afternoon while walking in a mall, I inquired from the chef of the restaurant I often frequented whether he knew of anyone renting out rooms. He asked me to come back the next day. I met him again the next day and he told me that he had a room at his apartment and that he would rent it out to me for RM150 a month. Someone had just moved out and the place had to be cleaned a little. I was desperate, so I immediately accepted the offer and that I would move in right away.

I walked around town nearby Mr Chen's optical shop in Karuna to look for other jobs and finally found one I liked. The store owners were a Muslim couple making bridal gowns and selling wedding gifts. I tendered my resignation at Mr Chen's store and started working at the bridal shop immediately after I moved into my new place.

Work was good and things were quiet at the apartment. Then tragedy struck on a weekend, on my day off. I was reading newspapers in the living room of the apartment when my housemate's friend entered the apartment. I continued reading the newspapers ignoring him as I did not know him. This stranger went straight to the master bedroom. He came out right away wearing just shorts and walked up towards me. He suddenly grabbed my left hand and tried to pull me into his room. I managed to pull myself away. He walked back to his room in a huff. I was scared and thought I should go back into my room. Quietly, I walked to my room but then, something made me turn back. I looked back at the strangers room and saw another guy in shorts. Just that I had seen this guy before when I missed the ferry to Langkawi. I thought 'it' might be a ghost since I only saw the back of this person every time and 'it' had a way of appearing and disappearing in the eeriest manner. Well you know the saying, 'Curiosity killed the cat.' I 'died' that day.

I was curious to know whether 'it' was a ghost or a real person, so I walked straight into the stranger's room. I looked around but this other 'person' was gone. Instead I saw pills all strewn across the dressing table. I was about to walk out when the stranger came out of the bathroom. He smiled when he saw me. I tried to run out of his room but for some reason I do not understand, I could not move a muscle. I was limp like a puppet on a string.

Knowing something was not right, I prayed in my heart, 'Precious Blood of Jesus, cover me!' To my horrors, there stood before me the ugliest demon with horns like a goat in place of the stranger. It had a shimmering blue light around it. It was ultramarine blue. The same kind of colour I had seen in the dogs eyes, Pippa, when she bit me. I kept blinking my eyes to make sure I was seeing right. I was suddenly overcome with fear, still wondering why I couldn't move or speak. Then the stranger spoke. He asked me to pick up the floor mat and smell it, which I did. I had become his puppet. 'What is happening to me?' I thought. The stranger then asked me to lie down on his mattress and I followed his command like a puppet.

That night, I was raped three times by this stranger. At first, I thought that he was going to kill me. I was overwhelmed with a sense of fear. He hurt me. I passed out every time he 'touched' me. In my heart, I kept pleading with God to make him stop. The strangest thing was that I was not alone. I felt as though my body, spirit and soul had separated. I was covered by a 'divine being' and 'He' was protecting me. He was 'covering' me. At one point while I was awake, my usual loving 'Take care, I love you' self, turned into one full of hate. It became 'Take care! You better watch out! I'm gonna kill you!'

But then the 'Divine Being' whom I know is Jesus Christ controlled my mind and my emotions, and kept me calm. Something had entered me and was trying to possess me, but Jesus covered me. He was taking the strikes for me and I felt less pain. I could only feel peace and calm.

Whenever I awoke, I would keep on blinking my eyes as the stranger kept switching back and forth from the demon to a man. The demon's teeth and mouth were like 'black tar'. I was very tired, hurt and angry when he tried to rape me again. But I was suddenly overwhelmed by Jesus' divine presence again and I heard 'myself' whisper to this stranger these three magic words, "I love you."

Immediately, the stranger dropped me and I watched the devil turn its back on me in disgust. It turned away from 'me'. It turned away from God. Of course!... It was evil. It could not love. It was lustful. And it was lust of the eyes that got me into this tragedy in the first place. I was relieved when the stranger dropped me but also a little confused.

When I started coming to my senses, I began 'questioning' him, the stranger. I asked him for his name and age. To which he responded, "Michael! Everyone calls me Michael. I'm 43."

"Are you 63?" I questioned. Because he sometimes switched to look like an old man with tarred teeth. I can't remember what else I asked him but he must have thought I was crazy.

Michael woke me up and told me to get dressed. Still fearful of him and under his 'spell', I obeyed. In fact, I obeyed his every instruction. I had become his 'slave'. When we got to his van downstairs the apartment, I tried to resist. I knew it was wrong to enter into a 'stranger's car' and I was afraid. But when he came near, I always had a sense of fear that he would kill me. So I obeyed.

Michael then drove me to a restaurant. There he ordered a whole steamed fish for me to eat. He said that he had a 'meeting' that night so he didn't touch any food while we were there. I was afraid at first and thought that he might poison me. He kept on persuading me to eat. Michael told me that I had slept for six hours straight and asked about my work. I told him that I worked in one of the shops in Karuna and he offered to take me to work the next day. Now, we had a normal conversation and I ended up eating the whole fish.

The next day, he drove me to work and brought me home after work. The day after, I insisted on walking to work myself. On my way to the bridal shop, my workplace, I chanced upon a 'church', 'Jesus Saves Mission'. They had service on Thursday and I was not going to miss it. Thursday came and I walked myself to church that evening. There were only about eight people attending the service including myself and the pastor. Even so, the hymns were lively. I was so glad to be there. They even invited me to their Christmas lunch at the Thai restaurant on the ground floor nearby.

Michael picked me up after church service because he wanted to introduce me to his daughter. When we got to the eatery, I don't know why I could not even look at his daughter. Something within me made me feel angry towards Michael and his daughter. She was only four years old. I didn't want to know any of his friends or family. His daughter didn't seem to like being in his presence either. Again, I felt like wanting him dead. Later that night, he spoke to me. He explained that he was a divorcee and that he was looking for someone to look after his daughter. He made it clear that he wasn't interested in marriage. I could only listen quietly. I didn't say a word. Then, he apologised for what happened that night. I had no reaction. Michael never touched me again and thankfully we slept in separate rooms.

That weekend, Michael took me to the supermarket to buy some groceries. I suddenly felt like running away but when he stood towering over me, I was again overwhelmed with fear. I felt like there was a magnetic force over my head. Something was trying to control me. I hated walking in front of him because each time I would feel something pulling over the crown of my head.

Back at the apartment, Michael pointed out to me that I had been eating worms. My eyes were blinded with darkness. I looked carefully at the banana in my hand which we bought from the supermarket and sure enough, there were worms in them. I didn't squirm or flinch. I had no reaction whatsoever but I kept wondering, 'Why couldn't I see the worms before?' I asked myself.

That night, I called my cousin Aaron and told him what had happened. My cousin advised me to get out of the apartment and come home to Penang as soon as possible but I did not know how. I felt like I had no way out. I felt trapped. I thought that Michael would kill me if I tried to 'run'. Aaron's advise remained in my heart. I thought hard about it. I just needed the courage to leave…

I remember purposely leaving my passport on the kitchen table to see what Michael would do. Sure enough he picked it up and went through it. He did not see me hiding behind the door. I wanted to know if he was a trafficker or pimp since he did not share much about his work even though I had asked him.

The next evening, Michael took me out. We were met by two foreign men. He told me that they were his 'boatmen'. They started conversing in a foreign language which sounded like Cambodian. The boatmen were definitely Asians but they were not locals.

The following week, I attended church service at 'Jesus Saves Mission' again. This time I told Pastor Tung and his wife about Michael and asked if our 'relationship' was normal. They were very worried for me and insisted to speak with Michael so they could understand what Michael wanted with me. My heart leapt in relief. They did not judge me and at least I had found some people I could trust and rely on. Pastor Tung's wife handed me RM50.00 to buy my ferry ticket back to Penang. They wanted to be sure I was safe. They waited for Michael to come and Pastor spoke with him. I heard Michael telling them that I was crazy and that he did not know why I called him 'Uncle'. Yes, I know I had been acting strange since the day I was bitten by the dog and more so when I got raped. I called him 'Uncle' because his face kept switching back and forth from a forty-something to a sixty-something year old man.

I thanked Pastor Tung and his wife for their help and told them I would be going home on Christmas day after the lunch. Michael said nothing and took me back to the apartment.

On the weekend, I got myself a ferry ticket to Penang. I contacted my parents to inform them that I would be coming home. I told my father that this man, Michael had harmed me and that I was scared of him. I could feel pain in my father's voice. I did not want to let him worry but who else could I turn to or trust? My parents called up Aunty Shuang-Li to check on me and they wanted to know more about what Michael had done to me. I spoke with Aunty Shuang-Li but I do not understand why I was again overwhelmed with fear that Michael would kill me. I told her that he could hurt her if she came to the apartment. She thought I was out of my mind and was talking nonsense. It is true. I wasn't making sense at all. I was too frightened.

Coming Home

December 25, 2006,

On Christmas morning, I walked to the only Catholic church in town for Christmas Mass. I felt a real need to attend 'church'. The local folk at the market gave me the directions to the church as I hadn't been there before. I got there early. During the sermon, I tried hard to listen to the priest and get a gist of what he was trying to impart but I felt like a zombie. Nothing was going into my head. As I was leaving the church building after mass, I met Tania, an ex-staff of Lang Animal Shelter. We exchanged greetings and wished each other well. I remember wishing in my heart that I could feel Christmas again. It just didn't feel right.

I met up with Pastor Tung, his wife and the other members of 'Jesus Saves Mission' church at the Thai Restaurant, just below the church. Christmas lunch was really good. I felt accepted even though I wasn't a member of their church. I felt I belonged there. We were only a small group of people and I felt peace and love amongst them. Pastor gave thanks and blessed the food. We had a scrumptious spread of Thai food. It was different from the same traditional Christmas meals I used to have at home.

February 5, 2020,
I managed to gain contact with Ps Tung and his wife again after their event organiser chose my workplace to hold their conference. Ps Tung has since moved out from Langkawi and is now the pastor for his Kuala Lumpur and Ipoh church branches.

> I have been so blessed to have met them at 'Jesus Saves Mission' and God has been so good to me. I wish them well and I hope that their church grows in abundance and that God will show them His favour as they increase in numbers and become fruitful in spirit. I pray that they will always have opportunities to share the gospel of peace with others. They have been a blessing to me.

Pastor Tung and his wife drove me to the Langkawi Ferry Terminal after lunch. I boarded the ferry to Penang. My parents were at the ferry terminal on Penang Island waiting for me. They were pleased to see me but didn't say much during our drive back to our home.

Back home, I found that my parents had prepared a room for me downstairs next to the dining hall and kitchen. It had been my sisters' room before. I moved all of my belongings into their room. My two elder sisters, Shannon and Joan, were still working in Kuala Lumpur, the biggest city in Malaysia. Roger, my younger brother, was now working in a factory as an engineer. His job paid well because he had to handle big projects. James, my youngest brother, had gone to USA to further his studies and was now working there. I hadn't seen or heard from him since 2003. Last I heard from him was when I sent him a package of Malaysian food pastes. My father had wired some money to him for his studies. Christmas was quiet because my siblings were all away. It was just me and Jonathan, my eldest brother.

I informed my parents about my plans to return to Langkawi to collect the remainder of my belongings. They were both surprised and angry that I still wanted to go back but I was adamant. I didn't want to leave anything behind. My parents immediately contacted Aunty Shuang-Li to arrange accommodation at her place for one night. All was settled. We would go to Langkawi end of December 2006.

The day before we went to Langkawi, Michael called me to see how I was doing. He told me that I was always welcome to stay at his place. If only I had the guts to tell him off. Michael had left strange instructions for me via the phone. He wanted me to put on the red slippers in his bedroom before I left Langkawi. I told him I would be back to collect my belongings. I was clear-headed now and I did not want anymore trouble. So I did not obey his instructions when we got to his unit. I didn't even want to open his room door to see if he was in. I just wanted to get out of there quickly, put everything behind me and get on with my life.

> **As I recall, Michael was the guy by the poolside at GC Hotel, who pretended to be of royal blood, back in the year 2000. I also remember that Michael has six fingers on one hand. Matthew my ex-boyfriend was also born with six fingers and six toes on each hand and foot.**

I tried to stop my mother from opening Michael's room door but I was too late. She had opened Michael's room door to have a peek. Thankfully, she didn't go in or put on the red slippers and thankfully, I didn't have the urge or curiosity to do so either. I didn't want whatever evil was lurking in there to follow us back home. Ben, my housemate, the chef returned to collect the house-key from me. I had settled my rent for the month.

My parents helped me carry all my belongings downstairs where Aunty Shuang-Li was waiting for us. We stayed with her for the night. The very next morning, Aunty Shuang-Li followed us back to Penang.

Back in our home in Penang, Aunty Shuang-Li and my mum sat me down in the dining room and advised me to look for a job in Penang. My parents wasted no time looking around for jobs for me. Barely a month had passed when my father came home with news that there was an opening at Wayne Logistics. Our neighbour, Mr Joseph Wilson, was the Managing Director of Wayne Logistics and he was prepared to offer me a position in his office at the Penang Cargo Terminal. I immediately contacted Mr Wilson to set an appointment for an interview. Thankfully, I got the job. I was overjoyed at being given the opportunity to work with Wayne Logistics on such short notice.

Mr Wilson personally drove me to work on my first day and introduced me to my colleagues. The following day onwards, I drove myself to the cargo terminal. My job as Customer Services Executive entailed me to follow up on our customers complaints, claims and outstanding payments. At times, I had to travel to their factories in the northern region.

Back home, I started getting nightmares about the devil trying to harm me. I could even feel something on me when I slept at night. Once, 'it' even tried to strangle me and 'it' only stopped when I cried out to Jesus for help.

At my workplace, I felt something tugging at my bra straps. My bra suddenly came loose and I had to rush to the ladies to fix it. In the toilet, a 'force' pushed me up against the wall. In anger, I said, "No!" and it stopped.

I was having a hard time trying to figure out what was happening to me that I couldn't think clearly. I started staying back till late in the evening at my workplace. Sensing something amiss, Mr Wilson called me to his office one afternoon. He brought out his bible and held it up. He advised me to read the bible. I kept quiet. I didn't even own a bible then. The only time I had read any scripture was when I subscribed to 'God's Loving Promises' and 'The

Sayings of Jesus' on beliefnet.com, while I was attached to Black Cat Logistics back in 2002.

Sometimes, Mr Wilson would drop in the office to see how I was doing. On two occasions, he bought me oyster noodles for dinner. Although I was grateful to Mr Wilson, I knew I couldn't stay long at Wayne Logistics. Something wasn't right and I felt miserable. I felt burdened and weighed down.

I called it quits when I started getting warts on my stomach and genitals. I was terrified as I thought I had contracted AIDS. I tendered my resignation right away. I worked for Wayne Logistics for only four months, from Feb 21, 2007 till June 26, 2007.

Feeling fearful of my health, I went for a full medical check-up at PEN Medical Clinic. I told the nurse who inspected me that I was raped and she advised me to see a psychiatrist. The results showed that I was perfectly healthy and that I didn't have AIDS. Still the warts didn't go away. Instead they spread to my face. It was ugly. I had these thick black warts all over my face, stomach and genitals.

Since the medication from PEN Medical Clinic didn't help clear the warts, I went to Burmah Clinic to be examined again. I stopped by the Catholic church nearby to see my parish priest, Fr Murray, before going to the clinic. I remember telling Fr Murray about the vision I had of the demon being enthroned while I was at Machang Stone Valley. I also told him about my dreams and nightmares in 2004. He told me that my dreams and nightmares were probably about me and that I had to pray to God to discover the meanings to the dreams and vision. He advised me to pray about them as he could not discern their meanings.

After getting some cream from Burmah Clinic for the warts, I walked to Baptist Bookstore to get a bible. I had remembered Mr Wilson's advice to 'read the bible'. This bookstore has got to be the oldest Christian bookstore in town. And yet, I had never stepped inside the store before. Timidly, I walked into the bookstore and asked the shop assistant if they had a bible for beginners. A lady who was also browsing around was kind enough to introduce me to the New Living Translation Bible by Tyndale. She explained that it was the easiest to read and understand. It was only MYR67.00. I thanked her for her help and drove home with my new bible. I bought my very first bible on July 9, 2007.

Without any assistance or guidance from anyone, I started reading the Bible. I had unpacked all my belongings which I brought back from Langkawi and made a calendar with 'The Sayings of Jesus' and 'God's Loving Promises'. (I still keep them neatly in a file). For the next four months, I stayed home without work reading the bible to occupy my time. I helped my mother to wash and hang the clothes out, and fed the cats.

During this time, my elder sister, Joan, came home for a visit. She brought with her a gift for me. It was a bible. The exact same bible that I had bought for myself. In it, Joan wrote in her own handwriting, the words "For the Gift of You".

Joan later found out from my mother that I had been raped. She went ballistic when she knew of my genital warts. I tried to tell her that something else was happening to my body. Something supernatural. I noticed that as I read the Bible, my warts were disappearing. Somehow, I couldn't get this through to my family members. My sister kept screaming at me for 'flirting' around. My father was silent. The only thing that kept me going was God's word. Somehow, I felt refreshed and connected to the Word that was my only hope and help. I felt encouraged to continue reading the Holy Scriptures and determined to finish reading the Bible from cover to cover.

The Holy Spirit is not just pure and holy. He is a powerful being. He was my helper and encourager during these times. I could feel the power of the Holy Spirit working in my body. God was cleansing me outwardly and inwardly. As the Holy Spirit counseled me, he told me that my DNA was being cleansed.

(Scripture Reading: Hebrews 4:12)

I was working at the airlines when I contracted the chicken pox virus at 21 years of age. Our panel doctor at that time wanted to help me so he recommended that I take 'Zovirax', a medication that would help suppress the symptoms of chicken pox. More than 10 years had passed and now the Holy Spirit was counseling me that all the 'dirt' was sticking to my bones and that God was healing and cleansing my bones and DNA.

When my face and body were finally cleared of the warts, I decided to go back to work. I worked for Baskin Robbins for two months before Joan asked me to follow her back to Kuala Lumpur to teach English at a Centre. My mother's good friend, Aunt Susannah, was a teacher at ELS in Kuala Lumpur. Her colleague was on maternity leave so they needed a replacement as soon as possible. I agreed to fill in this temporary position and followed my sister back to Kuala Lumpur where I worked for the month of December 2007.

Joan drove me to my new workplace in Kuala Lumpur for two days before allowing me to use her car to go to work for the whole month of December. I had two Korean students to teach. Aunt Susannah offered advice and guidance when and where necessary. She had studied in the same teaching college as my mum. Aunt Susannah advised me to sell my own car when I got back to Penang, after she learnt of my financial woes.

Joan was erratic. She would be nice one moment and shouting angrily the next. I decided to return to Penang as I didn't feel comfortable staying with Joan in Kuala Lumpur.

Upon returning to Penang, I met up with my cousin, Aaron, to get my daily dose of God's word. He showed concern about me and told me not to waste my life. He said that I ought to get married soon. He was truly concerned and he was not joking about me getting married. He brought me to the 'Salvation Bookstore' and asked me to pick out a tape that I liked and paid for it. The album that I picked was titled 'Shake The Dust Off'. It was my first Christian tape. At home, I played the tape over and over until the tape spoilt. I even borrowed some of Shannon's Christian tapes. One of our favourite albums was, 'The Power and The Glory' by Doug Holck and Tom Fettke. We got the tape from a close relative on my father's side. This tape inspired me to sing and make music unto the Lord.

I took Aunt Susannah's advice and sold my car. Using the money from the sale of the car to support myself, I also attended bible seminars and conferences. I did not work for almost two years from 2008 till 2009. I wanted to get 'well'. However, it was difficult trying to get my family to understand my circumstances and decisions. Both my mother and Joan were very critical of me. Even my relatives alienated me during our testive gatherings. In all these, I remained quiet. I did not answer back. I did not lose hope. My priority was to get well soon.

I kept a daily schedule for my chores and scripture reading that was divided into four sessions. Morning, Noon, Evening and Night. Usually after bible reading, I would do my chores or take long walks up to two hours depending on what my spirit compelled me to do and if time permitted me to do so. I became a doer of the 'Word' without understanding or being aware of what I was doing. I was being led by the Holy Spirit. I woke up as early as 5:00am and usually went to bed by 11:00pm. During my long walks and bus trips, I tried to collect as many brochures and leaflets from all churches within Penang. I not only attended their church services but I selected many seminars and conferences to attend.

Healing Begins

Sunday, December 30, 2007   *Isaiah 54*

I started recording the scriptures I read; my first entry being Isaiah 54. Just like in 2002, I began to feel the Holy Spirit speaking to me again. The Holy Spirit must have led me to read Isaiah 54 first. God knows our innermost desires. I was 32 years old; childless and still not married. I wondered if I would ever find someone suitable to be my husband. I was groaning when I read the scriptures but did not understand the reason behind it. The Holy Spirit then counselled me to bless my home-town, Penang, with these scriptures.

Apart from the holy scriptures, I was also reading other Christian books on prayer and healing. I dug up some of my parents' old prayer books: 'The Miracle Hour' and 'The Holy Spirit' amongst others. I was then inspired to register as a voter for our country's upcoming general election.

Tuesday, January 22, 2008   *Proverbs 6 & 8*

Monday, March 3, 2008   *Deuteronomy 1-8,*
                                13-15, 18-23,
                                Deuteronomy 27-28

Tuesday, March 4, 2008   *Jeremiah 29*

Saturday, March 8, 2008

I went to cast my votes in the General Election. Penang was won over by the Democratic Action Party by a landslide of votes. It was an unexpected but glorious change.

Tuesday, March 18, 2008   *Deuteronomy 10-12*

Wednesday, March 19, 2008   *Mark 19:28-48, Mark 20-21*

Friday, March 21, 2008

I attended 'Good Friday Service' at Dewan Sri Pinang, organised by the Penang First Assembly of God church. **Preacher being Rev Rajan Benedict, speaking on the theme of Isaiah 53:5.**

I came to know of this service from a leaflet I got from one of the Christian Bookshops I patronized. I also got some leaflets of seminars and conferences from different Christian churches. One upcoming Conference was the 'International Prophetic Conference' to be held from 10th till 13th December 2008. I did not know what it was about but the picture of the eagle on the leaflet appealed to me.

Friday, March 28, 2008   *Jeremiah 1 & 2*

Saturday, April 5, 2008   *Jeremiah 3-6; 7:1-15*

I remember driving aimlessly one night. This was before I sold my car in 2008. It was about 10:00pm on a Saturday night and I was speeding past the Western Road cemetery. I was in turmoil. I felt like killing people; just wanting to knock somebody down with my car. Then suddenly, calm and peace took over me as I took a bend.

"Where are all the people?" I asked myself, noticing that the roads were empty. My car had come to a sudden halt as I pulled over to the side of the road. I rested my head on the steering wheel. Immediately there was a knock on my window. It was a policeman.

"What is wrong?" he asked.

"I broke up," I cried, lifting my head up, sobbing uncontrollably.

I thought I would get into trouble but the police sped off on his motorcycle and was gone.

It had taken four long years for me to get over Daniel. My heart was still pining for him. I realised then that I was parked at the exit of the 'Moral Uplifting Building' where we were supposed to be married. We had stopped calling each other. I believed he had moved on. Now it was my turn.

Wednesday, April 9, 2008	*Jeremiah 7:16-34*
Thursday, April 10, 2008	*Jeremiah 8:1-17*
Saturday, April 12, 2008	*Jeremiah 8:18-22; Jeremiah 9-12*
Wednesday, April 16, 2008	*Jeremiah 12:14-17; Jeremiah 13-17*
Sunday, April 20, 2008	*Jeremiah 17-23*
Monday, April 21, 2008	*Jeremiah 23:33-40; Jeremiah 24-29*
Tuesday, May 27, 2008	*Job 38; Colossians 1-4*

I was now sleeping in the living room of my parents home because Roger had taken the room downstairs. He was now back in Penang working on big projects for a factory in Bayan Lepas.

After reading the bible one evening, something made me pick up the leaflet on the International Prophetic Conference. I turned to the back of the leaflet and there were contact numbers of the organisers of this event. So I called Madelaine. Turned out, she was Joan's classmate in high school. We arranged to meet up at a small restaurant nearby the next day so that I could register for this event.

I think it was either in May or early June that I went to meet her. At the restaurant, she introduced me to Bro Jerry, a minister of the Healing and Deliverance Ministry at Kensington Park Baptist Church. Bro Jerry had made that small restaurant his 'office' since it was nearby the church. It was also a walking distance to my parents' home.

After having a short conversation with him, he invited me to attend my first ever healing service. I remember being late for my first healing service. It was held in a small room upstairs the building within the church grounds. I made it a point to be early for the next healing session. The second session was held in the church and this time I was early.

Bro Jerry spoke about God's love using the holy scriptures. He prayed over those present and broke the curse of the generations over our lives. I felt so peaceful. At times, I would be groaning but I didn't understand why, at first. Before the service ended, we were advised to collect a piece of paper from the back of the hall which had scriptures written on them. We were to look up those scriptures in our bibles, read and meditate on the word of God for God's healing power to manifest within our souls and spirit.

I remember going back at about 10:30pm to find that my parents and brothers had already gone to bed. Everything seemed so peaceful and calm that night. I really felt God's presence that night.

Over the next few days, I had to include the list of scriptures from Kensington Park Baptist Church's Healing Ministry into my schedule.

The following is the list of scriptures given by their church for healing. Entitled 'The Miracle Of Positive Confession':

ANXIETY

Matthew 6:25-34;
Philippians 4:6-7, 13
Psalm 27:1; Philippians 4:8-9

HEALING

Exodus 15:26; Isaiah 53:4-5;
Galatians 3:13-14; Romans 8:11;
3 John 2; Proverbs 4:20-23;
Psalm 107:19-20; Mark 16:17-18;
Mark 11:22-24; John 14:12-14;
John 16:23-24

GUILT

Romans 8:1-2; Ephesians 6:16;
Isaiah 59:19; Isaiah 43:25-26;
Jeremiah 31:34; 1 John 1:9;
Proverbs 28:13

GOD'S FAITHFULNESS

Psalm 92:1-2, 12-15;
Hebrews 10:23;
Psalm 1:1-3; Isuiuh 40:29-31;
1 Corinthians 1:9;
1 Corinthians 10:13;
Proverbs 18:10; Psalm 118:17;
Isaiah 30:15

FEAR   *2 Timothy 1:7; Romans 8:15;*
                                1 John 4:4;
                                1 John 4:18; Proverbs 28:1;
                                Isaiah 40:10-11; Isaiah 43:1-2;
                                Psalm 91; Isaiah 54:17

Wednesday, July 9, 2008   *Ezekiel 2*

Thursday, July 10, 2008   *Ezekiel 1, 3-7*

Through reading the healing scriptures which the healing ministry had prepared for us, I was introduced to the Book of Psalms. Reading the psalms brought me much comfort and joy.

Friday, July 11, 2008   *Psalm 51*

Thursday, July 24, 2008   *Psalm 2, 19, 35, 79, 104*

Friday, July 25, 2008   *Psalm 5, 12, 23, 25*

Friday, August 1, 2008   *Book of Jude*

Tuesday, August 5, 2008   *Psalm 18*

Since I was not working during this time, I helped out with the household chores, feeding the cats and watering the plants. I remember my father asking me for help to rake the leaves in the garden. My parents had more than thirty potted plants in the garden. There were about ten potted plants behind the swing and the rest around the 'rambutan' tree. Raking the leaves meant that I had to remove the potted plants from around the rambutan tree and then rearranging them again. I only did this twice because I realised how difficult and heavy this job was. My father had been tending the garden for forty years and had managed to keep the garden neat and clean all the while. 'Oh! How my back ached!' I continued to rakes the leaves in the garden but stopped moving the potted plants. It was hard work.

I continued to attend the healing services at Kensington Park Baptist Church (KPBC) every month.

As it was getting dark one evening, I stepped outside our backyard to get some fresh air and to admire the beauty of the night sky. I watched some stars twinkling and started to count them. For a moment, I noticed that the stars aligned. All of a sudden, this blue ultramarine light joined the stars to form a larger star. I felt uneasy, so I quickly went into the house locking the back door behind me.

Through some research, I found out that the stars had formed the 'Star of David'. This star was on the flag of Israel. Why then was I afraid?

Friday, September 19, 2008   *Psalm 103; Haggai 1 & 2*

Wednesday, October 1, 2008   *Genesis 1-3*

On the next healing service at KPBC, in the month of October 2008, I spoke to Madelaine's husband, Gabriel about what I saw in the night sky sometime between August and October 2008. Gabriel advised me to keep a journal and to write in my journal the things that I saw and encountered in the spirit, supernatural things that happened in my life especially the healings that took place and also my testimonies. Taking his advice, I started writing down about my past dreams, nightmares and visions using a simple examination pad. Thankfully, I had recorded my readings of Bible scripture too. Well, most of them.

One hot and lazy afternoon, I walked out to our front yard. In the garden, I looked up into the bright, blue sky. The clouds parted and I saw the beautiful rays of sunshine shining downwards to our rambutan tree. I don't know what made me think of watering the plants as I usually watered the plants in the mornings and evenings. I turned on the tap and aimed the water hose at some plants on the ground in front of the rambutan tree. The money plant started shaking and a mirage appeared before me. To my horrors and disbelief, there in place of the money plant was a huge green anaconda coiled up on the ground. Terrified, I turned away to go back to my house but something made me turn to look back. Turning back in a split second, everything was back to normal again. The 'mirage' of the green anaconda had disappeared. It looked so real. The leaves of the money plants were also shaking.

"What are you trying to tell me?" I implored of the Lord, putting back the water hose neatly in its' place.

The clouds turned dark and it started to pour down heavilly. I quickly walked into the living room and continued my bible reading.

I remember taking out Coretta Scott King's article 'How We Open Our Hearts To God' and reading it one evening. It had started raining heavilly and as I read the article in the dining room, God's voice thundered in the storm and I heard crickets 'singing' to the sentences which were being read out aloud. I took note of those phrases and sentences. As I was doing that, I had a vision of 'Black People' singing in tents. They were praising and worshipping God in shelters in the midst of the storm. I was amazed by this revelation.

Using my computer, I highlighted those phrases and sentences in red and bold red. I had the article laminated.

There is much truth in what is written in that article and God is pleased when His church 'Arise' and stand up for the truth. God is a just God! He is our Provider and Deliverer! God is our Breakthrough!

Sunday, November 2, 2008	*Exodus 15:22-27*
Wednesday, November 5, 2008	*2 Samuel 22*
Saturday, November 8, 2008	*Isaiah 55;* *Ezekiel 13-14;* *James 1-5*
Tuesday, November 11, 2008	*Isaiah 63-66*

I often thought about the meaning of the mirage of the anaconda that appeared at the money plant under our rambutan tree. I recalled how my parents used to argue over their finances when we were just kids. Every time I thought about it, I would get depressed. So I went over to an internet cafe to research on anacondas and was surprised to find some news about 'Operation Anaconda' in Afghanistan. The U.S.A. were pulling out their troops from Afghanistan and this operation was called 'Operation Anaconda'. This started in 2007. I prayed about it and prayed for the safety of the troops from U.S.A.

Using Tasha Armour's book on 'Ribbon Weaving' for arts and crafts, I came up with the idea of ribbon weaving on bookmarks. I chose the colours of the bookmarks and ribbons to match our Penang State flag and our nation's flag (Malaysia). I was inspired by the blessings from the holy scriptures in Isaiah which the Holy Spirit led me to read. So each bookmark had a personal handwritten scripture of Isaiah's blessing on it. Each bookmark had a different design. Not one single one was the same.

Wednesday, November 12, 2008	*Revelation 10, 11, 15*
Monday, November 17, 2008	*Mark 3:22-36; Mark 4*
Tuesday, November 18, 2008	*John 1-21*
Thursday, November 20, 2008	*Romans 1-11*
Friday, November 21, 2008	*Psalm 61*
Monday, December 1, 2008	*Revelation 20-22*
Tuesday, December 2, 2008	*Revelation 14:17-18; Revelation 16-18*
Thursday, December 4, 2008	*Ezekiel 16:35-63; Ezekiel 17, 18, 24*

At my next healing session at KPBC, Madelaine advised me to read aloud the scriptures in the bible because it was meant to be read aloud. This was so that our spirits could hear and grasp the meanings of scripture and it could bring positive changes to the atmosphere.

Monday, December 8, 2008	*Mark 10-12*
Wednesday, December 10, 2008	*Psalm 90, 91, 92, 94*

I arrived early at the Charismatic Church of Penang (CCOP) to register for the International Prophetic Conference. The service started at 7:00pm with blows of the shofar sounding.

'Wow! What a wonderful noise!' I thought.

Everyone stood up to sing praises and to welcome the presence of our King Jesus. I watched and tried to follow the hymns and worship songs being sung as the worship team led us from the stage.

I remember there was one particular song that was led by an Australian preacher and the lyrics went something like this...

"There is no one like You, Jesus!" And this line was repeated over and over in the chorus and towards the end of the song. At first, I humbly praised God with this song but the more everyone's voices were lifted up and their hands raised praising Jesus, the angrier I felt inside. I started to question in my head, "Am I not like Christ?"

I was unsure of my thoughts and feelings. I sat down for a moment but stood up again ignoring my thoughts. In my heart I felt it might have been pride within me. I knew the anger welling up within me was not 'me'. I left the hall at 10:00pm to catch two buses to return home that night.

The next morning, I went with my father to town. He dropped me off at the bus station to catch the bus to CCOP. There were three sessions that day. Two in the morning and one after lunch. Thankfully I had arrived on time.

During our break at 2:00pm, David a member of Tabernacle of Worship church challenged me to walk to CCOP to prove that I love Jesus. I kept quiet but thought about what he said.

Thursday, December 11, 2008   *Acts 1-7; Acts 28*

After a late evening, I caught two buses back to my home. I awoke late the next morning, much to my dismay. I rode on a bus to town and decided to walk about 18km to CCOP from the pier, since I was already late.

Halfway into my journey to CCOP, I came across some needles and some rubbish on the grass in front of a temple along the road. It must have been left behind by some drug addicts. I prayed about it and asked God to bless and sanctify that area because that area was known to be an accident prone area.

I had already missed the first two sessions when I arrived at CCOP. I joined the third session before we went into our break. I had to shower and change before the night session. I had come prepared bringing some change of clothing for the night session.

Friday, December 12, 2008   *Exodus 14; Exodus 23:20-33*

In the Wilderness

Friday, December 19, 2008   *1 Chronicles 29:10-20;*
Psalm 86, 88

Saturday, December 20, 2008   *Psalm 87*

Around the end of 2008, my parents and I went down to Petaling Jaya (PJ) to visit Joan for the holidays. We stayed at Shannon's apartment in PJ but she had to travel to the U.S.A. for work.

Upon reaching the apartment, my parents and I found out that strange things were happening there. Joan told us that every time their female cat gave birth, the kittens would be found only with their heads and without their bodies. Shannon and Joan suspected that one of their male cats was attacking and eating the kittens' bodies. Shannon had two male cats and one female. At this time, their female cat had just given birth to a new litter of kittens just before we came down for a visit. They were probably about a week old.

I thought that I could get some rest after travelling from Penang to PJ but I was wrong. We had all retired to sleep; my parents in one of the bedrooms and I, in the living room, when we were all awakened by Joan's screams. She had found the kittens mutilated again. No bones. Only their heads remained.

Joan came out to the living room and shouted at me to get out of the apartment. She blamed me for the deaths of the kittens. She was yelling at me at the top of her voice to get out so I hastily got my things and left the apartment.

I was deeply hurt that my parents hadn't intervened. Maybe it was late and they were too tired from the five-hour drive to PJ. Maybe they were afraid of making the situation worse with Joan.

I did not know my way around in PJ but I remembered Shannon advising me how to get to the monorail station from her apartment. So I headed to the monorail station on foot. I cried all the way there. I felt rejected by my own family. It took me about 20 to 30 minutes to reach the station, and it was about 11:20pm when I took the train to the bus station at Pudu. At Pudu, I bought a bus ticket straight to Penang Island. I reached George Town, Penang between 4:00am and 5:00am.

Since it was too early to catch the public transport back to my parents' home in Tanjung Bungah, I had an early breakfast at a 24-hour eatery near the bus station. God was with me. He had been with me and kept me safe from harm and danger throughout this journey. I am ever grateful and thankful for His divine protection and covering.

Christmas came and went. I had longed for a joyous Christmas like in my childhood days but for three consecutive years, the Christmas season seemed like hell on earth.

Our family always made sure that we visited our paternal grandmother at her home on Christmas morning. Grandmummy was now 88 years old. She had slight dementia so my father asked me to check on her from time to time. Grandmummy stayed alone and usually walked down the road to the old market to buy her lunch. She loved her daily walks to the old market and could always find her way back. Sometimes, some kind strangers would send her home as they knew where she lived. Mostly everyone in the neighbourhood could recognize her as they had seen her walking to and from the old market every day. Many were amazed at her strength because she could take the slope up and downhill faster than younger people could.

I am grateful to God for blessing Grandmummy with a long, fruitful life. Grandmummy was very independent. Deep down, I wished I had her resilience. Her strength to endeavour through all obstacles and hardship. Sometimes, I left her home disheartened because Grandmummy could not recall who I was. Sometimes she couldn't even remember her own children: my father, uncle and aunt. I tried reading scriptures to her.

I remember her always asking me for 'good news'. I did not think much about it then but now I realise that in her spirit, she probably meant the 'Good news' about Christ Jesus. Maybe her time was coming and God was preparing to receive her. Who knows?

The year 2008 drew to a close and we welcomed 2009. Another year had gone by.

Thursday, January 1, 2009   *Psalm 72; Titus; Revelation 20, 21,22*

Friday, January 2, 2009   *Psalm 67*

Saturday, January 3, 2009   *Psalm 95, 96, 97, 98, 99, 100, 101*

Sunday, January 4, 2009

I continued to attend the healing and deliverance services at KPBC on the first Sunday of each month. After reading scriptures on healings given by KPBC, I was led by the Holy Spirit to read on further, scriptures on the following words, from the concordance of my NLT Bible:- brother, clay, self-control, anger, grumble, grumblers, grow, archangel, babies, baby, rock, seraphim, cherubim, child, childlike, children and witchcraft.

Monday, January 5, 2009 *Isaiah 60, 61, 62; Mark 4*

I used my free time making bookmarks with verses from Isaiah. All scriptures given to me by the Holy Spirit were good blessings for the nation of Malaysia. None of them were bad.

Tuesday, January 6, 2009 *Numbers 9:15-23; Ezekiel 14-16*

Sunday, January 11, 2009 *Mark 5:12-39; Mark 6-18*

Thursday, January 15, 2009 *Hebrews 1-13*

Saturday, January 17, 2009 *1 Samuel 27 - 1 Samuel 31*

Tuesday, January 20, 2009 *Exodus 31:12-18; Psalm 111; Mark 2:23-28; Mark 3; Hebrews 6-11*

Wednesday, January 21, 2009 *Mark 1 & 2*

Friday, January 23, 2009 *Proverbs 9; Isaiah 40-44*

Saturday, January 24, 2009 *Psalm 29; Hebrews 6*

During one of my visits to my grandmother's house, she told me that she had seen a valley of dry bones in her dreams. She seemed saddened by the fact that she had not been well enough to perform her daily tasks as before. She went on to tell me that she had not gone to clean Grandpa's grave for some time now as she had been under the weather. She asked if I could clear the weeds from my grandfather's grave and I assured her that I would take care of it for her. This gave me some ideas. I was in love with the Word of God. The psalms being my personal favourite because I could relate to how the psalmist must have felt. I also loved Hebrews because who Christ is, is revealed in this book and I thought Ezekiel was the most powerful book ever, as I had seen storms brewing and winds changing after reading parts of this book. I also knew that God was raising His army and that the dead could rise and speak. Why? Because each time I read Ezekiel 34, 35, 36 and 37, there would be thunderstorms and wondrous sights in the skies. And the next day, I would read of graves unearthed in the newspapers. I knew God was moving. In Mexico, graves of innocent victims of drug cartels were unearthed and in Bangladesh about 200 graves of victims of massacres were unearthed. Because of the power manifested through reading these scriptures, I wanted to do something good for my grandmother.

I went to a nursery to buy four potted 'Lavender' plants, to represent the four winds in the four corners of the world and one potted plant with red flowers to be planted in the middle of Grandpa's grave to represent God as center of us all. Also to represent the new heart, the heart of flesh. I got a huge spade and some tools for digging and planting and using Jonathan's car, I drove to the grave site.

First, I pulled out the weeds from Grandpa's grave. Then, I used the huge spade for digging up the surface of the grave. Next, I planted the four 'Lavender' plants on his grave - one on each corner of the grave to represent the four winds of the fours corners of the earth. Finally, I planted the plant with red flowers in the middle. As I was about to finish, I saw a white wriggly worm. I thrust the spade right into it. I believe I had cut it into half as immediately as I had struck it, there was a sharp pain in my abdomen. There was a sudden rumble of thunder in the distance. I spoke to God to hold on for awhile before he brought the rain. I was done, or was I?

The pain in my abdomen left immediately as it came. I said I was sorry but I could not help it as I could not stand creepy crawlies. Picking up my bible, I turned to Ezekiel 37 and prophesied about the valley of dry bones. It started to drizzle as I quickly cleared my stuff and left the grave site.

I also noticed that each time I walked to my grandmother's house, I had changed route from my usual short cut. I wondered why I made turns to certain lanes before reaching her house. It may have seemed I was lost. I was walking 'like a mad person'. But truly I was being led by the Holy Spirit. I decided to investigate this by walking down these roads one day. I found out that the names of the roads were actually 'directions'. Directions on the compass, like 'South-West', 'South-East', so on and so forth.

Thursday, January 29, 2009	*Psalm 37; Proverbs 15; Mark 4*
Friday, January 30, 2009	*Psalm 24; Mark 4*
Saturday, January 31, 2009	*Leviticus 7:22-27; Leviticus 19; Deuteronomy 32*

I had also started attending 'Night Worship' sessions on Wednesdays at the Tabernacle of Worship. Feeling desperate one afternoon, I rang the doorbell of their office.

I wanted to speak to their pastor. Steven, a member of their congregation, set an appointment for me to meet Pastor Sarah the next day. I was told to bring along my bible. The very next day, at the appointed time, I was there at their office with my bible. Pastor Sarah asked me to turn to the book of 1 John. She explained that it was the book of love amongst Christian believers. She guided me to read the Book of 1 John six times while I was there.

When I first started reading 1 John for the first two rounds, I felt as though the words of the bible were floating and getting mixed up so I could not read the scriptures properly. I saw the words literally floating and moving around just like in the movies. It was hard for me to just read one round of that book. Let alone, six rounds. I was there for almost two and a half hours. Pastor Sarah then advised me to read the final seventh round at my home. She then gave me instructions to read this same book, 1 John, seven times a day for six more consecutive days.

When I got home, I prepared myself to read the seventh round of 1 John for that particular day. After finishing the final round, I was groaning and my legs suddenly felt so heavy like an elephant's. Something made me drag my feet straight to the front gate. I opened the gate. I thought I was going out for a walk but the heaviness from my legs disappeared when I opened the gate. Something within me made me close the gate before me. So I did not go out. Instead I walked back into the house. I had thrown out a dark spirit which was like a Behemoth, a heavy 'dinosaur like' spirit. I believe this spirit is the one that caused Christians to be blinded to the truth and lazy to read the 'Word of God'. I had never encountered such a supernatural encounter within my body before so I was determined to finish the course of reading the book of 1 John for seven times a day, for another six consecutive days.

Sunday, February 1, 2009   *1 John 1-5 {Day Two}*
Revelation 20, 21, 22

After reading the Book of 1 John for seven times in a row, I began to see mirages of vipers but they were not so clear. They did not harm me but I could feel them slithering under my feet like wisps of air. All the more I was determined to 'get well' by getting rid of this evil through reading and meditating in God's word. So for the next two days, I immersed myself with the Word of God.

Monday, February 2, 2009   *1 John 1-5 {Day Three}*
*not recorded

Tuesday, February 3, 2009   *1 John 1-5 {Day Four};*
Psalm 22; Psalm 24;
Mark 5-9; Mark 13-16;
Hebrews 2-4; Hebrews
12-13

Wednesday, February 4, 2009   *1 John 1-5 {Day Five};*
Psalm 103

Thursday, February 5, 2009   *1 John 1-5 {Day Six}*

On Day Six of reading the Book of 1 John, something supernatural happened. My fingers in both hands curled up like an old man's and my voice changed to sound like that of old men. At each round, it was a different voice with a different accent. So there were six to seven different men's voices with six to seven distinct accents. And as I read each round, my fingers curled up like an old man's as I underlined the words of the bible in 1 John with my fingers. It was as though my body had been taken over by other 'spirits'. My voice became normal again after the completion of all seven rounds of the Book of 1 John.

*Please read, **2 Corinthians 5:4; Romans 6:6** and **Galatians 2:20** regarding putting off of our 'old selves' (preferably in the New Living Translation). In some parts of other bibles, they mention getting rid of our 'old men' and clothing ourselves with our new bodies in Christ Jesus.

The verses I love and remember most are, 'God is Love!' and 'God is Light!'

(Further Scripture Readings: 1 John 4:7-9; 1 John 1:5)

Friday, February 6, 2009   *1 John 1-5 {Day Seven}*

Saturday, February 7, 2009   *Psalm 23; Psalm 26; Psalm 27*

Sunday, February 8, 2009   *Job 7; Psalm 147; 1 Corinthians 6-15*

Tuesday, February 10, 2009   *Galatians 1-5 {x7 rounds}*

Because I had experienced the sevenfold power behind the Word of God when read seven times, I read the book of Galatians seven times in a row. The key message that I got from that book was that as believers, we become children of the free woman (Sarah).

Wednesday, February 11, 2009 *Psalm 128; Psalm 131; Psalm 136*

Sunday, February 15, 2009   *Ephesians 1-6*

Wednesday, February 18, 2009 *Daniel 1-12*

Friday, February 27, 2009   *Ezekiel 37*

As I read Ezekiel 37, I prophesied to the four winds because I was enamoured with this description of the Holy Spirit. It drew in heavy rain clouds and the weather changed drastically.

Sunday, March 1, 2009	*Habakkuk 1-3;*
	Colossians 1-4;
	Philemon
	Romans 12-16
Saturday, March 28, 2009	*Romans 12-16*
	Obadiah
Sunday, March 29, 2009	*Obadiah*
	Malachi 1-4
Monday, March 30, 2009	*Malachi 1-4*

I continued with my long walks every chance I had, usually after reading scriptures. I remember walking past the fire station along Tanjung Tokong Road on my way home one afternoon and seeing a heart in the clouds. It was very clear and blended well in the grey clouds. I had just been to an internet cafe and was reading on the principles that made up the 'pillars of our country, Malaysia' and the lyrics of our national anthem. Something just did not add up. I had become angry and restless again after reading the lyrics of our national anthem, so I left the internet cafe.

> **I believe the part which got me angry, was on 'the spilling of my blood' for my country. Something within me could not accept it at that moment. It was the devil in me. The same devil that tried to stop Christ from doing the will of God, that is dying on the cross for our sins and reconciling us to Abba Father, our Creator. Many of us have become cowards. Not speaking up for the truth. God's truth. Something or someone doesn't want us Christians to be prepared for martyrdom.**

NEGARAKU

(Lagu Kebangsaan Malaysia)
(Malaysian National Anthem – in our National Language,
Bahasa Malaysia)

Negaraku
Tanah tumpahnya darahku
Rakyat hidup bersatu dan maju
Rahmat bahagia Tuhan kurniakan
Raja kita selamat bertakhta
Rahmat bahagia Tuhan kurniakan
Raja kita selamat bertakhta

Literal Translation in English
(Malaysian National Anthem)

My country
The land where my blood has spilled
The people living united and progressive
May God bestow blessing and happiness
May our ruler have a successful reign
May God bestow blessing and happiness
May our ruler have a successful reign

LAGU NEGERI PULAU PINANG

(Penang State Anthem – in our National Language, Bahasa
Malaysia)

Selamat Tuhan kurniakan,
Selamat Pulau Pinang,
Negeriku yang mulia,
Ku taat dan setia,
Aman dan bahagia,
Majulah, Jayalah,
Negeriku yang ku cinta,

Bersatu dan bersama,
Untuk negeri kita.

Literal Translation in English
(Penang State Anthem)
May God grant safety,
Safety to Penang,
My noble state,
To which I am loyal and faithful,
Peaceful and happy,
May you progress and succeed,
My state which I love,
United and together,
For our state.

Malaysia's National Principles
RUKUN NEGARA

BAHAWASANYA negara kita Malaysia mendukung cita-cita hendak mencapai perpaduan yang lebih erat di kalangan seluruh masyarakatnya; memelihara satu cara hidup demokratik; mencipta masyarakat yang adil di mana kemakmuran negara akan dapat dinikmati bersama secara adil dan saksama; menjamin satu cara yang liberal terhadap tradisi-tradisi kebudayaannya yang kaya dan berbagai-bagai corak; membina satu masyarakat progresif yang akan menggunakan sains dan teknologi moden.

MAKA KAMI, rakyat Malaysia, berikrar akan menumpukan seluruh tenaga dan usaha kami untuk mencapai cita-cita tersebut berdasarkan atas prinsip-prinsip berikut:

- KEPERCAYAAN KEPADA TUHAN
- KESETIAAN KEPADA RAJA DAN NEGARA
- KELUHURAN PERLEMBAGAAN
- KEDAULATAN UNDANG-UNDANG
- KESOPANAN DAN KESUSILAAN

Malaysia's National Principles
(Literal Translation in English)

WHEREAS OUR COUNTRY, MALAYSIA nurtures the ambitions of: achieving a more perfect unity amongst the whole of her society; preserving a democratic way of life; creating a just society where the prosperity of the country can be enjoyed together in a fair and equitable manner; guaranteeing a liberal approach towards her rich and varied cultural traditions; and building a progressive society that will make use of science and modern technology.

NOW THEREFORE, WE, the people of Malaysia, pledge to concentrate the whole of our energy and efforts to achieve these ambitions based on the following principles:

- BELIEF IN GOD
- LOYALTY TO KING AND COUNTRY
- SUPREMACY OF THE CONSTITUTION
- RULES OF LAW
- COURTESY AND MORALITY

Wednesday, April 1, 2009 *Psalm 51; Philemon; 2 John; 3 John*

Verse 10 of Psalm 51 struck me. I felt a deep cut in my heart and was deeply convicted by the Holy Spirit. I, a sinner. I was groaning from within me as I read this psalm but still I didn't understand the reason behind it.

(Scripture Reading: Psalm 51:10)

Friday, April 3, 2009 *2 Samuel 21; 2 Samuel 22*

Tuesday, April 14, 2009 *Hosea 11*

Friday, April 17, 2009

I attended the 'New Tribes Mission Conference' at the Penang Christian Centre. The theme was 'Reaching Unreached Tribes'. Sadly I was not well enough and equipped to minister to others although I wanted so badly to be part of their missions group. The conference ran for three consecutive days.

Saturday, April 18, 2009   *Psalm 42; Psalm 43; Psalm 47*

Tuesday, April 28, 2009   *John 1 & 2; Hebrews 1 & 2*

*Journal: I also started reading on 'The Person' of the Holy Spirit again. (He is the third person of the Trinity & He knows as a person: mind)

Wednesday, April 29, 2009   *John 1 & 2; Hebrews 1 & 2*

*Journal: The Holy Spirit (HIS PERSON: He feels as a person - emotion)

Thursdsay, April 30, 2009   *John 2, 3, 4; Hebrews 1 & 2*

*Journal: The Holy Spirit (HIS PERSON: He acts as a person - will)

Friday, May 1, 2009   *John 4; Hebrews 1, 2 & 3*

*Journal: I attended the Eagles Team Leadership Summit held at the Charismatic Church of Penang (CCOP). The theme was 'The Future of Leadership'. At this training, I befriended two participants who asked me for transport from their homes to CCOP to attend the second session and I obliged. We had almost reached CCOP when my car ran a flat tire. A kind Malay man stopped to help change the flat tire. As a token of my gratitude, I gave him RM10.00.

We were late for the second session that day but thankfully, we were all in good spirits.

Saturday, May 2, 2009   *John 5 & 6; Hebrews 1, 2 & 3*

*Journal: "Shoo! Scram!" I was awakened at 4:30am by Roger's voice from downstairs. He was trying to shoo away one of our pet cats that got into his room. It was raining and I wanted to go back to sleep as it was still early but I could not ignore God's call. I heard the thunder rumbling. My eyes lit up and I felt fresh and wide awake. I sat up on my mattress and said a short silent prayer. Then, I opened my bible and read John 5 & 6. I could not really grasp what I was reading but my heart was filled with joy. I continued with Hebrews 1, 2 and 3. This time, my mind was more alert. I wanted to get more sleep before the Leadership seminar so I asked God to help me wake up at 7:00am. At 7:00am, I was awakened by the soft rumbling of thunder and flashes of lightning, but I was still in a dreamy state and 'Jonathan's' name kept playing in my mind. I drifted off to sleep again and awoke suddenly at 7:50am. I knew I could not reach the seminar on time but I was not going to absent myself from the seminar. I asked my father to send me to the bus stand when he awoke. It had begun to rain. We left the house at 8:15am and my father dropped me off at the bus stop by the pier.

I was the only passenger when I got on the bus to CCOP. The journey was smooth as there was not much traffic at that time. I arrived at CCOP at about 8:50am to find the speakers answering questions from the floor. I decided I just had to buy their CDs because I had missed two sessions and I did not want to forget the lessons being taught throughout the two days of the seminar.

On my way home after the seminar, I stopped in town to buy some materials for my arts and craft work. I had sold some bookmarks at our 'Coffee Morning' organised by the Society of the St Vincent de Paul of our parish. These bookmarks bore the colours of both the Malaysian and the state of Penang's flags. Also, each bookmark had a handwritten scripture of blessing taken from Isaiah. The materials required for these bookmarks were sticky double sided tapes, ribbons, cardboards, scissors and stamps.

I was all tired and sweaty when I arrived home at about 6:00pm. I spoke to the Lord and promised him that I would pray from 8:00pm till 10:00pm after having my bath, dinner and getting some rest. I had been too busy the whole day to find time to pray. However, at 8:00pm, I was lazing around on the couch in the living room. I had forgotten my promise to pray. I received a call from one of the participants of the seminar and we talked for almost an hour. After that, I joined my younger brother, Roger to watch football. I was not even interested in football but just lazing around.

Suddenly, there was lighting and crashing thunder. I suddenly remembered that I had missed my prayer session with the Lord. I panicked and quickly searched for my books. In my schedule, I was to read about the Holy Spirit and study scriptures about the Holy Spirit. I looked for the book but could not find it. Feeling tired and sleepy was not an excuse for I could rest the next day. I felt God had something important for me to do, so I asked Him to show me. Calmly, I gathered my notes, stationery and bible and went to sit at my work table downstairs, leaving Roger and my father to watch their football match.

My heart sank when I realized that I had delayed my prayer session with God. I had kept God waiting and did not keep my word! Then, I asked God again, what He would like me to do. I heard a voice say, "Just give me an hour". I looked up and stared at the clock. It was exactly 11:00pm. I was about to open my bible to read the scripture according to my schedule but the booklet on the 'Miracle Hour' by Linda Schubert popped into my head. So I opened the booklet and looked at the section according to the hour. No. 11 was a section for 'PETITIONS'. Actually all twelve sections only takes an hour but I had changed it to suit my own style of prayer and worship. I took about one hour for each section. The opening for section 11 was a scripture taken from Hebrews 4:16. It also coincided with what I had planned in my schedule for the following day, Sunday. As I was reading through this section on petitions, thunder rumbled when I read the words 'health concern' and it struck my heart. I began to pray to God to bless anyone I could think of with good health. My family members, friends, acquaintances and for myself. I started suffering from sinus since my days at Black Cat Logistics. So I prayed about it. I prayed for God's protection over those who would be travelling for their pilgrimage to France. They would be praying for the petitions from our parishioners. I prayed that the Holy Spirit would be with them, to guide and protect them.

Sunday, May 3, 2009   *John 5 & 6*

I attended the healing and deliverance service at KPBC.

Monday, May 4, 2009   *Revelation 22:7-21;*
                               Hebrews 1, 2, 3 & 4

*Journal: As usual, I awoke at 8:30am. Said a short prayer and had a light breakfast before starting my chores. I spent the whole afternoon making bookmarks and prayer cards. My mother began grumbling angrily after receiving a phone call. She started throwing rubbish around me and called me a 'donkey'. She wanted me to leave the house and cursed my work. I shot back at her telling her I knew very well she did not want me to live because she complained about me even when I was away from home years back. I actually saw my mother manifesting. Once in the kitchen, her head became bigger and her face turned squarish. Jonathan too became hostile and threatened me. Went to bed at 11:00pm after a short silent prayer.

8.11.2020

Thankfully, I do not remember the threats uttered or the exchanges of heated arguments etc. However, I do remember the manifestation every time they got angry. Thankfully, under proper medication, I do not see these manifestations anymore but I am more lethargic. Whether it is a good thing or bad, I will still trust in God.

Tuesday, May 5, 2009   *Hebrews 4, 5, 6; John 6; Isaiah 50, 51, 52, 53*

*Journal: I borrowed Jonathan's car and drove to 'The Church of Our Lady' to meet their Finance Clerk, Penelope at 3:00pm. I handed her some registration forms for upcoming Christian conferences and seminars. As I was leaving their office, I bumped into Fr Murray. He was talking to a lady named Theresa and he introduced us. I excused myself to go to 'Max's Cafe' for a cup of 'joy', for I suddenly thought of having ice cream to lift my spirits that day.

When I reached the church gate, something made me stop. The light of God was shining brightly. I figured, 'I don't trust myself with my spending habits but it is always a joy to share your meal with someone, especially someone who is really in need. What have I got to lose? Why not? Theresa might be hungry! So I turned back and started walking towards her. Her face lit up when I invited her to join me for 'coffee and ice cream'.

We walked over to the cafe which was not far away from the church grounds. There, we met Bro Jerry and his wife, Megan. They had just finished having their tea. I ordered food for Theresa and myself, then walked up to Bro Jerry and his wife to just say 'Hello!' Bro Jerry was pleased that I was 'getting better'. He encouraged me to continue reading the Holy Scriptures and to attend the healing and deliverance services before they left the cafe.

Theresa and I sat and talked for more than two hours. My full focus was on her for the evening. I thoroughly enjoyed my meal. It was always good to have a warm bowl of soup with bread on any occasion, especially if you have someone to keep you company too.

We were talking and talking and suddenly I remembered that Theresa had to travel back to the mainland. It was already 6:40pm and I also remembered my schedule. I had left a lot of work hanging but I could not let her travel in the dark by herself, so I offered her a lift. She excused herself telling me that she had to meet a friend downtown so we parted at the bus stand.

I stopped at the nearest pharmacy to buy some Calamine lotion for my face before heading home.

> Lord, it is painful but I sincerely hope that Theresa and those suffering from cancer will experience your divine healing and just believe. May their faith in Christ, Our Risen Lord and Saviour, Our King from Heaven above, grow deeper and stronger. May the love, peace, joy and grace from God above be bestowed upon them. Save all souls, Lord! Save all souls! Lord, you never turned away anyone seeking for your divine healing. You are a gracious and loving God. You are faithful!
>
> Let me be an example, Lord, of your act of love and faith in God, Our Heavenly Father. Teach me O Lord, to be more like you. And use me! I ask these in the name of Jesus Christ, Our Lord and Saviour. Amen.

Wednesday, May 6, 2009   *Psalm 23, Psalm 62*

*Journal: At 4:00pm, I went to the Penang Christian Centre (PCC) to register for the 'Ablaze' Breakthrough Seminar. It was to be held at PCC from 19th till 20th May 2009, followed by a ten day prayer and fast with the church. Within an hour I was back home to continue my arts and craft work and daily chores.

Thursday, May 7, 2009   *Psalm 23, Psalm 27;*
     Romans 12, 13, 14;
     1 Corinthians 11, 12 & 13

Friday, May 8, 2009   *Isaiah 50 & 51; John 21;*
     Acts 6

*Journal: I attended a seminar by speaker, Pastor John Kitchen who was also promoting his book 'Revival of the Rubble', which happened to be the theme of this seminar. I knew I had to rebuild myself and needed personal revival. Registration for this seminar started at 6:30pm and at

7:30pm, we had a buffet dinner before our 'Praise and Worship' session at 8:30pm. That night, Pastor John Kitchen gave us the outline of the whole seminar. We were advised to go back to read Nehemiah so that we would be able to follow through the remaining sessions the next day.

Saturday, May 9, 2009

*Journal: I awoke at 7:30am. Took a quick shower and left the house at 8:20am without waking anybody up. I walked about 1km to the bus stop. It was a bright and beautiful morning. The bus ride was quick and smooth but just as we approached my destination, it started to drizzle. As soon as I stepped off the bus at the bus stand, it started to pour heavily. So heavy I did not dare run across the road to the hotel which was directly opposite the bus stand. I felt miserable because I didn't want to miss the praise and worship sessions. Then I thought to myself, surely God must have a reason for this sudden outpour. So I asked the Lord which part of me still needed cleansing. I had realised that when I had prayed 'The Lord's Prayer' the night before, God had spoken to my heart to 'Do His Will'. Feeling quite anxious and not wanting any evil thoughts or desires to overcome me, I opened my bible and read Isaiah 40.

At first, I was facing some houses behind the bus stand but when I ended declaring the word of God in Isaiah 40, I stopped right in front of a sign posted on the bus stand. It was an advertisement on condoms. I was distraught. I knew that God had forgiven me for all my past sins but I didn't like being reminded of them. Maybe I had to work on forgiving myself. This, I believe was His way of 'cleansing' me. God was also strengthening me. God loves His church, the body of Christ so much that He does not even want any member of the body to be stained. We are to be as pure brides when Jesus returns. And it is by His blood that we are cleansed and purified.

> I do believe, Lord Jesus. I believe that you died for my sins and you rose again from the dead. You are seated at the right hand of the Father, enthroned in Heaven. I believe you will come again, to judge all the living and the dead. I believe in the Father, the Son and the Holy Spirit. I believe that You are One!

Slowly, my head turned to another notice that said 'JALAN' which meant 'WALK'. I knew I was being guided by the Holy Spirit. I had mixed emotions because I did not 'enjoy' being reminded of my past sins but at the same time I knew that God was working in me. He was filling me with His Spirit and joy to face the future. I had to allow God to work through me. I was being disciplined. I was being chastened. I had to learn to trust and surrender to Him completely. To my amazement, it stopped raining.

Abba Father, had been faithfully showing me His glorious 'light' in the mornings and evenings so I wanted to test Him today. I knew God had a reason for pouring rain down that day and I wanted others to see what I could see so that I could affirm that the light I encountered each day was from the power of our Almighty God and not any other power. So as I walked across the road and up to the hotel, I pleaded with Abba Father to show me His light at night so that I could affirm that I was still His child. I never want to be abandoned especially by God, the Father Almighty. When I reached the hotel, someone from the information desk greeted me with a smile and pointed me to the rest room.

After this morning, I stayed refreshed throughout all the sessions right till the evening. God bless all the kind souls that I met these past two days. Thank you, Abba Father, for the smiles on their faces that brightened up my day. From the road sweepers, bus drivers to my friends from church whom I met at the seminar. A friend from Kensington Park Baptist

Church dropped me home that evening. I took my shower, then went to Gurney to buy some stickers for my 'work'.

While I was walking back to the car after leaving Gurney Plaza that evening, I looked up at the sky to see a bright full moon and there was the light of Christ shining around it. Surrounding the moon were clouds with a bright light shining through them. It was just marvellous. Too beautiful to describe in words. That night, I remembered to thank God for that awesome miracle and for answering my prayers.

When, I got home that evening, my parents were not home. They had gone to the south side of the island to shop with relatives. That night, Aunt Trudy called to remind me about Mother's Day, the next day. I was so tired that I could only think of getting some rest. I had so much to do and so many tasks to complete each day. It was never ending. I wanted to go to KPBC for Sunday Service the next day. Mother's Day had been the same for us every year. I only knew that the best gift I could give my mother was peace. Normally, I just kept out of her way. I wished that God would rekindle the fire of the Holy Spirit within her and grant her a heart of flesh to desire the living God, our Risen Christ!

Sunday, May 10, 2009   *Isaiah 54*

*Journal: I wished our 'Bright and Morning Star' a very good morning. Aunt Trudy came over for a short visit after our church service and our Mother's Day celebration at KPBC, to wish my mother a 'Happy Mother's Day!' I ended the day singing praise and worship songs from 8:00pm till 9:00pm.

Monday, May 11, 2009   *Ezekiel 37:1-14; John 3:5-8;*
                                      Mark 1:9-11; John 1:32-33

*Journal: I found myself suddenly awake just before dawn - staring up the ceiling. I was still lying on my back on the mattress on the floor as I looked up the ceiling. Red clouds formed and filled the whole living room. I do not recall what I uttered but I felt so peaceful. I raised up both hands and felt the Holy Spirit come down and resting on me. I fell into a peaceful slumber once again. I did not feel fearful because I knew I was and still am loved by God.

In the afternoon, I started to plan my schedule for the rest of the week. I called up an organization 'MAHAS' to find out more about their seminars and workshops on 'Train the Care Givers of the Elderly'. In the late afternoon, Pastor Winnie from a Christian Church on the mainland came over for a visit. She invited me to join her cell group every Friday nights at 8:00pm but I had to decline.

Tuesday, May 12, 2009   *John 7; Hebrews 4, 5, 6, 7*

Started my day reading scripture and meditating on the prayer 'Radiating Christ'. I planned my schedule for the week.

2:30pm   Lunch
3:00pm - 4:00pm   Rest

Continued with my schedule and worked on my arts and crafts. Read and did my homework on 'The Holy Spirit' - His Person; His Names, before I went to bed.

Wednesday, May 13, 2009   *John 1, 2, 3, 4, 5, 6, 7;*
Hebrews 1, 2, 3, 4, 5, 6, 7;
Malachi;
Psalm 19, 51, 60, 61;
Isaiah 54, 57, 58, 59

*Journal: On the morning of 13th May 2009, I was reminded of God's grace and eminent light on the night of 9th May 2009. I cried tears of joy as I recalled that day. I can call Him, 'Abba Father' as I am His child and that He loves me still. I was given the reassurance by the Holy Spirit of God's faithfulness and love even though I was a sinner. I wish that by this message, everyone who is searching for love will find Christ and that in knowing Him, believe. And that in believing in Him, they will know for sure that God will never abandon His children, especially those who draw close to Him. Seek God with all your heart. As children of God, we must always believe that in God, all things are possible. Test Him! He always listens to our prayers. All that I had experienced on 9th May, was God's divine love. He was cleansing me. He was purifying me. He was chastening me. God loves us so much that He doesn't want us to be stained by sin and guilt.

- Read Psalm 19, meditated and stressed on verse 14;

- Meditated on Psalm 51

11:00am - Met Ming-Mei at Kensington Bookstore. She agreed to assist me on the sale of my arts & crafts at the bookstore.

- Read John 1-7 at the 'Church of our Lady'.

Upon Ming-Mei's advise, I went over to check out the other Christian Bookstores at a shopping mall next to the church. While I was on my way up to Salvation Bookstore, I bumped into Jaden, a member from Tabernacle of Worship. He seemed sincere and concerned about me. He wanted to know my progress on spiritual matters so I shared with him a little about what I had done the day before. I showed him my arts and crafts work and explained to him that I was led by the Holy Spirit to remove the pictures of two dragons in my certificate which I had received during my travel to Beijing and climbing up the Badaling portion of 'The Great Wall of China'. I replaced the two dragons with pictures of two great angels and transformed the certificate by adding some scripture on it. The scriptures that I was led to choose for this project were **Nehemiah 3:16; Nehemiah 1:10-11 and Revelation 11:15.** On each side of the certificate, in place of the two dragons were pictures of angels bearing trumpets. We parted and I went ahead to the book store.

There was a vacancy at Salvation Bookstore for the position of Sales Assistant. Tried my luck there. Went to Evangel Bookstore which was located just above Salvation Bookstore. There were so many interesting books to read and the bookmarks were so attractive. I picked out some bookmarks for myself and my family members. My eye caught some Chinese paintings framed and decorated on the walls in this shop. I asked the person minding the counter what the Chinese characters meant and he showed me the translation which were written below the pictures in small prints.

As I was browsing through the store, I came across a book on 'Prophecy'. I flipped the pages of the book and stopped in the centre page to read through some parts of the contents. I felt confused after reading a passage from Revelation 20. Verse 10 stood out. In an instant, I felt something overpowering me. The skin on my face tightened and became stiff as though it was pulled back and I clenched and bared my teeth as though I had fangs. I felt very uncomfortable. Banging the book on the shelf, I stormed out of the bookstore. When I got downstairs, I started to walk with a limp all the way back to the 'Church of Our Lady'.

- Read the book of Malachi, followed by Hebrews 1-7.

- I walked back to Kensington Bookstore to speak to Ming Mei, telling her what I had experienced at Evangel. I felt so much better after talking to her. I left the store in high spirits and high hopes.

Thursday, May 14, 2009   *Psalm 4, 12, 19, 119; Hebrews 7 & 8*

Felt really tired today. Unable to focus.

Friday, May 15, 2009   *John 9; Hebrews 9*

Saturday, May 16, 2009   *Ezekiel 34, 35, 36; Hebrews 9 & 10*

*Journal: I returned to the internet cafe nearby the fire station to do some research. On my way home that evening, I noticed the beautiful pink clouds in the sky. After passing by the fire station, I looked up into the sky and saw a beating heart in the sky surrounded by pink clouds. I quickly walked back to study the scriptures I had read earlier in the morning. **I found God's word 'spoken' and revealed to me in Ezekiel 36:25-27 and then I understood what the beating heart was. God had given me a 'new heart'. He had replaced my stony stubborn heart with a heart of flesh, an obedient heart.**

(Scripture Reading: Ezekiel 36:25-27)

How good is our Lord? He had given me a second chance. No matter what happens, no matter where I am or where I go, I will always heed the Word of God which brings me 'Life'! No other teachings in this world can teach me what the Word of God has taught me. No other teaching has brought me life except the Word of God, for the Word of God IS Life!

(Scripture readings: 1 Peter 1:23; Hebrews 4:12)

Jesus is the Word of God! **(Scripture Readings: Revelation 19:13)**

Jesus is the way, the truth and the life!

(Scripture Readings: John 14:6)

Finally, I understood why I had been groaning all this while. I had been groaning in the Spirit. The Holy Spirit was helping me and encouraging me. He was praying for me from within me. Then I understood why I was having heart murmurs and palpitations. I understood that the Holy Spirit was interceding for me as I read God's word. **(Scripture Reading: Romans 8:26).**

This is so real. At one time, my heart even developed lips of its' own. Many people would have rushed to the hospital or thought they were going crazy but I tell you the truth, my heart had lips of its' own.

Sunday, May 17, 2009	*John 10 (X 7 times); Hebrews 10; Revelation 10 & 11*
Monday, May 18, 2009	*Psalm 20 & 82; John 11; Hebrews 11; Isaiah 61, 62 & 63*

Spent the day learning on magnifying the name of our Lord - Psalm 20! Went to bed early

Tuesday, May 19, 2009   *Proverbs 3; Isaiah 51, 52, 53 & 54*

Read Proverbs 3 & Isaiah 51 before going to the Penang Christian Centre (PCC) for the Ablaze Breakthrough Seminar organised by the AG Prayer Commission and Northern District Council of Malaysia. The speaker was Barbara J. Yoder from USA. She is known for her prophetic ministry and apostolic breakthrough anointing and is author of 'The Breaker Anointing' and 'Taking On Goliath'.

I attended two sessions of Barbara's talks that day. One in the morning and one in the afternoon before we broke for lunch. I went home for lunch and rested the whole afternoon. When I awoke, I was kept busy with household chores till about 7:00pm. I made sure I read my daily scriptures for the day before I took the bus to PCC for the Night Meeting. I read Isaiah 52, 53 and 54 that evening before I left my home.

It was dark and I was running late. I walked down the slope and took the short cut to the bus-stop. As I turned around the bend at a cross-junction entering a housing area, I stopped because the dogs under a car startled me. They started howling eerily and scurried away from me. Just then, a motorbike came from the opposite direction heading towards me. Its' headlights shone at the ground and I was shocked to see a huge snake in front of me. It was black and white in colour and its' head was as big as a cow's. The snake slithered towards the river but disappeared before my very eyes. It was an evil spirit.

Afraid, I wanted to turn back home but I felt I had to attend the night meeting. It was a short trip to PCC. I got off the bus and sat at the back of the hall. After that night's session, one of the seminar's facilitators walked right to the back of the hall and approached me. She asked me to write down my sisters' names on a piece of paper and handed me a pencil. I wrote their names down. She then asked me to take a look at what I had written. I looked at the paper and read Shannon's name. My eyes suddenly opened up as though I had been blinded before. I read the next name I wrote down, 'Debel'. Why did I write the devil's name instead of my second sister's name? The lady left me and immediately I was surrounded by other church members who were known to me. They asked me to join them that night for supper. They even offered to send me home that night.

We all left the hall and I followed them to Northam Beach Cafe in one of my friend's cars. While we were gathered there together, I started trembling and shivering like a drug addict. One of the elders of the church saw me trembling and she gently wrapped her shawl around me to comfort and warm me. I felt loved by these group of caring Christians. After supper, Aunt Trudy and her daughter, Abigail, sent me home that night.

Wednesday, May 20, 2009

I attended Session 4 of the Ablaze Breakthrough Seminar from 9:30am till 11:15am. This was followed by Session 5 which covered a Healing and Anointing session that ended at 1:00pm. As I was too tired that day, I did not attend the Night Meeting. Fortunately, I could watch the replay of all the sessions on DVD as I had bought the recordings of the sessions of this Ablaze Breakthrough Seminar. God's word is indeed powerful. I pray for more breakthroughs.

For the next ten days, I fasted and prayed along with those who had attended the Ablaze Breakthrough Seminar.

Thursday, May 21, 2009 *Acts 1; Revelation 12 & 22*

Day One : The Kingdom of Jesus
            Pray For The Nation To Be Transformed

*Journal: What a beautiful and peaceful day it is! End with the Lord's prayer.

Friday, May 22, 2009 *Acts 1, 2, 3; Psalm 138, 148, 150*

Day Two : Standing Strong
           For The Fire Of Prayer To Sweep The Nation

Saturday, May 23, 2009 *Acts 2;*
                          Psalm 44, 45, 46, 47, 48, 69
                          & 70

Day Three : Standing Strong
             For God To Pour Out His Spirit Upon All

Sunday, May 24, 2009 *Acts 3*

Day Four : Turning Back To God
            For Many To Turn From Sin To New Life In Jesus

Monday, May 25, 2009 *Acts 1, 2 & 3; Galatians 1~5*

Day Five : The Peace Of Christ
            For Relationships To Be Restored

Tuesday, May 26, 2009 *Acts 2, 4 & 6; Psalm 103; 1 John*

Day Six : The Rising Generation
           God's Purpose For Families And Young People

Wednesday, May 27, 2009 *Acts 1, 2 & 3; 1 John*

Day Seven : The Call Of God
For The Nations To Hear The Voice Of God

Thursday, May 28, 2009   *Acts 4 & 5; 1 John*

Day Eight   : The Glory Of Jesus
Displayed In His People

Friday, May 29, 2009   *Acts 4 & 5; 1 Timothy*

Day Nine   : Healing Through Jesus
For Christ To Bring Healing

Saturday, May 30, 2009   *Acts 3*

Day Ten   : The Blessing Of Jesus
For Promised Blessing In All Nations

Sunday, May 31, 2009

Attended my first Bible Study Class at KPBC from 9:00am till 10:00am; followed by church service and fellowship. Was there till 2:30pm. I rested the whole day as it was my Sabbath. My day ended with thanksgiving and praise.

Monday, June 1, 2009

'Bless this home, O Lord, I pray,
Keep us safe by night and day.'

*Journal: Thank you, Jesus for the wonderful miracles you perform and display for us through your creation. Thank you for the morning sky, the cheerful chirping melody of the birds of the air, the sounds of people going to work- peacefully, the sounds of LIFE!

We had a short visit from our relatives who lived nearby. In the evening, I did some arts and crafts work. I stepped outside to watch the world go by. There were a myriad twinkling stars that night. Some were very clear, they looked so near that you could just reach out and touch them. They were all so bright and beautiful, they reminded me of glow worms and fireflies.

Thank You, Jesus, for this awesome sight. What a wonderful moment. May I always cherish these moments forever in my heart. May the peace of Christ blanket our home. PEACE, BE STILL! Amen!

Tuesday, June 2, 2009   *Psalm 91, 105, 109, 148 & 150; John 8, 9 & 10 - Prayer & Fasting*

Thank You, Jesus for listening to my prayers. Thank You for a beautiful morning. Your light, O Lord, is awesome, bright and beautiful. In You, there is no darkness at all. All praise the Lord, for He is good! Praise The Lord, Our Mighty Saviour! The One who is, who was and who is to come!

Wednesday, June 3, 2009   *John 11; 1 John 5:20; Hebrews 12:12; Philippians 3:21; Philippians 1, 2, 3 & 4; 1 Thessalonians 1:6; Exodus 6; Revelation 7*

Showers of blessings followed by bright sunny skies in the morning.

Thank You, Jesus, for sharing your word of life with me. Thank you for calling me to the 'Elijah Challenge'! Teach me, Lord Jesus; teach me, please! I want to cast out demons and heal the sick. Help me to discern the truth! O Lord, take Your place in the throne of my heart. I surrender myself to You! Thank You, for being my friend and counselor!

- Attended the 'Elijah Challenge' Training Seminar at PCC from 8:00pm till 10:30pm.

Thursday, June 4, 2009   *Psalm 27, 73 & 95;*
Isaiah 49; Joel;
Ephesians 2:18; Hebrews 4:16;
Hebrews 13:5; Colossians 3:2;
Psalm 94:14; 1 Corinthians 7:35

- Attended the 'Elijah Challenge' Healing Seminar and Rally' from 7:30pm till 10:30pm.

Friday, June 5, 2009   *John 12; Psalm 1, 2 & 3;*
2 Kings 4;
2 Kings 13:20-21; 1 Kings 17;
2 Kings 17

I remember having a conviction after reading Psalm 73. **(Scripture Reading: Psalm 73:23-26)**. God is faithful!

- Attended the 'Elijah Challenge' Healing Seminar and Rally at PCC from 7:30pm till 10:30pm

Saturday, June 6, 2009

Attended the 'Elijah Challenge' Healing Seminar and Rally at 12:00pm. Participants of the 'Elijah Challenge' Healing Seminar and Rally were sent out in groups of threes and fours to homes at the Rifle Range Flats. We were told to put into practice what we had learned from the seminar. At 3:00pm sharp, I met up with two of my group members at the market downstairs the Rifle Range flats. We bought some fruits for our hosts who were already informed of our visit to their homes for prayer.

During this practicum, we visited three homes. We stayed for 15 minutes to half an hour at each home talking to our hosts, most of whom were suffering from illnesses. They welcomed us to pray for them. I remember praying these words at the last home we visited, 'The Kingdom of Our Lord Is Upon You'. As we stepped outside their home, I saw spirits in light blue lights, all lined up at the entrance. They floated into the air one by one as we bid farewell to our hosts and left the premises.

That night, we met up again at PCC to share our testimonies. I spoke about my declaration about God's Kingdom being upon our hosts and what I saw after that. I learned that day, that declarations made in faith are very powerful weapons for God's children. Whether those who heard my testimony believed me or not does not matter. All that matters is that we advance God's Kingdom and we pledge allegiance with God.

Tuesday, June 9, 2009   *Ecclesiastes 1-10*

Wednesday, June 10, 2009   *Psalm 118*

Thursday, June 11, 2009   *Psalm 120, 121, 122, 123, 124, Psalm 125, 126, 127, 131 & 136*

Friday, June 12, 2009   *Leviticus 26; Judges 15; Psalm 144; Ezekiel 9*

Saturday, June 13, 2009

- Attended another seminar. This time, on deception, entitled 'Deception - Exposing The Work Of The Enemy'

Monday, June 15, 2009   *Psalm 19*

Tuesday, June 16, 2009 *Psalm 51, 52, 53, 54, 121, 123 & Psalm 141; Proverbs 19*

Friday, June 19, 2009 *Proverbs 3*

Attended 'Destiny International Women's Conference' at Harvest Christian Centre.

- Felt vulnerable. Could feel wisps of air, like snakes slithering beneath my feet as the speakers spoke on stage.

Saturday, June 20, 2009

Attended the 2nd day of 'Destiny International Women's Conference'. I was numb, emotionless as I watched a participant crying as she shared with a speaker about the death of her husband due to cancer. It had been four years since his death but she was still feeling the pain. Why was I so numb? I hope I wasn't judging her. God, I pray not!

Sunday, June 21, 2009 *Psalm 55, 56 & 57*

Wednesday, June 24, 2009 *Psalm 137, 138 & 139; Isaiah 56 & 57; Revelation 19*

Thursday, June 25, 2009 *Numbers 14; Job 3 & 4*

Friday, June 26, 2009 *2 Chronicles 28; Nehemiah*

Saturday, June 27, 2009 *Job 5, 6, 7, 8, 9 & 10; Acts 8, 9 & 10; Proverbs 1; Psalm 140, 141, 142 & 143; Revelation 14:13-16; Revelation 15*

Sunday, June 28, 2009   *1 Chronicles 28 & 29;*
Nahum 1-3;
Acts 13, 14, 15 & 16

Monday, June 29, 2009   *Psalm 14 & 15;*
1 Peter 3:8-22;
1 Peter 4 & 5

Tuesday, June 30, 2009   *Job 17; Zephaniah 3;*
Psalm 125, 126, 127,
128 & 129;
Revelation 11:15-19

Wednesday, July 1, 2009   *Zephaniah 1 & 2;*
Acts 11 & 12;
2 Peter 1, 2 & 3

Friday, July 3, 2009   *Psalm 18, 42, 62 & 63*

Sunday, July 5, 2009   *1 Samuel 15,*
1 Samuel 19 & 20;
Acts 20

Monday, July 6, 2009   *Psalm 119:57-112*

Tuesday, July 7, 2009   *Joshua 1;*
Psalm 116, 117 & 121;
2 Corinthians 1-13

Wednesday, July 8, 2009   *Psalm 25, 26, 27 & 147*

Thursday, July 9, 2009   *Revelation 22*

Friday, July 10, 2009   *Psalm 119:113-176*

Saturday, July 11, 2009	*Psalm 4; Psalm 68*
Sunday, July 12, 2009	*Psalm 4, 5 & 6*
Monday, July 13, 2009	*Genesis 4-31; Genesis 33-35; Deuteronomy 32; Psalm 1, 2, 3 & 4; Hebrews 10:19-25*

Had an early start in the morning of July 13, 2009. I wanted to be prepared for 2009's Bible Conference. The conference would be held at Trinity Methodist Church on July 18, 2009. The theme chosen for that year was 'Joseph: Overcoming Life's Challenges'.

5:00am - 12:00pm	Spent the whole morning reading scriptural verses from Genesis 4 till Genesis 35, skipping Genesis 32
12:00pm - 1:00pm	Brunch
1:00pm - 2:00pm	Deuteronomy 32
2:00pm - 3:30pm	Listened to Hosanna Music (Praise & Worship songs)
3:30pm - 5:00pm	Break
5:00pm - 6:00pm	Listened to Broadway musicals
6:00pm - 7:00pm	Scripture Reading: Hebrews 10:19-25
8:30pm - 9:00pm	Read Psalm 1, 2, 3 & 4
11:00am - 2:00am	Prepared my schedule on Book of Job & Genesis for the next day, July 14, 2009 before calling it a night.

Tuesday, July 14, 2009

9:00am - 10:00pm	Started my day with daily chores; showered; washed clothes.
10:00am - 11:00am	Continued daily chores; Fed cats
11:00am - 12:00pm	Had a meal; Prepared monthly schedule; Prayer and meditation.

12:00pm - 1:00pm	Psalm 4, 5 & 6. Mark 19; Luke 19
1:00pm - 2:00pm	Homework on 'The Holy Spirit - His Person'
	He acts as a person (will); Deuteronomy 33& 34
2:00pm - 2:30pm	Psalm 8 & 9; Isaiah 14;
	Reading from 'Our Daily Bread'
2:30pm - 4:00pm	Prepared monthly schedule; Prayer and meditation; 2 Chronicles 12:5-23; 2 Chronicles 12; 2 Chronicles 15
4:00pm - 5:00pm	Scripture Reading: Genesis 37
5:00pm - 6:00pm	Scripture Reading: Genesis 38
6:00pm - 7:00pm	Scripture Reading: Genesis 39
7:00pm - 8:00pm	Prepared monthly schedule; Prayer and meditation
8:00pm - 9:00pm	Scripture Reading: Job 13, 14, 42; Matthew 7
9:00pm - 10:00pm	Job 1, 2 & 3
10:00pm - 11:00pm	Job 4 & 5
11:00pm - 12:00am	Read Psalm 7 & 11 before retiring for the night.

Wednesday, July 15, 2009

8:00am - 9:00am	Good morning, Lord Jesus!
	Source of David and our 'Bright and Morning Star'! Prayer and Meditation!
9:00am - 11:00am	Daily chores; Washed and dried clothes; Fed Cats
11:00am - 12:00pm	Prepared schedule
12:00pm - 1:00pm	The Holy Spirit - His Person
1:00pm - 2:00pm	Scripture Reading: Job 5, 6 & 7
2:00pm - 2:30pm	Scripture Reading: Job 8 & 9
2:30pm - 3:30pm	Lunch; Homework on 'The Holy Spirit'
3:30pm - 4:00pm	Tea Break
4:00pm - 5:00pm	Listened to music: Russel Watson
5:00pm - 7:00pm	Scripture Reading: Job 10, 11, 12, 13 & 14

7:30pm - 8:00pm   Psalms
8:00pm - 9:00pm   Scripture Reading: Genesis 40
9:00pm - 10:00pm   Scripture Reading: Genesis 41
10:00pm - 11:00pm Psalms; Revelation 4, 5 & 6.

Thursday, July 16, 2009   *Genesis 42 & 43;*
Job 15, 16, 17, 18, 19, 20 & 21

Friday, July 17, 2009   *Genesis 32:24-32; Genesis 44;*
Exodus 21:12-30; Job 22-31;
Exodus 24, 25, 26 & 27; Psalm 18

Saturday, July 18, 2009   *Genesis 45; Job 32-37; Job 39-42*

I attended the Bible Conference 'Joseph: Overcoming Life's Challenges' at Trinity Methodist Church. I remember how proud I felt as I entered the church. Full of knowledge of God's word because I had read the scriptures and done my homework. I didn't want to be left in the dark about what the preacher was going to preach about. The moment I opened the door to enter the hall, pride set in. I had the urge to debate with the preacher. Thank God, I took captive of my thoughts and stopped myself. I knew clearly that I was there to learn and not to 'challenge' others.

Sunday, July 19, 2009   *Job 38*

Monday, July 20, 2009   *Psalm 28, 32 & 33;*
Haggai 1 & 2

Tuesday, July 21, 2009   *Psalm 34*

Wednesday, July 22, 2009 *Proverbs 4, 5, 6, 7 & 11*

Thursday, July 23, 2009   *1 Samuel 2; 1 Samuel 3*

Monday, July 27, 2009

10:00am - 11:00am	Psalm 110; Psalm 47
1:00pm - 2:00pm	Break
2:00pm - 3:30pm	Went to the State Registration Office in George Town to check the contents of my identity card and to ensure that my religion states that I am a Christian, a follower of Christ and God's child.
3:30pm - 7:00pm	Shopped for stationery for my arts and crafts work. Went to Gama, Prangin Mall and Macalister Road.
7:00pm - 8:00pm	Got some cards laminated for my arts and crafts work.
8:00pm - 9:00pm	Showered: Rest & Relax!
9:00pm - 10:00pm	Psalm 69
10:00pm - 11:00pm	Scripture Reading: 1 Samuel 1

Tuesday, July 28, 2009   *Isaiah 6-13; Isaiah 24-28; Isaiah 30; 32, 33, 35, 36 & 37*

Wednesday, July 29, 2009

5:00am - 6:00am	Scripture Reading: Luke 1; Isaiah 12 & 13; Mark 1 & 2
6:00am - 10:00am	Went back to sleep!!!
11:00am - 1:00pm	Daily chores: Fed Cats; Swept Floor; Washed Clothes
1:00pm - 2:30pm	Prayer in Solitude: Pray for change and healing; Praise and Worship Music; Carry the Call
2:30pm - 3:00pm	Daily Chores: Hung out clothes to dry
3:00pm - 3:45pm	I listened to music: Christ Crucifixion - our healing and change
3:45pm - 4:00pm	Break
6:00pm - 9:00pm	Listened to music: Praise & Worship; Hosanna Music with Don Moen.

Victory in God's Hands

Saturday, August 1, 2009   *Esther; Exodus 34;*
                                  Psalm 19 & 36;
                                  Romans 12-16

Good morning, 'Bright and Morning Star!'

I remember how I used to drive around housing areas looking for places to rent around this time. Sometimes, I wished that I would find my true love and settle down in a quiet neighbourhood. There were a few places I admired. One was an apartment for sale/rent at Rainbow Hill overlooking the sea. It was situated in a quiet neighbourhood, right in the corner down the road.

Wednesday, August 5, 2009   *Revelation 8 & 9*

Thursday, August 6, 2009   *Isaiah 44:21-28; Isaiah*
                                   45, 46, 48

Friday, August 7, 2009   *Psalm 119:1-56;*
                                   Proverbs 22, 23 & 25

Saturday, August 8, 2009

Mrs Patsy Wilson, my neighbour, took me along to the Church of Our Lady to attend a bible seminar on 'The Man From Tarsus: The Life & Message of St Paul'.

Sunday, August 9, 2009   *1 Thessalonians 1-5;*
                                   2 Timothy 1-3

Attended the 2nd day of the bible seminar on 'The Man From Tarsus: The Life & Message of St Paul'. This time I went on my own using Jonathan's car as I had planned to attend church service at the Holy Trinity Church. Halfway through the seminars, I got restless and decided to get some refreshments. I was sitting alone at the side of the hall and a gentleman came over to join me. In his hand, he held a book. He called himself Joshua and opened the book to show me his recent baptismal celebration at this church, Church of Our Lady.

Joshua's eldest sister-in-law had compiled and arranged the photos of his baptism into a photobook. It was the most beautiful thing I had ever seen in such a long time. Fr Matthias was the priest who gave him the blessing that same year.

I would have loved to stay and chat with Joshua but I had to excuse myself to go to Holy Trinity Church for Sunday Service at 5:30pm. To me, Joshua's baptism seemed extra special.

Monday, August 10, 2009   *Proverbs 14;*
1 Timothy 2:1-4;
Psalm 14, 15, 47 & 75

Tuesday, August 11, 2009   *Psalm 42, 43, 47 & 75;*
Micah 1-7

Spent the day making bookmarks for our Independence Day.

Wednesday, August 12, 2009   *Romans 12 & 13*

My mother and my cousin, Yen Yen, took me to a house just down the road. They told me that I could get 'help' from the woman who lived there. We walked into a dark and creepy

165

living room. I had a very eerie feeling about this place. I was furious when I found out that the woman was a tarot card reader. Only the 'blind', those living in 'spiritual darkness' would go there.

My mother and Yen Yen kept persuading me to let the woman read my cards. They kept on insisting that I touch the cards. My mother and Yen Yen didn't want to budge from their seats. They said that the woman could tell me my problems and provide a solution.

I was mighty upset that my mother would corner me like this. To make her happy, I touched the stack of cards with my finger and asked if we could leave the house. I was feeling very uncomfortable there. Immediately, the tarot card reader pulled out a card and said, "You have to see a doctor!"

I brushed it off as nonsense. I just wanted to leave that house because I knew it was wrong to be there.

In the evening, I went through some old photographs for my arts and crafts work. Had some trouble with Roger and my parents. I walked to the nearest police station in the district after they provoked me. I was feeling emotional at that time.

It was about 9:00pm when I got to the police station. I sat in the station for a while until a tall, young lady officer came up to me. She could see that I was distraught so she invited me out for a drink. We walked over to a food outlet opposite the police station where she bought me a cold beverage. She was very gentle and calm and lent me a listening ear as I poured out my story of being raped in Langkawi in 2006. I wanted justice to be served but it was too late. She listened, then gave me some advice about starting a new relationship. I felt much better after talking with her. I assured her that I would be alright and after thanking her, I walked back home. I was there for nearly an hour.

Thursday, August 13, 2009

I was supposed to attend a Care Group meeting at Holy Trinity Church but something dreadful happened that morning. I woke up feeling joyful as I thought about how God had inspired the psalmist to describe joy in songs as leaping gazelles. I felt light as a gazelle.

As I remember vividly, my mother was walking down the staircase and I was skipping happily behind her. She was about to step into the kitchen when I suddenly snapped. I lost control when I stepped into the dining room. Grabbing my hi-fi (CD & DVD player), I smashed it to the ground in front of my mother's feet. I was about to pick up a glass jug and smash it too when a gentle voice stopped me.

'She is your mother!' the voice whispered to me gently.

There was a sudden pain in my heart. 'But she's hurt me so badly,' I thought to myself, nursing the pain in my chest. Unable to contain the seething anger within me, I ignored the gentle voice and smashed the jug onto the ground. A dim, white light flashed in front of my face and I was normal again.

Shocked but thankful that no one was hurt, I quickly walked upstairs. I wondered where that white light had come from so I began to trace my steps. Roger told Papa to call the police. Then he and mummy pounced on me. Mummy pressed her knee on my back while Roger pressed the veins on my hands. I screamed in pain pleading with them to stop hurting me.

The police arrived and persuaded me to ride in the 911 ambulance to the hospital to be evaluated by a psychiatrist. My parents drove themselves to the hospital. At the hospital, I was placed under observation in a room with a psychiatrist. She didn't say a word to me. Neither did she look up to acknowledge me. Her head was buried in some paper work at her desk. I waited for more than fifteen minutes not doing anything. Fed up, I walked out of the office. I couldn't find my way out of the hospital. It was like a maze. I was about to enter the children's ward when two staff in nurses uniform walked past me. I turned to follow these two male nurses and suddenly I reached out to grab the back of the Indian male staff's neck. I did so because I felt that he was 'hurting' the children.

My father caught up with me and tried to block my way. The police arrived and escorted me to the ambulance which took me to the Women's Psychiatric Ward about 5km away from the general hospital.

Upon admission, my blood sample was taken. I was given supper and medication before bedtime. Since I had been on a fast before my admission to the Women's Psychiatric Ward, I told the nurse that I preferred to be on a vegetarian diet when given the choice between a meat or vegetarian diet. Then I was locked up in a cell along with the other girls - Asha, a teenager and Eunice, a former worker at Toy's R US, made me feel welcomed there.

Friday, August 14, 2009

The nurses at the Women's Psychiatric Ward woke us up at 5:00am for our morning bath. After that, my blood sample was taken again by a nurse and I was given medication. I sat up the whole day observing the other inmates and I prayed the 'Lord's Prayer' in my heart. I got to know another patient Yogini during our dinner.

Saturday, August 15, 2009

I started menstruating about 2:00pm so I told a nurse about it. They continued to put me on medication and I noticed that it affected my menstruation. I had suddenly stopped menstruating. I thought that perhaps I was too stressed out. By the third day, I was comfortable with Yogini, Rifat, Asha and Eunice.

I had gotten to know most of the other girls in the following days and I was comfortable with all except Chai and Li-Na. Both of them were quite unpredictable.

- Li-Na would be very childlike at times but would mostly distance herself from the others. She alienated herself and would get angry so I kept away from her most of the time. I would sometimes share my food with her.
- I was unable to get Chai to talk. She would get very angry when I tried to strike up conversation with her. Very silent.
- Dannavandana: Or Diane. I learned from Aunt Jessica that Danna was prostituted by her own husband to his 'friends'. She looked possessed. Her eyes were always rolling and she loved to remove her clothing and walk around naked.
- Yogini: She witnessed her own elder sister commit suicide. Her sister had a lot of problems with her husband and jumped off a building, taking her own life.

I could only think of the 'Lord's Prayer' for protection and to bless these girls with.

Tuesday, August 18, 2009

10:00am — Dr Anna told me that I could be discharged and that my parents had to sign me out.

6:00pm — Papa and Mummy visited me but told me that I couldn't be discharged.

Wednesday, August 19, 2009

5:00am — My blood sample was taken before my bath

5:00pm — Papa & Mummy visited me. They informed me that I needed to see Dr Cheong before getting discharged. I was a little agitated because Dr Cheong had said that I could be discharged already.

Friday, August 21, 2009

10:00am — Dr Cheong personally informed me that I could be discharged.

My parents arrived before 7:00pm to discharge me. My mother informed me that I needed to go for a brain scan at CITI SCAN on 3 September 2009. I spent a total of eight nights and nine days at the Women's Psychiatric Ward in Penang in 2009.

Saturday, August 22, 2009   *Proverbs 21*

Sunday, August 23, 2009

I took a bus down to George Town at noon to buy a burger for Yogini. She didn't seem pleased to see me when I went to the psychiatric ward to hand her the burger. I knew she wanted to get out and go home but what could I do? After I left the ward, I walked over to the Holy Trinity Church to learn about the Alpha Course. I attended church service there.

Friday, August 28, 2009 *Psalm 11; Mark 1 & 2*

Saturday, August 29, 2009 *Amos 9*

Monday, August 31, 2009

It was Malaysia's Independence Day. I had woken up too late to catch the crowd at the 'Merdeka Parade' to sell my Independence Day bookmarks. When I got to town, the crowd had already dispersed so I jogged at the Esplanade for an hour from 9:00am till 10:00am. After that, I took a bus back but stopped at the beach behind ECO Hotel, Tanjung Bungah to have a swim. A stranger I met bought one bookmark from me.

Tuesday, September 1, 2009 *Luke 21:25; Luke 21:9;*
Revelation 1 & 2;
Revelation 2:1-7;
1 Kings 8 & 1 Kings 9

Thursday, September 3, 2009 *Mark 22*

Sunday, September 6, 2009 *Mark 23*

Attended the 5:30pm church service at Holy Trinity Church

Monday, September 7, 2009 *Psalm 22 & 31*

Tuesday, September 8, 2009 *Proverbs 23, 24 & 27;*
Mark 24

Sunday, September 13, 2009

Attended the 5:30pm church service at Holy Trinity Church.

I attended the 5:30pm church services every Sunday for the months of October & November 2009. Their resident pastor was preaching mightily on the seven churches from the Book of Revelation. I joined them in praying for causes and for the nation of Malaysia.

Wednesday, October 14, 2009   *Psalm 108*

Following the footsteps of my father, I joined the Society of St Vincent de Paul (SSVP). I remember selling all of my bookmarks at their 'Jumble Sale' held in the Church of Our Lady. Madelaine and Gabriel who ministered to me at KPBC bought two bookmarks from me. When they asked me why I chose the scripture verses for Malaysia and Penang, I could not answer them. Neither could I explain what the Holy Spirit had revealed to me about Malaysia and Penang but I knew the prophecies in Isaiah were all good and for the good of our people and country.

Sometime in October or November 2009, the members of the SSVP from the Church of Our Lady organized a trip to learn more about the Tzu Chi organization. Coincidentally, Joshua was also a member of the SSVP. He had joined the society in August 2009. I was a passenger in Joshua's car, along with five others, on our way to the Tzu Chi facility in Macalister Road.

When we arrived at the Tzu Chi building, we were greeted by a senior staff member of Tzu Chi at the main entrance. She looked resplendent in her blue cheongsam. She took us on a tour around the facility. Some areas were cordoned off. I wondered if they had trap doors and secret passages. There were just so many 'doors' in this facility. The tour ended with a video session of the history of Tzu Chi and a tea drinking session. Drinking tea is a form of art. The idea of starting Tzu Chi actually originated from a Catholic nun. The founder of Tzu Chi is Master Cheng Yen.

From this visit, we learnt that Tzu Chi was usually the first to send aid and support to the victims of natural disasters globally. We also visited Tzu Chi's Haemodialysis Centre in Gottlieb Road to learn more about their works and services.

Friday, November 13, 2009

Attended a seminar entitled 'Spiritual Discipline & Renewal' at Copthorne Hotel.

Saturday, November 14, 2009

Attended the 2nd day of the seminar 'Spiritual Discipline & Renewal' at Copthorne Hotel. The speaker mentioned that most people were going about their daily lives like headless chickens. He meant that they had no plan or had lost their purpose in life. I recalled the dream I had in 2004. I still could not understand this dream but I knew my purpose was to build and advance God's kingdom here on earth.

Friday-Sunday, November 27-29, 2009

More than 100 members of the SSVP from throughout Malaysia, convened at a retreat centre in Port Dickson for SSVP's annual retreat. Joshua and I were lucky to be included in this retreat since we were new members at that time. The theme was 'Deepening Our Discipleship as Vincentians'. I watched and followed my father giving out food rations to the poor families in our district as I was growing up. I wanted to follow in his footsteps but I wanted so much more than that. I wanted to know my God: I wanted to know Jesus more; I wanted to taste the goodness of our Lord. Fr Murphy was our facilitator.

During our meals, Joshua would reserve a table for us so we could talk privately. I wasn't too sure about starting a relationship but he seemed like a perfect 'gentleman'. We exchanged phone numbers so we could stay in touch after the retreat.

Friday, December 4, 2009

I attended the 'Advent Retreat For Young Adults' which had the theme 'While Shepherds Watched Their Flock By Night'. This retreat was held at the Kensington College General of Penang and was facilitated by Fr Murray of Church of Our Lady. Two participants of this retreat had just joined the seminary and were in their first year to becoming priests. In this retreat, we were told to anticipate the return of our Lord and King, Jesus Christ. We had to prepare our hearts for His Second Coming to receive His Bride, the Church.

Saturday, December 5, 2009   *Psalm 139*

2nd day of Advent Retreat For Young Adults.

Theme: While Shepherds Watched Their Flock By Night.
We were shown videos to remind us of the basis of our faith: the Cross.

Sunday, December 6, 2009

3rd day of Advent Retreat For Young Adults.
Theme: While Shepherds Watched Their Flock By Night

Wednesday, December 9, 2009   *2 Thessalonians 1-3;*

Thursday, December 10, 2009   *Psalm 133, 134 & 139*

Friday, December 11, 2009   *Psalm 52, 53 & 54*

Saturday, December 19, 2009   *Judges 13*

It was around this time that I found out about a vacancy for the position of Parish General Clerk in the church bulletin of the Church of Our Lady. I called their office and was given an appointment for an interview.

Wednesday, December 23, 2009   *Judges 16:28-31*

I received my letter of offer from the Church of Our Lady, which stated that I had gotten the job as Parish General Clerk and that I was to begin my new job on 2 January 2010. I was overjoyed at being given this chance and grateful to Fr Murray and the church committee members who had selected me.

Thursday, December 24, 2009

It was Christmas Eve once again. Joan had come back for the holidays. Both Joan and Roger were engrossed in watching the World Tours, tennis matches. I was more excited about receiving guests into our home for Christmas so I got busy cleaning the house.

Friday, December 25, 2009

I had dressed up after arranging the furniture in the living room of my parents' home and was sweeping the floor in the living room when Joan came upstairs to watch her tennis match. I wasn't sure if it was the semi-finals, finals, live or replay matches. Joan switched on the television and slumped across the sofa. I hurriedly swept the floor. Unfortunately, I had blocked Joan's view. She flew into a rage and attacked me physically. I raised both hands to defend myself from her blows and she quickly grabbed my right hand and bit my hand at the exact spot where I had developed a mark after being raped in 2006. The mark was like a rash with dots that looked like a VGA port.

Crying because Joan's actions hurt me, I left the house and walked straight to the beach behind ECO Hotel.

Still sobbing as I walked along Elephant Walk Road, I looked up into the sky and saw pink clouds. The little pink clouds formed like 'little sheep'. One was bigger than the other.

I cried out, "The mother sheep would never leave the baby sheep!"

I couldn't understand what all that was about but I was simply led by what I felt in my heart.

There were not many people at the beach that morning. I walked straight into the sea until the sea covered me up till my shoulders. I was looking into the direction of the open sea, thinking how beautiful it was when my right hand started 'slithering' like a snake. Out it went! Some strange snake-like force was expelled from me. I saw this demonic spirit slither towards the deeper part of the sea. I wanted to follow it, almost forgetting that I could not swim. It left behind a blue dot. Something prompted me to turn back and head towards the beach. I thought that the 'blue dot' could have been a box jellyfish. Very deadly. Luckily I was not stung by it.

Turning back to the beach, I looked up into the sky. The sun was shining on my face. I knew at that moment that I had been 'delivered'. God had triumphed once again! I had triumphed over the serpent spirit! How I longed to see the face of my deliverer. My faith is in Jesus Christ! I knew that Jesus had delivered me but I could not see His face. However, I knew that He was with me.

When I got home, my mother frowned at me repulsively. Another year, another lousy Christmas with the family. I got some cash and my bible and left the family home once again. This time, I made my way to the Hibiscus Bus Station in Kedah. Why did I choose this destination? Maybe Langkawi was calling me again. However, this time I did not bring any luggage or change of clothing with me. I was being led to do what the Word of God told me to do. This time, I checked into a new motel nearby the bus station. I just needed some time alone with the Lord.

It was about 6:30pm when I had reached the Hibiscus Bus Station in Kedah. I could have gone to Langkawi but I said, 'No!' to Langkawi, this time. I bought a pair of undergarments at a supermarket close to the motel. Then I had my dinner at a fast-food restaurant close to the bus station. When I came back to the motel, I washed my clothes and used a towel to dry them. Then I hung out my clothes to dry in the bathroom after having my bath. I spent the night reading my bible until I got tired and slept till the next morning. I awoke at 5:30am and got dressed. My clothes had already dried by then. I thought there would be buses about but it was really quiet outside. The main door of the motel was still locked. I didn't want to go out using the side door as it was still too dark outside and I wasn't familiar with this area. At about 7:00am, I went out and bought a bus ticket to return to Penang. Then I checked out and headed home.

Wednesday, December 30, 2009 *Lamentations 1, 2, 3, 4 & 5; Obadiah; Jonah 1-4*

Friday, January 1, 2010 *Exodus 20; Amos 1-9*

Saturday, January 2, 2010

Started work at Church of Our Lady under the care of Fr Murray.

Tuesday, January 5, 2010   *Psalm 71*

Saturday, January 16, 2010   *1 Peter 1, 2 & 3*

Some time in March or April 2010, some parishioners from the Church of the Holy Spirit approached Fr Murray for permission to conduct the 'Alpha' course at the Church of Our Lady. As soon as Fr Murray gave the green-light, Joshua and I quickly registered ourselves for this course. We wanted to deepen our faith in Christ and we hoped that by doing so, our spiritual lives would grow and our relationship would be strengthened. Joshua would faithfully visit me during my lunch hours at my workplace. I had to help with the purchase of course materials for this first Alpha course. Besides the Alpha Course, Joshua and I also joined a year long course on 'Discipleship'.

Tuesday, April 6, 2010   *Exodus 10; Psalm 84*

Wednesday, April 7, 2010   *1 Kings 18:41-46;*
                                   1 Kings 19;
                                   1 Chronicles 22

Saturday & Sunday, May 29 & May 30, 2010

1st Alpha Weekend Away {A Holiday With Jesus}.

It had been a wonderful weekend for both Joshua and I. I can remember vividly that this was the weekend when I received the gift of tongues. Stephen, one of the facilitators, was gently coaxing me to just roll my tongue. Then he said, "Speak," and I 'spoke'.

"You've got it!" exclaimed Stephen. "Praise God!"

He advised me to keep practicing speaking in tongues before leaving me to minister to the other participants. I was overjoyed. Surprised and perplexed at first, because I thought I could not get this gift since others from other Christian churches had prayed over me to get this gift before. But I hadn't received the gift of tongues then. Praise God for His wonderful gift of the Holy Spirit. The Holy Spirit is my 'Wonderful Counselor', 'Helper' and 'Encourager'.

Even after my complete deliverance, I continued praying faithfully to God for strength and for God's guidance and protection. I also continued to pray for my family's salvation, for the sick and for victims of trafficking.

Sometime in 2010, I had another dream. In this dream, a woman was following a 'stranger' through a damp, musty cave. She felt cold so he lent her a blanket he had brought along for this trip. He was guiding her through this dark and gloomy cave. He seemed to know where they were going and could see better than her in this dark cave.

"Where are you taking me?" she asked.

"Be quiet! We're almost there," he retorted, quickening his pace.

They continued walking until they saw a dim light in the distance. It was the moonlight. They had finally reached the mouth of the cave. Suddenly, they heard the sound of a baby crying.

"The sound is coming from there!" they both remarked, pointing to something on the ground not too far from the cave.

They hurried over to where the baby was crying but were aghast by what they saw. The body of the baby was all butchered up and covered in blood. It was left there to die. The woman cried in terror.

"Hurry! They're coming!" he warned her, running back to the cave. "We have to leave now," he said, rushing her.

Looking up toward the hills in the distance, the woman saw a line of fire torches making a trail downwards, towards them.

"We can't leave it here!" the woman cried out, as she stood over the dying infant.

"What would you have done?" he sneered.

The woman quickly pulled out the blanket and wrapped the child with it, cuddling it close to her breasts. The dream ended abruptly just as she had wrapped the baby and embraced it.

I woke up in cold sweat, sobbing and pleading with Jesus to save my child. I wanted my child to be with Jesus. This had been my prayer over time. My prayer for the child I had aborted in 1999.

Was this dream about child sacrifice? Who were those people with the fire torches? What happened to the baby? Somehow, I felt assured that God had saved my child. This may have been God's answer to my prayers. God had given me a chance to 'rescue' my baby from being sacrificed to the evil one.

I saw a similar picture in the newspapers of the hill and the line of fire torches trailing down the hill. It was about a ritual celebrated in the Middle East but I didn't have much information about that 'celebration' except that the picture was in broad daylight. People carrying fire torches during the day? Whatever next? Does this mean that sin is no longer hidden in darkness. Either sin has been exposed or people commit sin openly now because sin is widely 'accepted'.

Wednesday, June 16, 2010 *Exodus 10; Psalm 84*

I arrived early for work as usual around 7:45am. Upon settling down at my desk, I noticed a note and form which Penelope, my colleague had left on my desk. The note said that the funeral parlour next to our office was occupied and that the mother of the deceased would settle the payment later that day. I looked on to read the name of the deceased on the form and had a rude shock.

'It can't be! What kind of a sick joke is this?' I thought, thinking how sick people could be. I read the form again carefully to make sure I was not mistaken. Name of deceased, 'Jude Chong...'. Date departed, '15 June 2010'. Jude was my first love. We dated while I was in upper high school. It was certainly his full name and date of birth on the form.

"No, how is this even possible? Fr Murray said that only Catholics were allowed to use this parlour," I whispered to myself in that dark quiet office. I hadn't even switched on the lights.

'Maybe it is just someone with the same name,' I thought, taking the form with me and walking out of the office to the funeral parlour to investigate.

It was so quiet and I felt so peaceful when I opened the door of the funeral parlour. I walked straight to the casket and looked inside. I was shocked by what I saw. I was looking at the face of an 'old man' with sunken cheeks. His skin greenish in colour. But then, when I checked the photo at the front of the coffin, it was Jude's photo.

'I don't understand,' I thought disbelievingly. I could not recognize Jude's face. 'How can this be Jude? What happened?' I questioned in my heart.

I closed the funeral parlour door and went back to my office. Shortly after, Penelope walked in. I told her I would handle the collection of payment as I knew the deceased. Later that morning, Jude's mother, Mrs Aubrey Chong came over to the office counter to make payment for the parlour. She was surprised to see me.

"I'm sorry about Jude," I said, "This is so sudden, What happened?" I asked.

"Cancer!" Jude's mother replied, maintaining her composure, "He couldn't eat. It was too painful. He only had one month," she continued.

Reality had set in. Jude was only 36. There was a peaceful calm all morning. I didn't feel angry or sad, I just felt peace.

Joshua came by for lunch and I broke the news about Jude's death to him. Joshua had never met Jude so he just listened. Joshua knew about my past relationships and he knew about the rape and abortion because I knew I had to tell him. I didn't want to hide anything from him.

At the church cafe, Joshua and I bumped into Jude's parents, Mr David and Mrs Aubrey Chong. I introduced them to Joshua and sat down with Jude's mother while Joshua went to buy us coffee and some bread. Jude's mother told me that he had wanted to see me before he died but it was too late. Jude's parents asked Joshua and I to attend the funeral the following day but we had to excuse ourselves as we had made plans to attend the annual Bible Conference at Holy Trinity Church. Coincidentally the Bible Conference was being held at Jude's parish and the theme for 2010 was on 'Forgiveness'.

One thing that kept bothering me was the dream I had about the headless chickens and the experiment carried out by the woman's husband and his 'friend'. Was the dream about Jude too? I also felt as though God was allowing me to find closure in my past to help me move forward to a clean start with Joshua.

Saturday, August 14, 2010

About fifty participants of the Discipleship Course gathered at the Church of the Holy Spirit to celebrate the 'Passover'. We had a real Seder meal then. We had already spent 17 weeks learning the Old Testament from April 2010 till August 2010. We had another 15 weeks of lessons to cover, ending in early December 2010, with a weekend retreat.

"I want to marry you!" Joshua declared, when we were together at his brother's place one day. I was ecstatic. I didn't even reply but Joshua knew he had gotten a 'Yes' from me from the way I smiled at him. I couldn't wait to tell my parents the great news. My parents, Mr Gerard and Mrs Mei-De McGregor, were overjoyed to hear the news. This was the moment I had been waiting for all of my life.

Joshua and I had been dating for almost one year. Although both of us didn't want to rush things, we knew that age was catching up on us. We lost no time in planning to make it official and to make plans for our wedding reception and dinner.

Saturday & Sunday, October 30 & October 31, 2010

2nd Alpha Weekend Away.

This time Joshua and I were in the committee to organize this course and to help facilitate the course.

December 10 - 12, 2010

DISCIPLE: Weekend Retreat at the Golf and Country Club, Kedah.

We had to travel up north to another state for our weekend retreat. Thankfully Joshua and I could find the resort. More than a hundred participants from throughout Peninsula Malaysia travelled to this resort to attend our last lesson and retreat. Our team from Penang put up two skits: one on 'The Wedding of Cana' and the other on 'The Raising of Tabitha From The Dead'.

Jude's passing made me feel that my time was up at the Church of Our Lady. A month after Fr Murray was transferred out to another parish, I sent in my resignation. I had served at the Church of Our Lady for only one year. I had accepted a job as a teacher for Kairos Academy, homeschooling ten children and teenagers.

Before I resigned from the Church of Our Lady in 2010, I prayed the following prayer based on the 'Word of God' taken from Colossians 4:2-4, an excerpt from RBC Ministries (Discovery House) prayer booklet published and distributed in 2006:

'Lord, I need to be a double listener:
to You and to the world.
May I communicate Christ clearly to others
so they understand'.

January 7 - January 9, 2011

Joshua and I attended the Engagement Encounter Weekend. We had a minor disagreement about having children. Joshua didn't want any children so I persuaded him to adopt. I couldn't force him. He had made up his mind.

Furthermore, he wasn't ready to take up any responsibilities of fatherhood and I didn't want to be alone again. So we kept the peace and continued with our relationship.

Not long after that, I received bad news that Kairos Academy was closing down. My employer, Pastor Rong-Yu had to return to her hometown in East Malaysia as her parents had both suffered injuries from falls. The good news was that she wanted to discuss the possibility of handing over the business to me. Pastor Rong-Yu's husband, Pastor Phua Ning assured me that they would provide proper guidance and advise along my journey. I was excited about it but Joshua was not too happy to learn about it. He reasoned that I did not have enough experience running a school on my own and he didn't want me to take this risk. Still I kept my hopes up high.

Another door of opportunity soon opened for me when a business owner approached me to become the manager of her language center. They had just opened their new centre in Tanjung Bungah, running Australian programmes for kids and I decided to try out teaching pre-school kids as well. Sadly this too came to an end when too many complaints came in about the programmes they offered. My employer was tasked to review their programmes and during this time, they decided to shelve the programmes I was involved in. I was paid handsomely for my work there and saved this money for my wedding.

Four years had gone by since I last met Aunt Susannah. I remembered her advice to take up a teaching course if I was serious about teaching English. Having taught at Kairos Academy, I found that I enjoyed teaching children and teenagers very much. I had found a new calling and I was in luck. There was a school in our district offering certified courses for teaching English so I wasted no time and enrolled for their Certificate in TESOL programme.

The Certificate in TESOL programme was packed with tutorials, examinations and a practicum at the end of the course. Classes at myTESOL were lively and fun. I made many new friends there. We exchanged many ideas through sharing our lesson plans. Within six months, we had completed the course and received our certificates. Most of us continued our studies with myTESOL at the Diploma level.

Wednesday, June 8, 2011

~Official Marriage Solemnization at the Registration Office in George Town.

Joshua and I were sworn into oath as a married couple. Our parents were witnesses to this event. After obtaining our marriage certificates, we adjourned to a hotel down town for a simple lunch to celebrate this occasion.

June 9 - June 11, 2011

~Holiday at Cameron Highlands with Joshua and my parents.

We visited the Strawberry Park, Boh Tea Plantations, vegetable markets and the 'Time Tunnel' museum. We also made a point to visit Uncle Aaron and Aunt Maggie while we were there. Aunt Maggie was my father's cousin. They had moved to the highlands in the 90's.

End June 2011

In my zeal to help Jonathan get healed and delivered in Jesus name, I registered both of us for the Annual Youth

Convention in June 2011. Sadly, when that weekend came, Jonathan backed out at the last minute, so I had to attend that convention without him.

During a praise and worship session at the Youth Convention, the band members were on stage leading us with praise and worship songs when the lead guitarist suddenly walked off the stage towards my seat. He looked faced down, then sat down in front of me. I could sense something amiss. All of a sudden, he raised his right hand like a cobra and maintained that position for a while. My heart was thumping hard. I was terrified. Fearful that the 'serpent spirit' had returned with a vengeance.

The young lad walked out of the hall and I followed after him. A group of men stopped him outside the hall and Fr Murphy rushed to the scene. The young lad 'fainted' and Fr Murphy laid his hands on the lad's head and prayed over him. I stood close by watching what would happen next. When the young lad got up, he said angrily, "I know a girl did this to me!" Still fearful but not showing any emotions, I walked back to the hall.

Later during lunch, I spoke with Marina and Eliza who were both from Bro Jerry's healing and deliverance ministry. Their team were on site to cater to our meals. I later found out that the band members had gone to the beach behind ECO Hotel. I could still laugh with them at their jokes but inside I was squirming.

I didn't want to boast about the evil one. I wanted more than anything to boast about what my Lord, Jesus Christ had done for me. But at that time, I was shrouded with fear.

In October 2011, Joshua was driving me and Jean, his sister-in-law around Tanjung Bungah looking for a place to call our home. He chanced upon the 'Apartment For Sale' sign at Rainbow Hill Apartments, the same place I had seen two years earlier but I remained quiet. He called the number on the banner and we waited at a cafe till the time to meet the real estate agent.

At the appointed time, Joshua, Jean and I went back to Rainbow Hill Apartments to wait for the agent. It wasn't long before the real estate agent came over to let us view the apartment. We were captivated by the breathtaking view of the sea from the car park. When I entered the apartment, I was sold completely. The living room was immaculate. The marble flooring looked new and clean. The bedrooms were spacious and to top it off, the apartment was fully furnished with cast iron furniture.

The living room opened up to a small balcony with a view of the sea. I didn't utter a word because Joshua didn't like being interrupted especially when he was thinking.

Joshua loved the place so he had his lawyer check on the place before he made his decision. Turns out the apartment was an investment for its owner who was a doctor and he had just moved into a bigger place. With everything in order, Joshua left no time in selling his property in Petaling Jaya to purchase this apartment up in Rainbow Hill.

Wednesday, December 28, 2011

The happiest day of my life! I woke up the earliest that day. My parents got up early too. The wedding reception wasn't until 11:00am. Peggy from the boutique was coming over to my parents house to do our make-up at 9:00am. When we opened the front doors of my parents' house, we found Jasper, our pet cat, Pistachio's sibling, sitting on top of the roof of the wedding car. It was as though he knew what was going on. He had never done that before. What triumphant joy! Just get me to the church on time!

The wedding reception was lovely and so was our wedding dinner. Everything went smoothly throughout the day as planned. I would have chosen **Ecclesiastes 4:9-12** for our scripture reading in church but I couldn't find the verses in my bible then. It must have slipped my mind when I was preparing the booklet. So we settled for the more traditional verses about husbands and wives.

We held our wedding dinner banquet at the Jade Palace Chinese Restaurant downtown. About 500 guests attended our dinner. Half were church goers. We had a traditional tea ceremony at 5:30pm before the dinner. I believe this was the Chinese tradition to welcome the bride and groom into the family and to allow the bride and groom to meet their families and relatives on both sides, especially the older generation or elders.

The dinner started at 8:00pm sharp. At 8:30pm, my father went up on stage to present the first speech of the night. He pronounced a blessing upon Joshua and me. He also highlighted a thing or two about wisdom. My father ended his speech by mentioning that I was a true judge of character and that he trusted my judgment.

Benjamin, my eldest brother-in-law, presented the second speech before Joshua went on stage to present the final speech. We expressed our heartfelt gratitude to our parents and guests for making this wonderful night possible. Dinner resumed right after Joshua's speech, stopping briefly again for the cutting of the wedding cake and a short toast before Joshua and I went around to take photos with our families, relatives and guests.

Dinner ended at 10:30pm with the bride and groom and their respective families bidding farewell at the entrance of the restaurant. What a joyous celebration! Both families were relieved that everything went smoothly as planned. I thanked God for blessing us with a peaceful celebration. I had prayed hard for unity between the two families and with our relatives and friends. I wished for God to unite our hearts and minds in One Spirit.

That night, Joshua and I went home to our new apartment in Rainbow Hill to begin a new chapter of our lives as a wedded couple.

Angels At Our Jubilee

January 2012

Two months had almost gone by since we moved into our new home. I continued to pray and minister to the Lord daily. I would play Joshua's Christian CDs in the living room as I soaked in the messages from the songs and hymns. I was especially touched by the song 'Draw Me Close' by David Huff in his album of the same title. I was brought to tears one morning as I sat on the couch listening to this song being played over and over again.

One hot afternoon, I had just come out of the bedroom after a shower when Joshua started mumbling about an eagle carrying a snake off past our balcony. He just stood in the living room staring out the balcony as he repeated what he had said to me earlier. I questioned him in disbelief, "What eagle? Where?"

Quickly peering at the balcony I exclaimed, "You're bluffing! I don't see any eagle outside."

"Really!" he adamantly insisted as he turned and walked towards our kitchen away from the balcony, "It flew past the balcony," he continued.

I hurriedly walked over to the balcony and looked out to the right, then to the left.

I was amazed by what I saw. This little eagle was carrying off its prey; a huge, dark, shiny black cobra firmly in the grip of its strong and powerful talons. I stood there watching the eagle fly away with its prey, twice its size; hanging loosely in the little eagle's grip.

Joshua returned with a drink in his hand and calmly sat down on the couch while I questioned him excitedly like a city girl who was in a country village for the first time. Only that we were not living in the countryside. Although we were surrounded by skyscrapers, we were lucky to have moved into this unit with a balcony overlooking the beautiful sea of the Pearl of the Orient.

"From which direction did the eagle come from? Where do you think it is going? How is it going to eat its catch? Or how is it going to feed its eaglets with its catch?" I 'interrogated' Joshua, expecting him to have all the answers.

I had in my mind a picture of the little eagle 'breaking' or 'slicing' its prey into many parts to feed its eaglets in their nest. I also felt my spirits lifted up. To me this was a good sign that God is with us...always. Good triumphant over evil.

Monday, March 26, 2012

I got a surprise visit from my father at about 9:00am.

"Where's Mummy? Why didn't you bring her along with you?" I asked my father. I felt it was strange that he had come alone since my parents always went everywhere together.

"She has some work to do so I decided to drop in and see how you were doing?" my father replied. "How's Joshua?"

"He's been drinking again. Papa, I didn't know what I was getting into until now. I feel like leaving him," I sighed heavily, half wanting to cry. "You know how he is! He's such an angry man. Everything I do here is wrong," I continued.

"You know he is a hurting man," my father added.

I could see the sadness in his eyes, so I quickly changed the subject.

"Papa, I want to look after you! Or would you prefer to live in a home?" I asked stupidly. My father sulked at what I had suggested.

In my heart, I knew I wanted to look after my father but I was stubborn and self-righteous. I thought I was the only one who could help him. I thought I had all the answers.

"I just came from the clinic. My kidneys are very painful," my father complained holding his sides.

"You better get it checked at the hospital!" I urged him.

Ignoring what I said, my father spoke up, "I have been with your mother all these years and I know this for a fact. Even in all this, you must know one thing, your mother is a good woman." With that, he got up from the couch and walked to the front door.

I let him out and watched him drive off, wondering if I had said something wrong.

Thursday, March 29, 2012

Around 8:30pm, I received a phone call from Roger asking me to let him and Uncle Ron into my apartment grounds. Uncle Ron had something to tell me and wanted me to meet them at the lobby downstairs.

When I came down, I saw Roger sitting down facing the sea. I greeted Uncle Ron who came over to me and asked me to sit down. Not expecting anything, I sat down. Then he gently broke the news to me.

"Your father passed away just a little while ago, in Shannon's apartment!" Uncle Ron said calmly.

I remained quiet for a while. Then I asked him, "Papa, passed away?" unsure if I had heard Uncle Ron correctly the first time.

"Yes! Your father passed away in PJ this evening," he asserted, then continued, "You better call Shannon to find out what they are planning to do."

"Thank you, Uncle Ron!" I expressed humbly before letting Uncle Ron and Roger out of the apartment grounds.

I didn't feel like crying as I was still in a state of shock. 'But I had only seen my father just a few days ago. He had been complaining about his kidneys. Why and when did he go to PJ?' I reasoned and deliberated for more than 30 minutes before I decided to call Shannon.

"Uncle Ron called you?" Shannon asked.

"He came over with Roger," I replied. "How's Mummy?"

"She's here with us," Shannon replied. "I need you to contact the undertaker in Penang to make arrangements for the funeral. We will be sending Papa's body back to Penang for burial. The undertaker here will handle that part. We should be back by 5:00pm tomorrow," she explained.

"I will call Jasmine tomorrow morning. She is from Eternal Bliss Funeral Home," I informed Shannon.

"Call her now. Then call me back!" Shannon demanded. Then she hung up.

I contacted Jasmine right away. I had gotten her contact through my work at the Church of Our Lady. I contacted Shannon again to let her know what was required by Jasmine in Penang. To which she replied that she would have to discuss with Mummy first. So we agreed to meet at my parents house by 5:00pm.

I waited for Joshua to come home and wondered how I would break the news to him. I was hoping that Joshua and my father would become good friends since he was fond of my father. I wasn't sure how he would take the news.

With deepest regret, I broke the news to Joshua when he came home around 10:30pm. He was equally shocked to receive the news of my father's demise since we had only gotten married three months ago. My father, Mr Gerard McGregor, had lived to walk me down the aisle.

The next morning, Shannon called me to pass on some information to the undertaker. Mummy wanted Papa's body to be at the family home until his burial and not at a funeral parlour.

After contacting Jasmine, I went over to the Church of Our Lady to notify our parish priest, Fr Matthew about the funeral date. We had arranged the wake services for three days at my parents' home and my father's burial on the fifth day.

Joshua was unusually quiet when he met the rest of our friends and relatives. But I was glad he was sober and willing to help us out in greeting the people who came to pay their respects. After all, he was family too.

I remember how hot the weather was before the priest came to bless the body for burial. It drizzled the moment Fr Matthew stepped out of his vehicle when he arrived at my parents' home. There was also cool breeze at the burial ground.

Saturday, June 30, 2012

Three months on, my grandmother, Grandmummy Sylvia passed away in a retirement home near ECO Hotel. I had thought that she would recover from her injuries sustained in a road accident but I was wrong. She succumbed to her injuries very quickly.

2012 was an especially busy year for me. The death of my father came to us as a shock. We had taken him for granted. I always thought my father would always be there for me. At 72, he was still climbing the mango tree to pluck its fruit. They say 'Silence Is Golden'. I can now understand what this means. While some saw my father's silence as his weakness, I saw it as his strength. God had given him strength to endure much suffering and hardship to provide for the family. He was always discrete and observant. He never wanted trouble for anyone. He was a true peacemaker.

I thank God for blessing me with such a wonderful earthly father.

I buried myself in my work, juggling three jobs at the same time. I was now teaching full time at a daycare centre working from 1:00pm till 6:00pm daily. I held this job since May 2011, while I was still attached to Kairos Academy which I covered from 7:30am till 1:00pm. At the same time, I was trying to complete my assignments for the Diploma in TESOL programme. I remember staying up late till 4:00am to work on my assignments.

I loved teaching the children at the daycare. I taught them Math, Science and English. Even though most of them were from broken homes, they were all well behaved because the 'naughty' ones were disciplined by our Principal, Teacher Jane. Apart from my full time job at this day care, I also had two part time jobs teaching English at Language Centres in 2012.

While I was juggling my work and assignments, Joshua approached me for help to apply for 'titleship' for his mother who was a well known figure in society. She had helped many charitable organizations and done charitable deeds herself. Her father was also the founder of the 'Home for the Infirmed and Aged' in Penang.

I was frustrated and voiced my concerns to Joshua about meeting the deadlines for my assignments. Even so, I had to help him with the application for 'titleship' for his mother because they trusted me. My work paid off as Joshua's mother was conferred the title of 'Dato' by the Governor of Penang in a ceremony attended by Joshua's family members. I had to miss this event as I was working on completing my assignments.

'The Death Penalty', 'The Abolishment of the Death Penalty' and 'Missing Children' were some of the pieces I worked on for my Diploma in TESOL.

Thursday, September 13, 2012

Finally, I received my Diploma in TESOL. All my hard work had paid off. I was most delighted at my accomplishment and that I could finally get some rest. Joshua was truly happy for me and joined in the celebrations with my other classmates at a restaurant in Feringghi Beach.

Sometime after Joshua's mother was conferred the title of 'Dato', Joshua's elder brother, Pastor Matthew and his wife, Megan invited us over to their house to attend their 'House Church'. I attended a few prayer meetings at their home but Joshua refused to go. At first, he allowed me to attend their gatherings and prayer meetings but then, he would get upset and sometimes even become hostile towards me and my sister-in-law, Megan. I could not understand why he reacted in such a manner.

To make matters worse, I had some inner turmoil within me. Every morning, I would wake up and start begging Jesus to remove my fears and evil thoughts that had returned to tempt me. I did not understand why I was getting 'unclean' thoughts; lustful thoughts of the flesh. I struggled to understand this and in my anguish, I asked Jesus,

'Haven't I been cleansed by Abba, Father? What is happening to me? Who is causing this? Why am I unable to ward off these attacks from the evil one? This is very unlike me...'

So many questions popped in my mind but I remained silent. I did not tell Joshua about this but I shared it with Megan who also became my prayer partner.

Then one morning, my miracle came. Jesus had heard my cries for help and His answer came through the mailman. I received my magazine of 'Our Daily Journey with God' by RBC Ministries for the second quarter of 2012 and I was amazed when I read the scripture on its cover. **It was Philippians 4:8.**

Also, on the cover of this issue of 'Our Daily Journey with God', there was a picture of a lady walking alone along the beach. This scene reminded me of the CD I had been playing on our mini hi-fi at home. This CD was produced by

Richard Lacy and Christopher Norton for Classic Fox Records or Kingsway Music and was based on the 'Psalms of David'. Everyone would have come across the beautiful poem 'Footprints in the Sand' written by Carolyn Joyce Carty. I first heard and read this poem when I was a teenager in secondary school or junior high school.

When this scene flashed in my mind in 2012, I humbly implored to our Lord Jesus to bring healing to our souls, especially to those in broken relationships. I also remember perfectly well what the spiritual director had said during my 'Engagement Encounter' weekend. He had told the participants of an encounter with a man while he was on board a flight. He had tried to strike up conversation with the man seated next to him and he had introduced himself as a 'Catholic' priest. The man next to him boldly told him that he belonged to the Church of Satan and that he prayed for relationships to be broken. That was the main agenda for 'his church'.

All of us, the participants at the weekend, gasped in horror and disgust.

I started meditating on this scripture in Philippians 4:8 daily and soon I found myself 'free again' and strengthened in the Lord.

Sunday, September 16, 2012

Joshua and I got to know about the 'Hope of Jubilee' celebration, in conjunction with our Malaysia Day celebrations. It was to be held at 7:00pm at the Church of St Anne, Bukit Mertajam. This marked the end of the 40-day fast for all churches in Penang.

Joshua and I were not aware of this event until someone from our parish advised us to join in the celebrations. That evening, we drove across to the mainland to catch this event. We got there fifteen minutes before the event started but the sanctuary was already packed. I had been looking forward to visiting this newly built church as I had heard how magnificent the structure was and how Fr Matthew had decorated the outdoor and interior of the church grounds with statues of saints and angels.

As I walked past the front entrance, I glanced at the two magnificent statues of Archangels (in blue and red armour). They stood on each side of the entrance and their white wings touched the ceiling of the porch. Both of the Archangels had swords clasped in their hands towards the ground.

Noticing that the front entrance was already crowded with people, Joshua guided me towards the side entrance. We managed to get our seats there.

The event began with children marching in bearing flags of all nations and singing the entrance song, 'A New Hallelujah' by Michael W. Smith. I felt blessings flow out every time the children proclaimed a country's name. I knew I just had to get this song.

The sanctuary was hot, stuffy and crowded. We were sweaty but we were glad to be part of this celebration.

It was only when I visited the church again that I discovered that the 'statues' of the 'Archangels' that I saw were actually real angels God had sent to protect His church, the Body of Christ during the 'Hope of Jubilee' celebration.

In place of the two Archangels were two white coloured statues of angels, holding books. They were half the size of the real angels that I saw during the Jubilee. I remember that they wore armours like that of Archangel Michael.

November 2012

I started ordering Christmas gift items for my family and friends via two Christian online bookstores. One from the USA and another, from a local online store. Among the gift items were books, mugs, stationery, CDs, DVDs, planners, diaries, devotions and two floor mats. The floor mats had scripture on them. I thought it was a great idea at first so I bought one for my home and another for my mother's home.

Although I wasn't in the mood for celebrating Christmas without my father, gift giving during this season was a tradition I liked to keep.

Christmas 2012 was very quiet. Joshua and I, picked up his mother and his aunt, Aunt Lucy to have Christmas lunch at my mother's home. If I can recall, Joshua and I attended church on the Eve that year.

Schizophrenia

January & February 2013

Joshua started binge drinking again. Twice he had to be sent to the hospital because he was without food for almost one week at a time.

I continued to work at the daycare. I had to take the bus whenever Joshua was binge drinking. Sometimes I would request for days off just to take care of him.

March 26-30, 2013

I was invited by my course facilitator to become a facilitator in the story-telling camps organized by the state government. We were to teach drama and story-telling to children from orphanages and homes. In the 1st Story-telling Camp in 2013, my team won the first prize for 'The Tortoise & The Hare'. These camps were held only during the school holidays when I got a break from the daycare.

May 2013

I kept receiving this message from Psalm 46:10. "Be still, and know that I am God! I will be honored by every nation. I will be honored throughout the world." At times I was afraid and anxious but I was reminded that God is bigger than all my troubles.

June 2013

As soon as Darlene Zschech's latest album came out, Joshua drove me to the Baptist Bookstore to get her CD, 'Revealing Jesus'. I wondered what he was so excited about. When I learned that Darlene Zschech had recovered from cancer, I used her song 'In Jesus Name' to pray and intercede for others suffering from cancer. Combining Paul Wilbur's 'Song of Ezekiel' and Darlene Szchech's song, 'In Jesus Name', I danced and 'fought' against cancer.

One night, I was playing Joshua's Christian CDs and dancing to them when I found myself fighting with 'Rebellion'. My hands clasp like the shape of the football trophy as I commanded the 'Spirit of Rebellion' to "Get Out!"

I also formed my own dance moves to honour God. There was a CD I used to praise and worship God in dance which had the words from the 'Book of Revelation' in it. They sang of the glory of Christ and how only Christ is worthy to break the seals and open the scrolls.

August 2013

Joshua, my husband had been drinking again. I had no one to help me to care for him. Each time his mother came over to see him, he would request for more alcohol and cigarettes and his mother would get her helper or relative to buy them for him. I would get angry with them and at one point I scolded his mother. It got to a point that I stopped them all from coming to the home. I was enraged.

When Joshua's eldest brother Benjamin called, I told him that I didn't like his mother feeding Joshua's addiction and that they should not bring his mother over to the home until Joshua got well.

I needed help but not their kind of help. I wanted so badly for Joshua to come out of his addiction to alcohol. Out of worry, Joshua's mother started calling my mobile and my mother's mobile. She would call us the whole day. We received more than a hundred calls a day that my mum called me up to scold me. I told her to shut her mobile for a while till Joshua got better. I had shut my mobile and that was why Joshua's mother started calling my mum. This went on for days. Joshua refused to eat and would lay on the bed with his bottles of dry gin and vodka next to him. Outside in the living room, I would pray to God for help. Finally after many restless nights, I cried out to God in a loud voice, "God! Show them that you are my God!"

There was peace and quiet in our home for a while. I was so tired I felt like crying. Looking out of our balcony overlooking the sea, I saw the bright sky suddenly turn dark. I thought it was going to rain but as I watched the dark clouds take form unlike any I had seen before, the sea was turned dark grey as though something was hovering over it. I watched as the dark grey clouds took form in a 'U' shape, like a thick pillar. The grey cloud hovered around the little island opposite where we lived. I was brought down to my knees and started to panic as I had never encountered God visibly in this form. I asked God to speak for I thought He was there to answer to my cries for help and laments the previous day. Joshua was not able to come out of his habit and oppression. No one had come to our aid and he was becoming abusive. He was fast asleep when God appeared. I knelt down to listen to God's voice. Then I heard a voice say, "Speak!"

I complained to God about the pain in my knees and the emotional abuse and pain I was enduring. My complaints then slowly turned to intercessions for my family, friends and extended families.

It seemed like thirty minutes of complete silence and attentiveness from the heavens...

After the thirty minutes was up, God again spoke.

With furiousness in His voice and in all His majesty, God spoke, "I AM THE ONE WHO HEALS. NO ONE ELSE. SEE I CAN REMOVE YOUR PAIN." Immediately I felt Him removing the pains in both my knees like chains being unlocked and lifted from both my legs. Then I heard the 'Advocate, the Holy Spirit', counsel me about the ones who practise the occultic arts. I could sense God's wrath when He continued as He spoke these words, "I AM VERY ANGRY WITH THESE FALSE PROPHETS. I WILL NOT GIVE THEM ANY MORE VISIONS."

I unlocked the sliding door to the balcony and went out to the balcony to get a closer 'look' at the grey cloud. Then the Holy Spirit touched my chin and lifted my head up so I was looking straight into the 'Eye of God', a huge bright light shaping His eye. At first, I just stared into God's eye. When I was aware of what I was doing, I quickly moved back into the living room. I wanted to hide but I knew God could see me. And I was still alive. So I went back to the balcony and looked up at the grey cloud and the 'eye of God'. Finally, in His audible voice, God ended with this message, "NOW GO. DO AS I HAVE DONE UNTO YOU." And the Holy Spirit counseled me once again telling me to 'LISTEN! GOD HAD GIVEN ME THIRTY MINUTES OF HIS PRECIOUS TIME. DO UNTO OTHERS AS HE HAS DONE UNTO YOU. FOR THE SAKE OF HIS KINGDOM'.

I was standing in awe and wonder in God's Holy presence. The great grey cloud swept over the sea to the right side, till the area near the Chinese Swimming Club. Then the skies cleared again and everything was back to normal.

I rushed into Joshua's room to check on him but he was fast asleep.

I felt so privileged to have such an encounter of God's holy presence. I recalled reading the Book of Psalms on such powerful encounters and how God answered David's cry for help. I was overjoyed in knowing that I am the apple of God's eye!

(Scripture Reading: Psalm 18:11-13; Psalm 33:18; Psalm 121:5; Psalm 121:7)

That night, I went back to sleep in the master bedroom next to Joshua. In the middle of the night I had a dream. In this dream, a gigantic green crocodile was 'struggling' in the sea. I remember myself asking the Lord, "A crocodile, but why Lord?" Still dreaming, a very strong and powerful man appeared in the dream, walking up to the crocodile in the sea and gently picking the huge monster with both arms. With that, the dream ended. I felt complete peace during and after this dream. GOD IS IN CONTROL. Praise the Lord!

The following day, Joshua woke up, took his bath and went out to eat. He was back to normal again, but for how long?

Over the next few days, I had made arrangements to attend computer classes with Aunt Lucy, Joshua's aunt. I learnt from Joshua that she had recovered from cancer. When she came to pick me up, she immediately started explaining herself about the time in May 2013 when Joshua, her nephew, started to drink. On this occasion, I had questioned them for buying liquor for him. Everyone was upset with me and my sister-in-law, Jean said that he had free will to come out of his drinking habit. Also they kept saying that I could not leave him as I should be responsible for him as a 'wife' should stay by her 'husband'.

As Aunt Lucy continued explaining herself, I remained silent and listened attentively. Then, she shared with me about the time she entered the Catholic church in England to pray for her sister when her sister was dying of cancer. Somehow after listening to her, I was able to gracefully share with her on the 'Book of Job'. To put things in short, I told her that many of her friends like Job's friends did not understand her real situation. Sometimes, diseases are cast upon us by Satan, our accuser and not because of our sins, as a testing to prove our obedience or allegiance to God. I told her that although her sister was not healed of cancer, her prayers to God brought life to her own self as she herself was saved when she had cancer.

I tried to encourage Aunt Lucy by trying to understand her better. I was further encouraged to know how little effort I had put in and by the fact that the Holy Spirit had done most of the work. I just listened as God commanded me to do unto others as what He had done unto me the day before. Thank you, Lord Jesus, for this precious gift. I need to practice listening more.

October ~ November 2013

During this time, Pastor Matthew and Megan, my in-laws, invited Joshua, his mum and me over to their house for a barbecue dinner. We arrived early to help prepare and lay out the food for their guests.

Many people turned up for this gathering. There were some new faces and some I had seen before but barely recognized them then. We were introduced to a pastor, our guest from Poland. I cannot recall his name but he had a very strong 'European' accent. As he was seated against the wall with his friend, a local pastor, I took a glance at our friend from Poland. I nodded and tried to look away. His eyes were deep dark black like precious onyx stones and they had a strange and numinous glow in them. He scared me so I quickly turned and walked away.

After everyone had eaten, Pastor Matthew invited our guest pastor from Poland to preach the word of God. His voice was powerful and distinct. Among us were unbelievers who had yet to come to Christ. Our guest pastor borrowed a bible and started to declare the word of God from Isaiah.

To me it was more like a show but since it was God's Word being preached, I listened on to claim God's promises and to be reminded of God's Word too. I watched as this pastor prayed over my friends and laid his hand on their heads to give them blessings. The others coaxed me to be prayed over so I went forward to get a blessing. With his right hand, he gently raised my left hand high up and using his left hand, he pressed his left hand hard on the crown of my head and commanded me to, "Be strong!"

> **June 12, 2021**
>
> **I must admit that something about that pastor from Poland 'scared' me. He looked exactly like the man in the painting 'Prince of Peace', painted by Akiane Kramarik. He also looked exactly like the man in my dream, who picked up the huge green crocodile. Over time, I have wondered about these words of scripture in Revelation 3:20. Could he have been the Messiah? I am quite aware that false Messiahs would come too. But who was he really?**

November 19-23, 2013

I was again invited to be a facilitator for the 2ⁿᵈ Story-telling Camp for children. This time my story was about bullying - 'Choices Of Heart'. I drew the idea and the title from the internet and chose this storyline about bullying because issues and cases about bullying were increasing in our country. Although my team didn't win this time around, I was requested to use back the same story for the third camp.

December 3-5, 2013

Breakthrough seminar by Pastor Julius Suubi at Traders Hotel, Penang.

I missed the first night of service as I had a minor 'incident'.

December 3-7, 2013

3rd Story-telling Camp - 'Choices of the Heart'

After the first day at camp, one of the facilitators, Norita, invited me and the other facilitators out for tea. We decided to go to Tesco's, just opposite the school where our camp was held.

As Norita drove us to the car park at Tesco's, she stopped to let a white van back his vehicle so that she could take his spot. Instead, the person in the white van signaled for us to pass.

"Norita! I think he wants us to go first," I remarked, seeing that the person in the white van was not going to budge.

A sudden gust of wind blew through the gaps of the windows of the car and I felt a sharp stinging pain in my left eye. I thought nothing of it although my eye was tearing.

Thinking that my eye would get better if I had a nap that afternoon, I slept as soon as I got home.

I had checked my eye in the mirror and tried to wash my eye with lubricant eye drops but nothing worked. It felt as though someone had thrown sand into my eye.

I woke up around 5:00pm to find that my left eye was sore and that I couldn't open it. I informed Joshua and he rushed me to a clinic in Burmah Road. I was lucky because there was no one in line that evening. Dr Teng swabbed my left eye with medicated cotton swab. He was alarmed when he didn't find anything. He warned us to consult a specialist or I would be blinded in my left eye.

Fearing the worst, we took Dr Teng's advice and drove to the General Hospital. A doctor there washed my eye with a solution but the burning sensation and irritation continued. When that didn't help, I was told to see their specialist, Dr Chan. Her office and treatment room was upstairs.

I didn't have to wait long to see Dr Chan but the pain was unbearable. When my turn came, Dr Chan, a very attractive lady specialist asked me to open my eye wide and look into a machine. She wanted to see what was causing the pain and irritation in my eye. It was difficult and painful to stare into the machine because of the bright light. Thank heavens it was a quick process.

Dr Chan drew a large circle on an eye chart. She told me that there was a 'cornea abrasion' as big as my pupil on my left eye. But we didn't know the cause of it. She then applied eye ointment into my left eye and gave me an appointment card. I was to return to see her on 5 Dec 2013, two days later, if my eye wasn't better by then.

All the time, I was covering my left eye with a shawl as there was a sharp pain every time the wind blew into my eye. It was almost 9:00pm when we left the General Hospital, so I decided not to go for the 'Breakthrough' seminar at Traders Hotel.

The next morning, 4 Dec 2013, I went to teach at the Story-telling camp as usual. It was difficult but I made it through that morning. Later that day, I insisted on going for the 'Breakthrough' seminar at Traders Hotel so Joshua took me there.

I went into the ballroom and sat right in front at the right wing facing the stage. The ballroom was filled with people. Every seat had been taken. Pastor Julius Suubi came on stage. His mere presence filled my heart with joy and hope. I learned of how he had come to Penang, Malaysia. A country foreign to him. All he knew was that God showed him an island shaped like a turtle. That we all know as the Island of Penang.

After his service, Pastor Julius Suuibi requested us to place our hands over the spot that needed healing. I covered my left eye with my shawl. Then he prayed over us silently in his heart. In an instant, the pain left my eye and I could open my left eye widely. God had healed my eye through the prayer of this man of God, Pastor Julius Suubi. I was so relieved and full of joy in Christ that I bought Pastor Julius Suubi's book on 'Government Anointings'. When Joshua came to pick me up, I told him that my eye was healed but he just brushed it off. Maybe he didn't believe me.

'What would it take for Joshua to believe in God's grace and healing?' I often asked myself.

The next day, I attended the Story-telling camp as scheduled. I didn't return to see the specialist as I believed that God had healed my eye completely. There was no more pain. I threw away the eye ointment too.

December 25, 2013

Mummy and Roger came over to see Joshua who had been drinking again. I wonder what goes through a person's mind that drives him or her to the bottle. I went over to my mother's house for Christmas lunch and Roger sent me back after that. My mother was kind and loving enough to pack Joshua's favourite roast pork and pineapple jam tarts for him. He was sober by 2nd January 2014.

March 25-29, 2014

Using the idiom 'Wolf in Sheep's Clothing', I rewrote the script for 'The Boy Who Cried Wolf' and came up with the title for the 4th Story-telling Camp - 'The Shepherd And The Wolf'. Sadly there was a minor hiccup when I forgot to give the 'Wolf' his sheep's costume on the actual day of the competition. So he was actually 'exposed' as a 'wolf'. Even so, I believed the children who attended this camp had lots of fun playing their parts and getting to know each other.

I was advised by one of my psychiatrists to bring two character witnesses if I wanted to stop taking my medication. Teacher Jane felt that my work had improved since I stopped taking the medication. I was more alert and my weight had gone down a little. She was full of support and encouragement when I approached her to be my witness. I had to persuade Megan, my sister-in-law to be my other witness. My psychiatrist spoke to them alone and decided I was well enough to be off my medication based on their word.

Between the months of April and July 2014, I had to admit Joshua to the hospital twice when he had drunk too much vodka and dry gin. During these times, I slept on chairs at the hospital lobby because I was too tired to travel by bus to and from the hospital and home. I had to excuse myself from the 5th Story-telling Camp which was held from June 3rd to 7th, 2014. Sadly after much deliberation, I had to make my decision to stop working at the daycare to look after Joshua.

I had been struggling with a messenger from Satan; a 'thorn' in the flesh since November 2013. It had come back. It found me again.

At night whenever I wanted to sleep, I would feel a spirit disturbing me in bed. I felt ashamed to tell Joshua about it and didn't want to worry him further so I moved into the guest room to sleep. I lied to myself and made Joshua think it was because of his drinking that I moved out of our bedroom.

I had been reading and meditating upon the psalms from the bible daily in the mornings. I would pray for up to three hours at my favourite spot, on the couch in the living room every time Joshua took his mum out for breakfast.

One morning, I heard a knock on our front door when I had just finished reading a psalm. So I went to answer it. I opened the door but there was no one there.

Then I heard a whisper, "Where are your enemies?"

To which I joyfully replied, "I have none! I have no enemies! God has driven them all away!"

And time and time again, I have pondered on this question. Not 'who', but 'where' are your enemies?

Going back to the couch, I opened my Bible. I thought I saw a 'Buddhist' or 'Taoist' monk in orange robes, sitting next to me as I was reading the bible. He said to me, "Come. Come. Let me teach you the right way to read the bible."

Then he disappeared. I thought I was losing my mind.

I tried so hard to pray and meditate in God's word like before but it was just so hard. Every time I opened my bible and tried to read the scriptures, I would feel a presence next to me. I chose to ignore 'the shifting shadows'. I kept seeing these black shadows throughout 2014.

May 2014

Our relationship mellowed over the weeks. And weeks turned to months. Joshua and I joined a retreat together at the Maranatha Retreat Centre in Merry Widows Creek. It was a beautiful place with serene surroundings.

Most of the sessions for this three day retreat were on meditations under the guidance of a priest. During one of these sessions, I saw a vision of a Boeing 777 soaring in the sky. It was such a peaceful feeling. I knew immediately that this was the Malaysian Airlines MH370 which disappeared. Then the scene changed to a Buddhist or Taoist monastery, located high up in the mountains. The monks were all seated cross-legged on the ground. All of a sudden, they stood up and their robes dropped off. They were then covered with a bright blueish-white light. Then these beings floated into the skies and disappeared into thin air.

'Are these the illuminated ones? What is this vision trying to tell me?' I questioned myself.

> I knew that MH370 had disappeared from the radar on 8 March 2014. No one knows what really happened to this plane. No one knows if there are any survivors. All 227 passengers and 12 crew were presumed dead. Some debris allegedly belonging to the plane were only found in 2020.

Another weird thing that occurred at the Maranatha Retreat Centre was when all of us were told to do some 'homework'. I was all alone in the classroom reading my bible when a giant black hornet came close to me. I could hear sounds like Buddhist or Taoist chantings...coming from the black hornet. When it flew away, the chantings stopped.

I had another vision at the retreat centre during our meditation before our priest ended the session. In this vision, there was a bright light in the sanctuary of God where we were all sat and my father-in-law appeared, standing before this bright light in the sanctuary. I didn't share this with Joshua as I was afraid he would get angry with me but I told my sister-in-law, Megan about it.

Once back home, I tried praying as I did before but I couldn't. Something was playing with my mind.

Thursday, August 7, 2014

Made a police report against Joshua at the nearest police station in Tanjong Tokong, at 7:00pm. The following is the translation of the report made that day:-

My mother-in-law called me around 4:00pm. I heard my husband vomiting in his room. After that, I heard my husband talking to his mother over the phone. He was angry because he didn't want to go to the hospital. After the call ended, his mother called me again. She asked me to call for an ambulance. We agreed to call Dr Hu from Island Hospital to treat Joshua. After calling the hospital to make the arrangements, I entered Joshua's room right away and helped to clean his face and nasal discharge (mucus). I packed his clothing but did not tell him that I had called for the ambulance. Joshua asked me to put his clothing back into the cupboard. I dared not go against him. As I looked out the window, I saw a car parked downstairs which I hadn't seen before. I wanted to enter the toilet but my husband prevented me from going in. He asked me to get out of his room. He shouted at me and walked to the kitchen. Without hesitation, I unlocked the front door. At the same time, I received the call from the nurse in the ambulance. They told me that they were at 'Diamond Valley'. My husband was angry and pulled me into the living room. I screamed in fright and in pain because he was holding me very tightly. He hammered the crown of my head towards the left side with his fist and punched my cheeks left and right. I punched his face and managed to free myself from his grip. I walked out from our unit and rushed straight across to Unit 1-4. I snatched a life-like python from my neighbour's front door and threw it down to the ground floor. The ambulance was now at the gate of our apartment. I saw my husband going down using the staircase. This incident happened at the Rainbow Hill Apartment.

I was given a slip by the police for a medical examination but I did not go to the hospital for a check-up. In fact, I forgot about the slip. The police had told me that my husband was at the General Hospital so I went there to check on him. Feeling too tired and miserable, I went home after seeing him at the hospital.

Friday, August 8, 2014

I went to the State Registration office for Marriages and Divorce to seek counseling from the Marriage Tribunal. I applied to have my marriage withdrawn. I was asked to attend my first counseling session from the Marriage Tribunal on 13 September 2014. Joshua was also asked to attend the counseling by the Marriage Tribunal.

Over the months, Joshua continued with his binge drinking. Twice, I had to stay at the YMCA, opposite the hospital where he was admitted. I felt supercharged to pray for Joshua then. But travelling to and from home, hospital and the YMCA was tiring. I had to clean up the 'mess' in our apartment.

After one such evening, I came home to take my shower. I had just visited Joshua in hospital and I only reached home around 8:00pm. I felt so tired and sleepy in the shower. I didn't have any strength left within me. All of a sudden a vision appeared in my mind. In this vision, I saw a young Chinese man; the same man in my dream who took me in a cave and brought me to the baby.

This time, he was teaching a young girl about the age of four years, karate or judo.

He instructed the child, "You should punch like this!"

Immediately as he said that, my right arm went through the shower screen and it broke. I was shocked and terrified. Thankfully the shower screen was part plastic and fiberglass. It wasn't glass. And thankfully I came out with only minor scratches on my arm.

I have my guardian angels to thank for keeping me safe that night. I gently pulled out my hand from the screen. If not, I would have suffered deep cuts from the sharp edges of the broken screen. God was with me. God is with me. May God abide in me as I abide in Him. Thank You, Abba Father, for your loving protection!

When Joshua came home, he was equally shocked to see the broken shower screen. I don't know what might have gone through his head then but he called the repairmen to replace the screen within a few days.

Sunday, August 24, 2014

Joshua was admitted to Island Hospital again.

After cleaning the apartment, I checked into the YMCA to be closer to Joshua. I found out from Jared that Renee Winston from USA was giving a talk on 'Women's Role In The Last Days'. Coincidentally it would be held at the YMCA. I attended her talk from 7:30pm onwards, on both nights, 29th and 30th August 2014.

Tuesday, September 2, 2014

Joshua was discharged by his doctor. He was afraid to go back to the apartment alone so he stayed at Matthew and Megan's house. My cousins from New Zealand were down for the holidays but I had to excuse myself from our family gatherings because I wasn't in any shape to meet anyone.

Saturday, September 13, 2014

I applied to the Marriage Tribunal officially. Joshua was not present for the first session. So they only heard from me.

Monday, September 15, 2014

Matthew texted me to inform me that Joshua was drinking again.

Wednesday, September 17, 2014

Matthew informed me that Joshua was admitted to the hospital again. Joshua had written down vulgarities on his bedroom door. I had to clean that up and also his vomit and urine before my in-laws, Benjamin and Jean arrived from KL.

Monday, September 22, 2014

Joshua was discharged.

Wednesday, October 22, 2014

After a week of binge drinking, without any food, Joshua was admitted to the Penang Island Hospital again.

Joshua had just become sober when he came home with distressing news. His father who was 91, was deathly ill. We visited his father in the hospital before he was discharged and taken home to be cared for by a nurse.

After just a few days, Joshua's father passed on. He had wanted Taoist rites so Joshua's brother, Rupert arranged the funeral. Every time Rupert held the joss sticks and prayed at the 'altar' a black hornet would appear. I could hear Buddhist or Taoist monks chanting each time the black hornet came near me. I had to excuse myself each time to pray on my own. Even though Taoist rites were performed at my father-in-law's funeral, I knew that he had gone back to the Lord because of what I saw in my vision at the Maranatha Retreat Centre in Merry Widows Creek some months before.

21 November 2014

'Abba, Father, You have shown me Your glory. You have spoken to me and You show me that You are in control over every situation. I do believe that You will answer me in Your time and I have knowledge and wisdom that You are the one who answers our prayers and that You watch over us all. Why then, O God, don't I feel the connection to my King of Kings and Lord of Lords, Jesus Christ, Your One and Only Son? Why don't I love Him as I did before? I have the knowledge that Jesus loves me but I want to know Him more. Jesus, I adore you, I appreciate you, and I love you! Please, Abba Father, remind us of Your love and sacrifices that Your Son, Jesus Christ poured out for us as this weekend we celebrate the 'Solemnity of Christ the King' in our church.'

After all the tears and thunderstorms, Brian Littrell's 'Welcome Home' CD caught my eye. I started to arrange the CDs in our television cabinet according to 'seasons'. Joshua has a hobby of collecting music CDs… and I have been thoroughly blessed by God through him and the prayers of intercessors.

I was again brought to tears when Brian Littrell's song 'Welcome Home' was played. It brought healing to my soul and I interceded for all especially those who were grieving the loss of their loved ones. On the same night, I immediately started working on this book project, again.

The following were the dates given to Joshua and me, to attend the Tribunal sessions:-

- Tuesday, October 28, 2014
- Tuesday, December 9, 2014
- Tuesday, January 20, 2015
- Tuesday, February 10, 2015

I could only make it for three sessions out of all five. Joshua never attended any of the sessions. I was devastated. It felt like he didn't care at all. He was out of the home most of the time. We rarely spoke to each other.

Tuesday, March 10, 2015

The Marriage Tribunal was over and I could either go back to Joshua or take the lift to an office on the upper level to see a lawyer if I wanted to proceed with divorce. I had to make my choice.

Feeling lost at that moment, I sat alone for a while at the waiting area. 'Did I really want a divorce? Where can I go from here?' These thoughts raced through my mind. As I sat there, I was overwhelmed with peace and something within me just thought of 'home'.

'I should go home,' I thought to myself. So I got up and went back home to Joshua.

One afternoon after washing up the dishes and cleaning up the kitchen, I got dressed to go out. I suddenly felt something burst or snap behind my neck. I immediately felt dizzy and sleepy and couldn't lift up my head, so I quickly entered the guest room which was the nearest to me, to lay down for awhile. I felt liquid rushing up to my brain. I fell asleep in a fetal position and the next thing I knew was Joshua had just come home. I heard him unlock the front door. I had been sleeping for exactly one hour. I called Joshua over to the room and told him about my neck. I managed to get up but my neck was bent stiff. I couldn't lift up my head. It felt heavy.

Joshua called Aunt Lucy for help. He didn't know what to do. We immediately went to pick her up, then we went straight to Island Hospital.

After registering myself, I went in to meet the doctor. Joshua and Aunt Lucy followed me in.

I tried to tell the doctor what I felt but Aunt Lucy cut in and told the doctor that I needed to rest as that was what she had been told by Joshua. She asked the doctor to prescribe muscle relaxant pills for me.

I told the doctor that I had insurance as I pulled out my card. I was ready to be admitted. However, the doctor didn't even examine me and dismissed me after prescribing three types of tablets to be consumed.

Once back home, I studied the medication that the doctor had prescribed me and found out that one of the tablets had severe reactions, so I threw that packet away. I only took two types of muscle relaxant pills which the doctor prescribed.

I noticed that my eyes couldn't turn sideways. I could only look straight. I exercised my muscles and forced my eyes to move around daily until finally, I felt normal again. This went on for about a month.

During this time, I started juicing and ate only my cooking. I loved to cook pesto pasta and tuna pasta. I also tried cooking curries but using pastes. I exercised a lot by taking long walks but something was drawing me to the beach too. Twice, I swam at the sea around 3:00am. I found my sports shoes missing once when I came out from swimming at the sea. Someone had stolen them so I never went back to swim at that beach again.

As my weight dropped to 49kgs with the juicing and exercise, my bones started to give me trouble. I felt as though someone or something was constricting me. I was in excruciating pain and thought that someone was trying to harm me. The pain was far worse than the time I had trouble with my left eye, the cornea abrasion. When I was with certain people such as Bro Jerry, the pain would go away. But with others it would be so painful, I sometimes cried. The soles of my feet were also painful that I had to stop my long walks altogether.

I stayed within the comforts of hotel rooms to help me write this book and would always choose hotels near churches. This helped ease my suffering and take my mind off the pain that I had been enduring. I'm still trying to understand what Paul wrote in the bible about the 'thorn in the flesh'. Was this what he was experiencing? Or was it temptation? Maybe it was a bit of both because I felt like lashing out at people when the constricting pain became unbearable.

Sometime in November or December 2015, Joshua started binge drinking again. I was so upset with him that I threw away his hardcover collection of Dalai Lama's books but kept the ones on Mother Teresa.

In my anguish, I cried out to God again like how I did before when God came down to our rescue. This time, the Holy Spirit led me to Joshua's CD rack. Joshua kept hundreds of CDs on the CD rack outside his room. I believe the Holy Spirit led me to pull out the CD which carried a curse, one which caused Joshua to drink. I just pulled out one particular CD from the lowest part of the rack. I, myself had never touched or listened to this CD. It had a picture of a man dying in bed with skeletons all around him. I burned the CD right away.

The next day, Joshua arose and took his bath. He stopped binge drinking for three straight years. However, he was mighty upset that I had thrown out his Dalai Lama hardcover collection.

In 2016, I had discovered how God had connected the Body of Christ through intercessors. When Paul Wilbur's albums came out, I listened and meditated upon the words that he spoke and sang in English and in Spanish. I realised that he had prayed for Julius Suubi to 'Arise' in his songs.

Apostle Julius Suubi first came to Malaysia in 2010 and had set up a 24/7 House of Prayer for the nations in his own country. I was led by the Spirit to read Revelation 21 and 22 and soon started working on my arts and crafts project to build 'The New Jerusalem'

Throughout 2016, I could not pray as before. Once, I felt something hovering above the crown of my head but thought nothing about it, always thinking positive that maybe God was giving me my reward. When I played the same CDs to praise and worship the Lord in dance, my left hand would hit my right hand and I couldn't coordinate the steps well as before. It just didn't feel right. I started to get frustrated with myself. So much so, that I shelved the whole project of building 'The New Jerusalem' as in Revelation 21 and 22.

In 2017, I had a big argument with Joshua. He just exploded one day. He was still mad at me about his Dalai Lama books. I had just returned from an outstation trip and hadn't unpacked my belongings. He demanded for my keys to the apartment, threatening me. He grabbed me and pushed me out of the apartment. He pushed my luggage out too and locked me out.

That whole week, I stayed in hotels in George Town using up all of my money. I had to close my insurance just to get some more money. Then one day, while I was searching for a cheaper hotel, I decided to walk into the St George's Anglican Church grounds and chanced upon their Heritage Cafe.

The cafe was run by Arlene Williams whom I befriended. We talked and she began to counsel me gently. I felt so much love in her presence. She was kind and gentle. Caring too.

While I was there, a police car pulled up at the cafe and Arlene went up to the officer. After talking to him, she turned to me and said gently, "Chevonne. Please follow this officer. He will take you to the hospital. You need to be re-medicated."

I didn't know what to say. But something within me told me I could trust her. In the end, I took her advice and went along with the officer to the Women's Psychiatric Ward.

I was readmitted and the psychiatrist contacted Joshua and my mother to let them know where I was. They had to sign me out when I was discharged...when I was more stable.

That night, a demonic spirit came upon me. I was too tired to fight and depressed about the whole situation that I let it have its way with me.

This time around, I didn't make friends with anyone. I slept most of the time. My bones were too painful. Most of the girls warded were only teenagers and young adults in their twenties.

The psychiatrists pulled out my old files and tried my old medication on me but it didn't work. According to one psychiatrist, I was hallucinating because I told her that I could sense a presence and see a 'tiger' spirit. They decided to give me monthly injections and replaced my old medication with a new one that seemed to work well on me.

I started to gain weight too. I was 49kgs when I was admitted and I believe I was 51kgs when I was discharged. I felt my legs ballooning.

My mother and Aunt Judith came to discharge me after more than two weeks in the ward. I was there for almost a month. I had told them about Arlene so they brought me to see her. I thanked Arlene for her help. We later found out that she was a trained and qualified psychologist from Australia. She was also a cancer survivor.

While I was glad to see Arlene and also to be out from the psychiatric ward, I was saddened by the fact that Joshua hadn't come to discharge me. I didn't feel secure in our relationship.

'Do we have a future together?' I asked myself.

When I got home, Joshua was there to welcome me back. He opened the door for me. I told him about Arlene and Aunt Judith. We made a point to visit both of them in the near future.

The constricting pain had vanished but I was gaining weight rapidly. Within a few months after being remedicated, I had gained more than 20kgs. I was now 78kgs. The psychiatrist evaluating me kept asking me if I was pregnant because my pregnancy hormones were getting higher. Sadly it was not so.

I felt miserable about gaining weight and I slept for up to 12 hours each day. One morning, I awoke to find that I couldn't remember what day it was, what I was doing there. I was almost about to succumb to anxiety but I said aloud to myself, "No!"

I forced myself to get up and knew I had to do something.

When I came across a bulletin about a Women's Bible Study Group, I decided to join the classes. We met every Tuesday morning for about 3 hours each week. I started to attend the meetings faithfully except for the days I needed to go to the hospital for my injections and psychiatric evaluation.

Doctors from the Penang General Hospital had diagnosed me as suffering from osteoarthritis. It was one ailment after another. I was prescribed Neurobion tablets, vitamin D and calcium tablets. I had high fever the first two days of taking these medication. My nasal passages were all clogged up with mucus. On the second day of taking these vitamins, I snorted out all the mucus and the nasal passages near my cheeks were all cleared. On the third day, my fever was gone.

Over the next few months, I realised that my sinus had disappeared. 'Could Neurobion be the cure for sinus?' I thought.

I had to buy Glucosamine tablets from pharmacies when the calcium tablets didn't work. The pain in my knees subsided too.

I was still overcome with fear and doubt after being re-medicated. Through immersing myself in prayer by attending the Women's Bible Study classes, I started having flashbacks of my childhood. God was reminding me of His presence throughout my childhood and how I chose to turn away from Him through my disobedience.

Memories of My Baptism...
A Blessing In Disguise

Flashback to December 1975...

It was 'Boxing Day.' Instead of preparing the usual traditional Portuguese dish, known as 'Debel curry' with the leftovers from Christmas Day, Mei-De was busy packing to go to the hospital.

At about 3:00am, Mei-De started experiencing labour pains and was rushed to the hospital. I was born early that morning on 27 December 1975.

> **It was only in 2007 that I learnt about this incident, after Aunt Susannah shared with me that she never got to eat my mother's famous 'Debel curry' because of my birth. She loved to joke about it.**

My parents were staunch Catholics. It is a norm for Catholics to baptize their babies a month after they are born. Following this tradition, my parents arranged for me to be baptized in their parish.

January 31, 1976

I do not remember clearly, receiving the sprinkling of water on my forehead. But, I remember waking up to the beautiful sight of trees, rustling in the wind and the sun smiling on my face as I was brought out of the church. I could feel the blustery winds caressing my face and I saw the leaves falling from the trees just outside the church building. I was comfortably snug in the loving embrace of my Godma, Aunt Mabel's arms. Upon seeing that I had awoken from my sleep, my mother and god-mother tried to hush me back to sleep.

I know that my memories are real because we had photographs of that beautiful and blessed day. In one photograph, my Godma was carrying me lovingly in her arms.

I believe I received a special blessing that day. A blessing, that not only had I been 'chosen' to enter into the Lord's house, but that, 'He will forever love me and abide with me as long as I abide in Him'.

(Scripture Reading: John 15:16-17; John 15:7)

Early Childhood …
Nightmares Begin

Flashbacks of early childhood days...

I was a year old when my family moved into our new home on a hill slope. It was just a minute's drive from our previous home.

I was very attached to Jonathan, my eldest brother when we were growing up. He would always keep me company and would play with me whenever he could. He attended the Penang Buddhist Association kindergarten where our aunt worked as the Principal. I was too young to attend kindergarten at that time so I usually stayed at home while Jonathan and our two elder sisters went to school. Roger, our younger brother, was sent to a nursery.

One fine day, I woke up to find the front door of our house opened. I could hear my mother talking to our neighbour outside so I walked out to her.

"Go back inside!" my mother urged me.

Just then, Jonathan's school bus came to pick him up. He came out through the front doorway and I stopped him. I begged him to let me follow him to his kindergarten. I did not want to be left alone in the house. I wanted to be with Jonathan.

"Go and ask Mummy first!" Jonathan insisted.

"Okay! Make sure you wait for me!" I exclaimed.

I tugged at my mother's housecoat to catch her attention and pleaded with her to allow me to follow Jonathan to school.

"You can follow him to school next year," assured my mother.

I took it as a 'Yes!'

"Mummy says I can go with you," I told Jonathan.

"You smell," Jonathan said as he gestured, waving his hand in front of his nose. "You better change your clothes."

He got on the bus and told his school-bus driver to wait for me. I quickly put on a shirt and a pair of shorts and got on the bus with Jonathan.

The teachers at the kindergarten did not suspect anything because Jonathan had told them that I was accompanying him that day. While Jonathan went for his singing lessons, I was left alone in the classroom. However, when the children returned, we all got a chance to play outdoors.

My mother soon realised that I was missing. She called up the kindergarten and upon checking, my aunt told her that I was safe with Jonathan. What an adventure! Kidnapped, by my own brother on my first day at kindergarten!

At three years of age, I could already recite 'The Lord's Prayer' by heart because my mother would say this prayer with me very often. While she taught catechism to upper primary school children every Sunday, I was left under the care of a gentle and soft spoken Indian lady teacher who taught Catechism to five year old children. I admired her long black hair all neatly tied in a braid and often wondered why my mother had cut off her beautiful long black hair.

I loved learning about Jesus and truly enjoyed singing children's songs and hymns about Jesus, especially His love for me.

> **I am glad that I was taught Catechism from an early age. Although not much was said about the power of the Cross, I would later learn about the power in His name and the greatness of His love. It was only from the millennium that I received the counsel from the Holy Spirit, who reminded me and taught me all about Christ Jesus.**
>
> **(Scripture Reading: Proverbs 22:6; Deuteronomy 4:10; Deuteronomy 11:19; Psalm 34:11; Psalm 78:5-6; Isaiah 54:13)**

I remember being given an activity book by my catechism teacher when I was five years old. Sister Anne, from the Good Shepherd Sisters Order, taught me catechism every Sunday morning for that year.

Sometimes, I would 'cheat' in my activities just to show that I loved Jesus more than the other children. On one page, there was a picture of a 'rosary,' only without the beads. Our task was to draw and colour a bead on the rosary for each good deed we performed. The day came, when we were to hand in our work to our teacher. I noticed that the girl next to me had more colourful beads on her rosary than mine. I quickly added on more beads to my rosary. I even enlarged the beads and made them more colourful. I started 'justifying' my actions by trying to recall my good deeds on that very morning.

My most memorable moments would be singing Christmas carols during the Christmas seasons, with my family and relatives gathered around our grandly decorated Christmas tree. We would always have lots of presents under the Christmas tree in our living room.

I will always cherish the moments spent with my grandmother. She would bring us to the supermarket one by one, to let us choose our gift for Christmas. She would then have those gifts wrapped and placed under the Christmas tree. Although I already knew what I was going to get from her, I was always excited about opening her gifts on 'Boxing Day'. To me, this was the way Grandmummy showed us her love. And I really felt loved by her. Not because of the gifts she bought, but because she really cared about my feelings.

I loved to hug dolls. One of the gifts I got from my grandmother was this huge strawberry shortcake doll. I remember one year when she took me to a supermarket downtown and asked me to point out to any toy I wanted. I was too shy to pick one so she picked out a soft, cuddly and sweet looking Eskimo doll. My face lit up and I guess she must have known I loved the gift she picked. She had it gift wrapped at the store.

Another time, Grandmummy bought a large tea set with trays on wheels and all. At first, I grumbled about it because it was different from all the soft toys I had received from her the previous years. I preferred to play with Jonathan's panda. But when he started playing with the tea set, I learnt from him how to pretend we were having real tea. He was always very patient with me and we enjoyed each other's company.

> **I still have the little musical box that Grandmummy gave to me as a Christmas gift and it is still in working condition. It plays the song 'Pearly Shells'.**

Jonathan and I would share our toys. However, I remember getting scolded by my parents for spoiling his soft toy panda. I had pulled the thread that formed its mouth as its down-turned lips made it look very sad. I thought we could stitch it back to make it look happy. I always wondered why the panda was brown and beige instead of black and white. But uugghh…, it did look ugly with the thread hanging loose. I think the panda must still be kept in a cupboard somewhere in my parents' home.

Jonathan was not one to get angry easily. He loved me so much that every morning when I sang to him,

"Are you sleeping, Are you sleeping,

Brother John, Brother John,

Morning bells are ringing, Morning bells are ringing,

Ding Dong bell, Ding Dong bell,"

to wake him up, he would get up and join me in singing this nursery rhyme and we would giggle happily. If he did not get up, I would tickle his tummy and he would have to get up no matter what.

Jonathan and I used to share a room when we were little. When I was three years old, I started to have nightmares almost every night. Night after night, I would wake up anxious, sometimes even crying. I would cry out to Jonathan softly to 'Wake Up!'. Whenever Jonathan awoke, I would point to the hinges of the window panes and I would see them turn into lizards.

"Can't you see them moving?" I asked.

But Jonathan could not see them. Each time, he would gently assure me that it was only a bad dream. These nightmares and visions went on for quite awhile before my parents had to move me to their room. They let me sleep in a cot so that I could not climb out. My father would also prepare my favourite beverage 'Milo' for supper each night so that I could sleep better. The nightmares and visions soon stopped after that.

Soon it was my turn to attend kindergarten. I was enrolled in the same kindergarten that Jonathan had attended before. I could not understand a word the teachers were saying as I did not have any knowledge of Mandarin.

Once during a music lesson, I had to stand at the back row on a bench with the other children. They were all singing Mandarin songs and I felt so lost and restless. A fair skinned Chinese boy standing right next to me caught my attention. I watched him singing. He looked so cute that I pinched him on his arm (twice, I think). A teacher noticed that we were fidgeting and were both distracted from our music lesson. I can't really recall what happened next but I was called down to stand next to my teacher as punishment.

My family would attend church services on Sunday mornings. When my father started serving as a Communion Minister during the evening masses, the family started attending church on Sunday evenings. Back then, the evening masses started at five thirty.

I had been eyeing Joan's flower girl pink gown, which was hung up in her wardrobe. I wanted to wear it to church. One Sunday evening, our maid helped me into the gown. I was thrilled to see that the gown fitted me perfectly. I thought my parents would be delighted to see their 'new bride' going to church but instead, my mother scolded me. She berated me and forced me to take off the gown and change into more casual clothing. My heart was crushed. That was just the beginning of more heartbreaks.

Opening Doors, Hardening Hearts

Flashbacks of early school days...

I was enrolled into a convent school where my mother was teaching when I turned seven in 1982. My parents couldn't decide whether to place me in that convent or in another convent in town where Shannon and Joan were studying at, so I was enrolled late into the convent. Due to my late enrolment into Primary 1 (Standard One), I was placed in the third stream.

In the first week of classes, I had to sit at the back of the classroom because the front rows were already taken. I was afraid and felt uncomfortable as the other students were taller and bigger than me.

I took an instant liking to a particular student who was small like me. Her skin was as white as snow and she had short shiny black hair. She was also very quiet. I plucked up the courage to introduce myself to her and soon, Sue Lin and I became good friends.

My mother was happy to learn that I was making friends. I grumbled to her that Sue Lin and I could not see the blackboard from the back of the classroom. I think my mother spoke with our class teacher to rearrange our seating. Within a week, we were moved to the front seats of our classroom. Every month, our class teacher would change our seating arrangements so that it would be fair to everyone and as long as everyone could see the blackboard. It did not matter to us as Sue Lin and I always got to sit near each other. We even made friends with the 'giants' in the classroom. Everything was blissful.

Then one day, something awful happened. I had cheekily drawn on Sue Lin's face with my pencil and it left a light scratch on her cheek. Her mother came to see my class teacher the next day and I was called out. My class teacher slapped me across the face in front of the whole class and Sue Lin's mother forbade me to talk with her.

The year-end holidays rolled by. The following year saw both Sue Lin and I, transferred to the first stream. Although I was very excited about making new friends and learning new things, I was also sad at losing Sue Lin's friendship.

There was a healthy mixture of various races in our class. I had three close Malay friends among my other Chinese and Eurasian friends. One of them whose surname was 'Khan' proclaimed that 'Genghis Khan' was her ancestor. She was always so cheerful and loved to make us laugh. We were bowled over by her crazy antics. I was also close to my Eurasian friends as we also attended the same catechism classes on Sundays. I was very unhappy when one of them had to move to another state down south, with her father. I only knew her as 'Geraldine' but I do not remember her last name. She had to follow her father to Melaka, where more Eurasians of Portuguese descent lived. Her father had gotten a new job there.

Here, I began to feel the pressure to compete with my peers in my studies. It was a huge struggle keeping up with the 'smart' students because I was too playful. I spent my recess playing instead of eating. Each time I prayed for good results, I would still perform badly. My grades were not improving.

My report card was due one day and I had forgotten to let my parents see it. So when my teacher called all the students to hand in their report cards at the very last moment, I did the unexpected. I signed my own report card. Of course, my teacher found out because she knew my mother's signature well. When she called my mother to come over to the classroom, she passed a remark to my mother saying that I was so 'bold'. I didn't understand what 'bold' meant and took it as a negative word because I knew I was in trouble.

Back home, I got reprimanded by my mother, who got my father to cane me. My mother nagged me for days about my grades. I just couldn't take it anymore. So to escape from this hell, I started dreaming a lot.

Soon, I started having mental blocks and found it harder to concentrate in the classroom while the teacher was teaching. My form teacher caught me staring out of the window a few times and complained to my mother. Changing my seats didn't help as I couldn't stop day dreaming in class. My teachers thought it was because I wanted to go out to play. But the real reason was that I often dreamed my parents would stop fighting at home.

Primary 3, Standard Three...1984

My parents had different opinions about my schooling and often argued over little things. My father wanted me to participate in sports but my mother did not. I loved running so eventually my mother relented. I got to take part in my school's sports events and started my training in athletics under the tutelage of our school's sports coach. I felt more freedom here doing what I enjoyed most.

We started with only three runners, myself included. The other two girls were my classmates, Ann and Fauziah. The three of us became bosom friends. We always challenged each other and gave our best. We never felt jealous or envious about our achievements. Instead, we encouraged one another and shared our techniques with each other.

Even with all my mother's constant nagging and admonishing, I have to say that I had a really happy and splendid childhood. My siblings and cousins were running around the house all the time. If we were bored of the same old games, we would create our own games. My elder sister, Joan, created 'Two Stones' or 'Two Pillows'. She sewed two little pillows big enough for us to hold in the palm of our hand and filled them with either uncooked rice or beach sand. We then invented 'moves' that would test ones speed and motor skills. We played this game in replace of the traditional 'Seven Stones' which was more common during our time.

When our parents were not at home, we would sometimes play 'Police and Thieves' or climb the hill just opposite where we lived. An old man who lived a few doors away from us, warned us about the cobras and pythons. We nicknamed him 'The Old Man of the Hill' because he was always clearing and planting up the hill and we didn't know his name. He forbade us to climb up the hill telling us it was dangerous.

Still, we did not take heed of his warning. We had a lot of fun climbing the hill and exploring nature.

One day, six of us went out to climb the hill without our parents' knowledge. There was a slippery bend around a corner near the cliff when we wanted to descend from the hill. Climbing up was easy but coming down was a struggle. We got stuck around the bend because small stones and sand were rolling down beneath us. We squatted and held on to the roots and branches of trees and tried walking like ducks around that bend. I couldn't get a grip of the branches because there were too many of us around that bend. I started sliding towards the cliff. Jonathan saw me sliding and moved so I could grab hold of the root where he had let go off. I turned to help him. His voice was shaky. I saw that he was sliding fast and tried to get hold of his hand but he slid and vanished over the cliff. We were all horrified. We shouted after him, "Jonathan! Jonathan!" But there was no reply. We tried to move down faster to get to him and to check if he was alright. My heart was pounding fast and I was in panic but I could not go any faster.

"Jonathan!" we all cried out when we got down the hill and searched for him. There he was, smiling at us. He was standing in front of a tree and brushing off the sand from his knees.

"What happened to you? Why are you smiling?" I asked, puzzled at his reaction.

Then he showed us his hands. His fingers were blistered and bleeding at the tips. He had used his fingers and nails to scrape his way, all the way down to the ground like 'Spiderman' sticking to the wall. And he landed on a tree covered with thorns. The tree had actually 'cushioned' his fall.

After that incident, Joan, stopped climbing up the hill with us. None of us ever told our parents what happened that day. We were all afraid of being punished. Punishment meant getting caned and scolding. Somehow as we grew older, Jonathan and I mastered the art of hiding my parents' canes. They would always have to buy new ones...which would later 'magically' disappear. I guess that is why my parents eventually stopped buying them and using them on us.

During the mid-term school holidays in 1985, my family and my closest aunt's family went up to Penang Hill for a bungalow stay. On this occasion, we stayed at the 'Fern Hill' bungalow for two nights. We loved the hill because it was misty and much colder than where we lived.

Being children, we brought up our game sets and comics to keep ourselves occupied. I was only ten, then. Jonathan was twelve and already very much into football. His favourite teams were Liverpool and Everton. He wanted to be the next football star like his idols 'Gary Lineker' and 'Ian Rush'. He had bought a football with his own savings and brought it up to the hill for this trip.

After returning from our walk on the first day, our parents, aunt and uncle went back to the bungalow to have their tea. While they were busy talking and reading the newspapers in the lounge, Jonathan and I stayed outside the bungalow to play with our siblings and cousins.

Before dark, our mothers called us in to have our bath and to prepare for dinner. Jonathan stayed out a little while, dribbling his football as I watched him. He accidentally kicked his football down the slope and it rolled into the thick jungle out of sight.

My brother was devastated. It was his hard earned pocket money and the football was still new. He was determined to get it back. He told me he knew where to find it. I did not want him to go alone, so I followed him into the jungle.

As soon as we got into the jungle, we tried looking for the football. Instead, we found that we were walking in circles. We tried to find a path out but we could not. I was getting scared because we kept returning to the same spot where there were bamboo trees in the middle. The cool mist surrounding us was blinding me and the atmosphere seemed eerie. We were lost. I was afraid because I could not hear a sound. Then, Jonathan started to lead me. He could hear my mother's voice calling out to us but strangely I could not.

Thank God, Jonathan led us out and that my mother and aunt came looking for us before it got dark. Heaven knows what might have happened to us if they did not realise we were missing. And how did they know where to look for us? God must have sent his angels to guide them to us. Praise the Lord for He is good. His unending love and faithfulness never fails. God sends his angels to protect his children.

We got up early the next morning so that we could watch the mist go down. We stayed indoors playing board games since we didn't have the football to play with. We were afraid too, of getting lost again. What an adventure!

In the fifth grade or Primary 5 (Standard Five), I had to sit for our government exam. I only managed to score an average and this really upset my mother. I was nearly in tears when my name was not called out for the 'A' class by our form teacher. I had to move to the next class with the 'average' students. We were deemed noisier and boisterous by our teachers, parents and other students.

Just after our final exams and before we were to enter sixth grade or Primary 6 (Standard Six), a party was held in our classroom. We were allowed to bring our own board games from home for the party. My classmate, Amber brought her 'Ouija' board. I knew in my mind and heart that it was not right to play this 'game' as my friends from church had mentioned it to me before. Their parents had warned them about it. But I was curious. I observed Amber, Tamara, Angela and Yi-Ching playing the game and listened as Amber asked the 'Spirit' some questions. It looked as though they were controlling the movement of the coin so I said to them, "You're just moving the coin on your own. I can see you pushing it".

"No, we're not! It's real. If you don't believe, come and try it," Angela exclaimed.

"I don't believe in ghosts," I retaliated.

"The spirit is controlling the coin. Don't believe me, put your finger on the coin," Amber responded.

They challenged me to lay my finger on the coin. And I did. Then Amber, who had summoned the spirit asked,

"Spirit of the coin, tell us your name."

I felt the coin moving as my finger touched it. Then it spelt out 'M-I-C-H... It was moving back and forth from 'E' to 'A'. I lifted my finger up because there were too many of us crowded around and I thought they were *pulling my leg*. I was a little sceptical and afraid at the same time. Some of us were 'pushing' the coin and we had to stop and start over. Amber had not removed her finger from the coin. As we were curious to know 'its' name, she repeated the same question. Together they repeated that step and the coin moved and spelt out 'M-I-C-H-A-E-L'.

I still did not believe them when Amber tried to send the 'spirit' back to its 'home'.

Wednesday, June 10, 2015

As I am writing this section, I am reminded of how King Saul summoned the seer to call up Samuel's spirit. However, we know that this act of consulting in mediums or invoking the spirits of the dead is an abomination to the Lord God Almighty. I have renounced all involvement in these acts of consulting the dead spirits once in 2002 and again in 2008~09 and will continue to do so as I intercede for others.

I also felt uneasy about the name Michael because the person who raped me in 2006 called himself Michael. I then thought to myself, 'The devil is a great liar because he is trying to discredit our Archangel Michael'.

Another thought that came to my mind was the faces of the people on the coins. During Jesus' time on earth, He taught the disciples to pay back to Caesar what belonged to Caesar. He meant that his disciples were to pay their taxes to Caesar who was living then. However, times have changed and in our present day, we are still using coins and notes bearing the face of our late king, the first king of Malaysia. So how do we pay him back? Is this why there is so much corruption in our country?

Should I then, carry a Polaroid camera so that I can take snap shots of the grocer or salesman and paste their pictures on the notes I am paying them with?

Sunday, August 1, 2021

Dear Readers,

I hope you will advise your children to stay away from such 'games' as the Ouija board, whether virtual or physical, as it was the spirit that lured me to participate in this 'game'. You know the saying, "Curiosity killed the cat."

Opening doors to these evil spirits only cause heartaches and heartbreaks. Amber came out of an abusive marriage. Tamara's marriage ended in divorce. I, myself have had my fair share of failed relationships. When I met Angela in 2003, she told me her life was a mess before she found Christ. And this is my testimony too. I had been in several broken relationships before I gave my life to Christ. Now, I have been married for ten years. Jesus Christ is my Saviour! He is my Redeemer and Jesus Christ is my LORD!

I hope and pray that you will find your love in Christ Jesus. He will bless you abundantly.

Love,
Chevonne.

Dreams and the Fantasy

Flashbacks of childhood days...

Things started to change dramatically when there were heated arguments between my mother and father. At that time I was too young to understand what was going on but I would always stay in Jonathan's room when things got too 'loud'. We immersed ourselves in mastering board games. Jonathan was an ace in chess, checkers and 'Chinese checkers'. Whenever our cousins came around, we would play 'Police & Thieves', 'Hide and Seek', 'One-leg' or 'Kah-Li-Toi' around our home or outside, along the road. Sometimes our neighbours and their school friends would play with us or join us at the playground nearby our home.

Jonathan attended tuition in a house just behind our row of houses. Usually before his tuition classes, I would follow him to the sundry shop nearby our home to buy all his card games and some snacks. I still remember the cards we used to collect on cars, airplanes, bikes, 'Pick Up Sticks' and also family card games like 'Happy Family'.

Later, I was to find out that Jonathan had been missing his tuition classes. My father was very upset and grounded him. He had been joining two boys from his tuition class to play at the video arcade instead of attending tuition. I confronted him about it but he just shrugged it off. It did not stop there because the two boys who were actually brothers living in our neighbourhood started coming to our home to persuade him to join them at the video arcade. Jonathan never allowed me to follow them. Our parents were not at home to stop him because they were usually busy working or monitoring the stock market in town.

One evening, my family prayed the rosary in our living room. I was happy when my father asked me to pray a decade of the rosary. When it got to my turn to pray, my mother scolded me for mispronouncing a word. I had said 'blest' instead of 'bles-sed.' I was deeply hurt.

I could never understand why each time there was an important and special occasion for me at church, my mother would make me cry on the day of the event. I remember crying all the way to church on the day I was to accept my first 'Holy Communion.' I was deeply hurt and felt useless.

At school, I played all the time. I hated to hear my mother nagging me all the time too but I just could not bring myself to study. I was easily distracted by play and television. I started to withdraw from my friends because of the constant scolding and caning from my mother. Even my friends were afraid of her. I became stubborn and would not study.

Then one day, my History Teacher gently advised me to study for myself and not for others. "Getting good grades will benefit you," she said. I could not comprehend what she said because to me getting good grades meant less scolding, peace at home, peace in my mind and peace in my heart. Teacher Nadira then persuaded my mother to speak gently with me and encourage me to study instead of nagging me. Finally, someone who truly cares. I scored a 100 percent in History in my class.

Sometimes my grades were bad and sometimes I thought they were good. Even when I scored 98 or 99 percent, my mother would still criticize me and berate me for being careless. It was always embarrassing especially when she scolded me in front of my teachers and friends. I remember getting trophies for Art and the Malay Language but nothing I did ever seemed to please my mother.

I remember always trembling when I received my report card or book. Each time I tried to let my father sign the report card, he would ask me to let my mother check it first. And each time she did, I would be in trouble.

It was also unfortunate that every time my family had to go to church on Sundays, my favourite cartoons would be on. I was crazy over 'He-man', 'She-Ra', 'Thundercats' and 'The Transformers'. We were always late for church because of me. I loved to imagine myself as the heroine in those cartoons. Furthermore, the menacing villains in those cartoons fascinated me.

There were other cartoons which Jonathan and I truly enjoyed. We made sure we never missed any parts and would follow them faithfully.

Saturday, April 11, 2015

I did some research on the cartoons that I used to watch in my childhood days to learn their effects on children. They definitely had an effect on me. Children love to role play and sometimes this could be the problem. Just be careful. In the 'Thundercats', the villain 'The Mummy' had an evil mantra. He conjured up evil spirits. We know that the 'Ancient One' in the Bible refers to God and God alone, but in the cartoon, the Ancient One referred to was the 'evil one'.

I don't know if anyone took notice, but these cartoons were turned into movies and were due to be released when the coronavirus (Covid-19) pandemic hit the world.

God IS a JEALOUS God! He will never share His light with darkness. God IS LIGHT; in Him there is no darkness. HE IS the TRUE LIGHT.

God brought me out from being a pawn for the 'Mummy' in 'Thundercats' and gave me His strengths as in 'Bravestarr', 'Paw Paw Bears' and 'Voltron' when I started attending 'The Prophetic Conferences' from 2008 onwards.

Now I understand what the psalmist must have felt when he poured out to God, "Even when I go up to heaven, You are there. And when I go to the graves, You are there."

God, You are Omniscient - All-knowing God!
God, You are Omnipotent - Have unlimited power!
God, You are Omnipresent - You are present everywhere!
You are the Almighty God, My Creator!

My group of friends would share our troubles with each other. To escape from our troubles, we created fantasies.

I started having recurring dreams about a 'Snake Prince'. These dreams turned to fantasies. The 'Snake Prince' had the ability to transform himself to a human being or python as he wished. In my fantasy, this 'Snake Prince' married two sisters. One blonde and one raven haired. I even made out one of the sisters to look like 'Elizabeth Taylor' the British actress, with her beautiful violet eyes.

Little did I know where these dreams came from and what they meant. Thank God, now I do.

Monday, August 2, 2021

I used to think that because good can triumph over evil, we could win over the 'evil one' and convert him to become good. Many people think this way and get caught up in worldliness.

As a child, I used to put myself as the heroines from the cartoons I watched in my dreams and now I realise how dangerous it is for one to do so.

The 'Snake Prince' is a python spirit, a religious spirit that many people have been oppressed with. It oozes with lusts of the flesh, eyes and power. It also darkens your mind so you do not truly worship God. You doze off when you try to read the Bible and you become disobedient towards authority, especially towards God and your parents.

Now I know that good and evil cannot mix. We are set apart for good works. We should set ourselves apart as examples of our faith in Christ Jesus.

If you are under oppression, make a decision to rise up against whatever is oppressing you. Get an elder or pastor of a church to minister to you. Do not be ashamed to ask for prayer and for help. God is your healer and deliverer. If you are alone, get a bible. Read and meditate upon the Word of God. God will not forsake you. The Holy Spirit will guide you. Put your trust in God.

It took me two years to read the Bible from cover to cover. I have not memorized all of it but I can remember some verses which the Holy Spirit convicted me about.

First Encounter with Evil

Flashbacks of highschool days...

In January 1988, I was transferred to another convent which was located in the heart of George Town. I was twelve when I started schooling at my new school, which was also the oldest girls' school in Penang. It was founded by three French nuns on the 12th of April 1852. My father explained that this transfer was to facilitate our transport arrangements, as my two elder sisters were also studying there.

I was reunited with some of my friends from kindergarten. Although I made some new friends at my secondary school, I wasn't close with any of them. I missed my friends from my primary school very much. I was quieter here.

Shannon and Joan had set an example by being elected as school prefects. It was not a surprise that I was nominated to become a prefect in 1989 and later became a senior prefect within two years.

I remember that the prefects would gather at the school's second porch every morning. There were two table-tennis areas and many benches to put our school bags there.

In mid-1989, Uncle Ronald, Aunt Karen and my cousins, Ivan, Anne and Anthony returned from the United States. They had been there for almost five years. Anne was enrolled in my school and placed in my class. I was overjoyed to have her in my class and introduced her to my friends.

Anne shared with me about her life in the United States and about the 'naughty' things they did in school and the wild parties they had there. Being young and naive, I related these stories about her to my friends. We laughed and cracked jokes about it. The next thing I knew, I was ostracized by my own group of friends and my cousin became part of their group.

A younger schoolmate told me that they were spreading rumours that I was deceitful and conceited.

Whenever we went to Sister Dempsey's class for catechism, they would not talk to me. They treated me as though I did not exist. I could tell from the look on Sr. Dempsey's face that she was not pleased. She obviously knew something was going on.

I felt great respect for Sister Dempsey. She was always gentle and gracious. Never angry even when we were late for her class. I thank God for her patience, her loving kindness shown toward us, her quiet demeanour and obedience, just like Mary, Mother of Christ Jesus.

Sister Dempsey taught us how to say the morning prayer. I have altered the prayer to make it personal for my relationship with Abba Father to grow in Christ,

"Lord, God Almighty, I offer You all of my prayers, words, works, joys, trials, sufferings, thoughts, actions, desires, worries, fears, anxieties and confusion, For the intention of your divine heart. Merciful God, let me not yield to temptation but deliver me from every evil. Lord, may You be adored, glorified, loved, praised and worshipped throughout the world, now and forever... I put all my hope, love, faith and trust in You. Please take charge of my soul and spirit. I enthrone You, Lord God Almighty, in my heart

and You are and will always be head of my home. In Jesus' name I pray."

Matters only got worse when my mother started to compare me with Anne. My mother adored Anne. Once when I was studying, my mother passed this remark angrily, "How come Anne gets thinner when she studies hard while you are putting on weight? Most people lose weight when studying under pressure. Are you really studying at all?"

I got so used to listening to the negative comments from my family members, school teachers, classmates and friends that I just did not care anymore. I did not realize that I had grown into a cold person. Though I loved people and wanted to help, I would always either think twice or just stand and wait for others to take the first step or make the first move. There was this protective wall I had put on. This was definitely not 'The Armour of God'. It was more like a defensive wall that said "Do not come near me!"

When my mother advised me to pray for my studies so that I would get good grades, I tried. When my grades did not improve, I scoffed at God. I even questioned his existence. I felt he was not real in my life. I didn't know how to connect with God then. I had forgotten how much I enjoyed singing praises to God as a young child.

My grades took a plunge from then on and so did my sports. I used to be good at athletics. I did not want to compete with Anne, so soon I was letting go of everything. I tried to join different societies so we would not clash. Although I never suffered from jealousy, my self-esteem suffered.

Every day it was just school, study, sports and homework. The same routine day in and day out. I stopped watching cartoons. I thought people who watched them were plain stupid and childish. I even stopped listening to music. So when my classmates were talking about Walt Disney's 'Little Mermaid' and singing and humming to the songs in cartoons and to the latest music on radio, I was always in a total blur. "Wait. Who? What song? I do not know that one.... Sorry, I can't sing along... I do not know the lyrics."

After achieving a distinction in Grade Five for my practical in piano, I begged my parents to stop my piano lessons. I have no regrets in making that decision.

Early one morning, my father and elder sister, Joan, had to go to the Penang Stadium for sports events. So I had to be dropped off at school as early as 6:45am. The sky was still dark when we reached the front gate of my school. I saw a man on a motorcycle drop off his daughter. She walked towards the front gate before me. As I entered, I noticed there was not a soul around. Neither was the security guard at his usual seat.

'Where had the girl gone? And where was the security guard?' I pondered.

I continued walking towards the first porch. It was just twenty metres from the front school gate. When I reached the first porch, I was taken aback. 'Why were there no lights at the table-tennis area? And where were all the students and teachers?'

I stopped at the first porch and glanced towards the second porch where the prefects usually met. The second porch was just another 30 metres from the first porch. I saw no one except a piece of black cloth blowing in the air. I thought hard, 'Where could they be? And what is that? Where did that cloth come from?' I stared hard at it.

I was just about to turn back to walk to the front gate when I noticed that the black cloth had grown large into a silhouette of a human being. It looked like 'Death' or 'Hades.' It had no face. And back then 'Lord of the Rings' was not even in the theatres or published in books yet.

Thoughts were running through my head. 'What if I ran back to the gate and walked in together with the girls getting off from school buses? Then, what if this spectre followed me from behind or appeared right in front of me?' I froze immediately. Cold sweat trickled down my spine. I was freaking out. Thoughts were playing in my head.

Slowly, I summoned the courage to take a step. Then the spectre floated up to reveal it had no feet. I felt that it wanted to challenge me. I stopped and muttered, "Jesus, please send a school bus! Please send a school bus!"

After what felt like four minutes had passed on, I heard a school bus door slam. I waited for the students to walk in so I could follow them. When the girls walked in, the sky suddenly turned bright. The spectre was gone. And there were lights and students at the second porch. I looked behind me. There were so many students.

'Where were they before? What had just happened?'

I walked to the second porch very slowly as I pondered hard. When I met Mei Lin, my classmate and fellow prefect, I asked her if she had seen me standing at the first porch and whether she had been at the table-tennis area earlier. She claimed that she had just arrived and that she just saw me as I entered.

I did not think much of it at first as I did not believe in ghosts. I still don't. (I only related this incident to my sisters after I left the convent in 1992).

Saturday, April 11, 2015 (whilst thinking back those times when I was going through hurts and frustrations in life)...

"Thank you, Lord Jesus for carrying me; for walking with me in the wilderness. Thank you for guiding my footsteps and lighting my path. Though I was not fully equipped with the 'Sword of the Spirit' and knew no other 'tongue', Lord Jesus, You were always there when I cried out to you for help and strength, for healing, deliverance and restoration and for peace. I only had to call Your name, 'JESUS'. Sweet Jesus, Most Holy God. Most Pure and Holy One of God. I LOVE YOU JESUS, BECAUSE YOU LOVED ME FIRST. Thank you for your unfailing and unconditional love. Thank you for loving me."

Rebellion

More flashbacks of my high school days...

I performed poorly in my final year in secondary school. My grades had plunged drastically from 'A's' to 'F's'. I remember how anxious I was whenever there was an examination.

I spent late nights watching soap operas like 'Dynasty', 'Colby's' and 'Falcon Crest' instead of studying. I was sick of memorizing every bit of my textbooks and was tired of my mother's constant nagging. To release my mind off stress, I threw away all of my textbooks before my final government examination in October 1992.

While waiting for my school results, I was hired as a casual worker for banquet functions at the Shangri-La Hotel. One of the casual workers there took an interest in me. He was Jude Chong. At first, I tried to avoid him but he kept on pursuing me and would sit next to me in the van on our way home. He shared his 'life stories' with me and I took pity on him.

Jude and I started dating after the Shangri-La's annual dinner for the banquet casual workers. However, our relationship was put to a test when my parents forbade me to go out with him. Aunt Susannah's sons, Jordan and Trevor spotted us together. They knew Jude from school. My parents forbade me to go out with Jude after Aunt Susannah warned them about him.

Jude and I were on a bus to town one day, and he was acting strange. His words suddenly turned harsh and thoughtless. He uttered the most unkind words since we met. I was deeply hurt and immediately knew something was not right. When the bus stopped at our destination, he got off hastily and walked his own way. I quickly walked in the opposite direction trying to hold back my tears.

For a while, Jude did not call me. My heart was crushed when I found out through his god-sister, Lynnette that he had dumped me for his ex-girlfriend who lived in another state down south. I never knew his ex. After two months or so, Jude and Lynnette persuaded me to return to him. Eventually, I forgave Jude and went to meet him and Lynnette at his home. It was the first time he had brought me to his home because he did not want me to know where or how he lived. It was a small place but very cosy.

Jude told me that he was upset that my parents would not give him a chance. He had been through many experiences where people labeled him a thief and a liar because of his 'past.' I knew of his past and did not judge him. I only wanted to help him but I did not want him to hurt me the way he did before. He assured me that he loved me and that he was very sorry for what he had said on the bus. And so that was what I thought and was led to believe.

My SPM final government examination results were out. I had missed Grade One by one mark. I only scored well in Geography and English. My father wanted me to work but my mother wanted me to continue studying. I wasn't sure of what I wanted so finally my parents enrolled me into a private school.

During the first year of my studies in sixth form, my cousin, Samuel, who was also studying in the same private school advised me to apply to be a prefect in this school. My answer was a straight 'No'. I was glad to have my 'freedom'. But, best of all, I would not have to remain in my sisters' shadow or be compared with them.

Things went very well, during my first year in high school. I took up Geography, History, Economics and Malay Literature. I loved my teachers there. They were a dedicated lot and made learning very interesting and enjoyable. All of my teachers were very lively and engaging. They managed to bring their stories 'alive' during their lessons. So everyone paid full attention and enjoyed themselves during their classes. For the first time, it wasn't all about memorizing the facts but understanding them. Although my favourite was still Geography, I was not pleased with my results. I had studied very hard for the paper but my results were not up to my expectations.

'How can this be?' I thought. I studied from many different revision books and I knew my answers were detailed and comprehensive. I compared my answers with that of another classmate who got higher marks than me. I found that our content were similar except that his answers covered five pages while mine was only three pages long. So much for neatness and tidiness. I guess I should have enlarged my writing a little bit so my teacher could 'see' more clearly.

Jude and I continued dating throughout high school. He would pick me up from school every day and send me to the public library to study. Over time, I got to know his mum. Jude's mother was good to me. I liked her a lot and respected her. They were Christians and I was Catholic. He brought me to his church at Reservoir Gardens one day. I was introduced to his church friends, elders and pastor. Not long after that, he told me his church pastor and elders advised him against our relationship because I was a

Catholic. They told him that there would be problems in our relationship. But which relationship is free of problems? He even told me that his 'friends' joked about sleeping around with their girlfriends and dumping them to 'teach' them a lesson if ever the girls' parents were to be against their relationship. I should have stopped seeing him then but I was deeply infatuated with him so I said nothing. Nothing because I could not understand the people he grew up with. His pastors, his friends and his father.

Even though my parents totally opposed our relationship, Jude and I continued to see each other. We started to frequent discotheques because we enjoyed dancing and the beat of the loud music played at the discos.

After we both stopped working as casual workers at the hotel, Jude started helping his friends at a very popular discotheque near Batu Ferringhi. He introduced me to his friend, Tom, who worked there as a disc jockey. Tom was a humble man who kept to himself most of the time. His passion was in the music he played. I liked Tom because he was a family man. He was also kind and patient towards Jude. It made me happy to know that Jude still had good friends.

Even so, our relationship wasn't always a bed of roses. Jude and I got into a lot of heated arguments mainly because I could not get a single truth out of him. He continued to lie and was always making up excuses. His attitude really angered me. However, after each argument, we would kiss and make up. Jude's mum persuaded him to return to the Holy Trinity Church. I attended church services with him on Sunday mornings. It was usually very crowded and I was introduced to some of his friends there. Jude would tell me light-heartedly about how Stephanie would cook for him and give him little cute gifts before he knew me. She used to be interested in him. So I asked him, "Why didn't you go out with her, then?"

He replied almost belching, "She's not my type."

But I thought to myself. 'She's such a sweet girl.'

In spite of all the warning signs, I carried on dating Jude. My thinking was very conservative. I thought of Jude as my first and only love. Then one day, he showed me a cupboard full of letters his ex-girlfriend had sent him. He had kept them all this while and was still corresponding with her. He asked me if he could go down to meet her in Kuala Lumpur where she was now working as a radio DJ and I felt obliged so I said 'Yes'. I felt it was the right thing to do. If he truly loved me, he would return. He did return after a week in Kuala Lumpur. His ex-girlfriend decided it was best for them to remain as friends. I believed it was due to the distance. Out of curiosity, I asked Jude why he still kept all the letters she wrote to him. He only smiled.

'Was he still pining for her?' I pondered. But we left it at that.

One day, when I was resting in Jude's home, he forced himself on me. He could not penetrate deep because I was not 'with him'. Afterwards he plonked down next to me, smiling and asked, "How do you feel?"

I was immensely disgusted and angry. I wanted to cry but could not.

'What just happened? Is this how love is supposed to feel like? My God, I am a Catholic! How could I let this happen? I know my friends were doing it but I would not. But...'

My thoughts and emotions were in turmoil. I was so confused.

cannot leave him now. I have to marry him,' I thought.

o I stayed on. Our relationship continued and so did our ove-making.'

became addicted to sex and thought it was normal. I nistook lustfulness for love. If we had respected each other, we would have refrained from having sex before marriage. Jude would have waited if he honoured God, honoured me and my parents. I had defied my parents. I rebelled against my parents and one thing led to another. I was sinning against God and I had lowered my standards to become just like everybody else. Most of my friends were doing it. Rebellion is not something to boast about. If you do boast, boast about the goodness of God. He delivered me from the serpent spirit! He delivered me from pride and rebellion.

Jude and I continued dating. Our relationship was on and off just like his job-hopping. I even overheard Lynnette, his god-sister, advising him to leave me. Feeling betrayed, I started to avoid her. Finally, when Jude could not secure a permanent job or rather stick to one, his mum's friend advised him to take up a course in 'Tourism and Hospitality'. She was willing to offer him a job at her company as a tour agent. Days went by and the December school holidays arrived. By then, Jude had already completed his course and was working at his mum's friend's company.

On one occasion, he was to deliver the passports of a tour group's members to the Penang International Airport in Bayan Lepas very early the next morning. He told me he would pick me up at six in the morning. Six o'clock came and I was ready. I waited and waited. I called him several times but there was no answer. Finally I got him. He had overslept. He was more than an hour late. I told him to go without me or he would be in trouble. Instead he rode his bike straight to my place in Tanjong Bungah from town to pick me up. He hadn't even showered or changed into his uniform. Together, we rushed to the airport to deliver the passports. When we arrived, he asked me to wait for him downstairs while he settled matters at the check-in counter. After about 45 minutes, he came downstairs. He looked relieved and his face was beaming. His friend, Anuar, a staff of Malaysia Airlines, had managed to secure seats and the connecting flight for all his tour group members. The tour group got on board the flight with a slight delay.

Christmas came and I was invited to Jude's company's Christmas party. It was humiliating when I got an alarm clock as a Christmas gift from his employer. Still, I forgave him.

Another year went by. I remember always getting into arguments with my mother because she wanted me to end my relationship with Jude. My parents almost stopped my schooling because they thought I would never make it. My father lectured me about how expensive my education was. He was already finding it difficult to put food on the table. Furthermore, they had to bear the cost of my eldest sister, Shannon's education at a local university. I was deeply troubled. I had already come this far.

End 1994

It was during this time that my eldest brother, Jonathan, was sent to Singapore to work as a technician in a factory. There was no one to confide in. I struggled to focus in my studies. I knew I would fail in Economics because it was my worst subject. I did not understand the terms in the Malay Language. I was cramming all I was learning into my head at the last minute. All the questions I spotted for my History examination came out. But I guess I could not spew out what I had crammed into my head. I only managed to scrape through with a pass in most subjects. And as expected, I failed in Economics. My mother was not too pleased with my results. She blamed it on my relationship with Jude.

I took up my first permanent job at a pewter company as their sales representative. I needed to gain some working experience and build up my self-confidence. I was very impressed with my boss. I loved the way she carried herself and how she spoke. She was strict but never harsh with any of the staff. I also loved the training I got at the pewter factory in Kuala Lumpur. I found their facilitators very professional. The training helped me a lot as I learnt more from them than I had learned in school.

Meanwhile, everyone was talking about the airline industry. It was a booming industry and everyone I knew wanted to join the airlines. My cousins were already flying with Golden Keris Airlines and Jonathan left his factory job to join the same airline as their ground staff at the Singapore airport. I wanted to try out but I loved my job and my boss. So I persuaded Jude to go for an interview instead. I was very happy for him when he got the job and thought it would be better for us as the prospects were good. I figured he would gain better exposure and learn to become more responsible and independent. He looked worried about us but I reassured him that things would be fine. I was with his mother to send him off at the airport. We stayed in touch through phone.

Jude would call often to tell me about his new job. He had been placed in the baggage handling department. Then one day, he called to say that he was coming back to Penang. I was disappointed that things did not work out too well for him there. I started to have negative thoughts about his attitude again. I did not know how to help him, to encourage him or to motivate him anymore.

When Jude returned to Penang, he found other jobs which were not paying so well. We discussed his spending habits so that he could make ends meet. I did not understand why he was always borrowing money from his friends. They were looking for me to pay up his debts. With all my thoughts and feelings worked up, I failed to appreciate Jude's cheerful disposition. No matter what life threw at him, he always had a cheerful face. He surprised me one day, when he took me to the 'Reptile & Orchid Garden' in Bukit Jambul. He told me how much he loved that place. There, we saw all types of snakes, birds, tortoises and even the giant sized 'dragon fish.' We sat at the pond to talk. The weather was hot but the huge trees provided much shade. I felt it was a good place to take a break from the hustle and bustle of the city.

Jude's other god-sister, Xin Zhen also approached me to help her find work at the hotel where I used to work. Through some connections, I managed to find out that there was a vacancy at the hotel's sales and catering department. She had been through a rough break-up with her ex-boyfriend. He had taught my brother, Jonathan, how to use Word and Spreadsheets. My friend, Heng, who helped Xin Zhen at the hotel was immediately smitten by her and started to woo her with flowers and gifts. Soon, they were courting.

In the same year, I decided to attend an interview when the local newspapers advertised for vacancies again with Golden Keris Airlines. This time, the vacancies were for positions based at the Penang International Airport. I was hired and tendered my resignation at the pewter company after having worked there for only eight months. My boss had a talk with me before letting me go. She reasoned that my starting salary was similar to what I was getting at the airlines. However, she understood that there would be better prospects at my new job.

Thursday, November 2, 1995

I reported to work at the airport with high expectations about learning new things and making new friends. My first impression of my colleagues was that they were quite unfriendly. Most just went about with their work and gave me a stare as though saying, 'You wouldn't last long.' One or two staff were even quite hostile. They gave me the impression that they were racist. The only person who welcomed me was our Supervisor, Paul. He was the one who arranged our roster. He greeted me with a smile and gave me a briefing of the duties I had to learn up and perform well within my probation period of three months. Paul assigned Melisa as my mentor. She had been working there for about two years then. We had to learn everything on the job and no formal training was given. I had to take down notes. Loads of them. It was very hard for me to take in all the details as things were very fast paced and I hadn't seen an airline ticket before this.

My first duty under the guidance of Melisa was documentation. We had to prepare all the relevant documents of the incoming and outgoing flights for the authorities such as customs, immigration, health department, travel control and also for the ships bag for our chief steward or chief stewardess to be handed over to our counterpart in Singapore. We only had about an hour to prepare our documents while the aircraft was on the ground. These I learnt to do quite well. It was the duties of tallying and segregating the tickets for the sales departments in Singapore and Penang that slowed me down. This had to be done very quickly after the plane took off and before it landed in Singapore. Also, because the staff always rushed to the canteen after each flight, I was rushed to complete my other side duties. Sometimes, I was told that they would help me with my duties after we came back but often times they would be too busy with their own duties when we got back. Sometimes tickets would go missing and the staff would blame each other. Or sometimes I counted the tickets wrongly. Melisa helped me to read the codes on the tickets when I explained my difficulty in segregating the tickets.

My first month on probation was a living hell. I had other loads of duties to learn and I hadn't even mastered documentation or check-in yet. There were a lot of codes to remember for checking-in passengers and baggage for departure. There was a lot of pettiness and gossip going around and I was caught in the middle of it all. These same staff teased me a lot because I smiled a lot. They kept on telling me that I did not have to 'pretend' to be good. I did not like the language they used but soon it all became a norm. They teased me about the way I walked and about the way I looked. I just smiled. It did not really bother me when I was given nicknames, but I did take offence when it came to body shaming. I think it started because I brought a book on 'Face Fortunes' to be discussed at work during our free time.

My focus then was being accepted by my colleagues. Friendship seemed very important to me then. I guess my superiors also had a difficult time with the staff. They raised their voices and had arguments over trivial matters like overtime, duty rosters and other staff problems. Every time I was questioned about my work, I became defensive. I was lucky to be confirmed as a permanent staff. The staff turnover was high. Many of my senior staff resigned and the airline was always hiring new ones.

> **I realise now that 'Face Fortunes' hurt people. There is no truth in it.**
>
> **No wonder God opposes all these 'fortune telling' materials and actions. I was wrong in believing them. We should never label people. It hurts them.**

Things did not work out between Jude and I. He had asked me to keep his salary for him since he was afraid he could not control his spending. I did not want to because I felt it wasn't a wise thing to do. I felt a person had to learn self-control. Still, he insisted. He pressed his money into my hands.

Not too long after that, Jude's mother called me into her room to have a talk with me privately.

"Have you been borrowing money from my son?" she questioned me.

I was totally shocked. My heart was crushed. "No," I replied.

"Well he says that he does not have enough money to spend because you are holding his money," she said inquisitively.

"He asked me to keep his salary once. But I have given it all back. In fact he is the one who keeps borrowing from me and I had to pay some of his debts," I explained.

His mother immediately called him into the room and questioned him in front of me. That day, we had a huge argument. I could no longer trust him. After four years of heartache, he still continued to lie to me. I felt betrayed. Jude and I broke off our relationship after this incident.

Back home, my father knew I was going through a break-up as he watched me with my face buried in the sofa. I was sobbing and trying to hide my tears. It must have hurt my father too to see me crying like that but he did not say a word about it.

Downhill ... The Good Life

Flashbacks of my young adult life...

I was young, free and single once again. Despite our busy schedule, my colleagues and I still found time to frequent the discotheques. I was often coaxed into joining them even though I did not really enjoy going dancing anymore.

Most of us were driven to work overtime because of the money. I remember working up till fourteen hours a day even on my days off. When I got too tired, I would reject the overtime. I guess that because we were all too busy for dating, we only went out with our colleagues. I, for one, had no life out of my workplace. My work was my life.

Every month, I would spend at least RM400 till RM500 on grooming myself. Back then, I enjoyed reading all sorts of magazines. I bought a lot of magazines on travel, home furnishing, 'Women at Work', 'Cleo', 'Marie Claire' and other women's magazines. I would reserve some cash for my father because I understood that he was finding it hard to pay for all the bills. I regret the time when I raised my voice at him when he said that I hadn't given him money for a particular month. He still had to pay for my eldest sister, Shannon's education at a local university. I did not realise how arrogant I was and how much sacrifice he had made in his effort to provide for us and keep the family together.

Thinking back, I realise how much hardship my father had to endure. Every time, there wasn't enough money to settle the bills, he would have to bear the brunt of it all. My parents continued to argue over financial matters and I remember my mother throwing her ring away twice. The third time, it may have fallen into the toilet by accident. My father had to open up the sewage tank in our backyard to get the ring back.

Usually when the home got too noisy, my father would ride his motorcycle to the coffee shop at the market. He got blamed for not being able to budget wisely. My parents continued to speculate at the stock market and to try their luck in winning at 4 digit numbers or the sweepstakes.

I remember being sent to Singapore on a few occasions in 1997 for training. On one of those trips, I arranged for my youngest brother, James, to fly down with me using my privilege staff travel ticket. I was hoping that we could meet up with Jonathan whom we had not seen since he left Malaysia to work in Singapore in the early 90's.

This time, my training ran for ten days, from 3 March till 12 March, 1997. On board the flight to Singapore, I made sure James buckled his seatbelt before we took off. Even during the flight, I made sure we both had our belts buckled up. It was a night flight and although I was a little tired out after work, I was glad that James and I could finally visit Jonathan.

The plane started shaking and the sudden turbulence almost jolted me out of my seat. My heartbeat was racing as I held on to my seat. The plane was still shaking and I remember praying to God in my heart trying to calm myself. When all was calm again, the captain apologized and announced that the plane had gone through an air pocket. He reassured us that it was quite common and that there was nothing to be afraid of. Some passengers were gasping as they picked their belongings from the floor.

here was a feeling of relief as I reached over to pick up my book.

Upon arriving at the Singapore airport, James and I quickly made our way to the hotel by taxi. We met up with Jonathan at our hotel that evening. I explained that I could only be with them during the following evenings after my training and asked Jonathan to show James around town during the day.

When I got back to the hotel the next evening after my training, James confided in me. He felt that Jonathan had behaved very peculiar all day. He explained that he was walking with Jonathan in town and around the block but Jonathan kept taking him in circles and was walking as though in a daze or trying to avoid someone or something at times. I could tell that James was truly concerned about Jonathan but I was not quite sure what exactly he had experienced that day and furthermore, I had always known Jonathan to be a person of strong character. I continued to listen attentively to James but I did not suspect anything amiss as Jonathan had seemed quite normal the night before. I reasoned that he may have been quiet because he was exhausted from work.

Jonathan turned up at the hotel but he excused himself saying that he had some work to do. James and I followed him down the lift to send him off. We were still trying to persuade him to join us for dinner. However, as soon as we got out of the lift, he hastily made his way out of the hotel. We tried to follow him but could not find him. James thought that he had seen Jonathan enter one of the alleys but we did not see him there and dare not go any further. Still not suspecting anything, we returned to Penang after my training had ended and life went on as normal.

A few months later, my father confided in me. He had received a call from Jonathan's landlady. According to Papa, Jonathan's landlady was worried about his strange behaviour. He had cut the wires from his computer and she claimed that he was talking to himself. I could only listen in disbelief as he seemed quite normal to me apart from the fact that he was quieter. However, I told my father what James had told me while we were in Singapore.

My parents wasted no time in deciding what to do. They flew down to Singapore to meet Jonathan's landlady and returned home to Penang with Jonathan, leaving behind some of his belongings. His landlady, who was a chief stewardess, had offered to discard the electrical things Jonathan had destroyed.

Jonathan had always been a gentleman. A 'ladies man'. He was never short of admirers because he was really good looking and well mannered. Jonathan was helpful and humble. However, I noticed a change in his behaviour. Jonathan seemed calm but fearful at times.

When Jonathan came home, both of us had to sleep in the main hall. The living room space was quite big. I usually slept on the couch. As Jonathan's bedroom was occupied by our younger sibling, James, he had to sleep on the floor next to me.

One night, I awoke to find Jonathan sitting upright on the floor next to me **with a blanket over his head and covering his whole body.** My heart almost leapt out of my chest. Imagine seeing that in the dark.

"Jonathan. Jonathan," I whispered, "What are you doing?"

"I'm scared," he whispered back, "Can't you smell it?"

"Smell what?" I replied.

"There's a putrid stench. It's following me," he cried out softly.

"Go back to sleep. There's nothing here," I gently assured him trying to calm myself at the same time. I was actually quite scared myself but I just could not understand what he was going through. I was in anguish every time I saw him suffer like that.

Another time, after I had finished my dinner, I walked into the living room to join Jonathan. He was sitting on a pouf and his eyes were glued to the television set. He was watching one of the episodes from the 'Hercules' series starring Kevin Sorbo. He did not even move a muscle when I called his name repeatedly.

"What's wrong?" I asked casually as I walked up to him from behind.

Turning to face me and pointing to the 'demon' with ram's horns on the television screen, he replied "He looks like my friend!"

I was horrified. I looked at the 'demon' on the screen. It was huge, had greenish black 'skin' and was hideous.

'Whatever does he mean by that?' I thought, 'How can that demon be his friend?'

Back at the airport, I requested to do more arrival duties as one needed to follow up carefully on the 'mishandled cases'. I call this department the 'Lost and Found' department because besides opening the aircraft door, receiving passengers and assisting them at the immigration and customs department, my duties also included assisting passengers with their mishandled luggage. Most of my colleagues avoided this department as there would be a lot of miscommunication when cases were being handed over to the next staff on duty. Also because many avoided this section, I would be able to find more 'peace' in this area. I received a lot of help from another colleague, Balaraj, a senior staff who 'specialised' in this area.

During our company trip to Pangkor Laut, I got to know Matthew from the cargo department. We soon started dating. He was also a Christian like Jude.

One day, when we were in his home, he asked me what 'love' meant to me. My reply was that when you love someone, you give your trust and respect to the person.

"Why?" I asked inquisitively.

Matthew replied, reciting a passage from the Holy Bible, "Love is patient and kind. Love is not jealous or boastful or proud or rude. It does not demand its own way. It is not irritable, and it keeps no record of being wronged. It does not rejoice about injustice but rejoices whenever the truth wins out. Love never gives up, never loses faith, is always hopeful, and endures through every circumstance."

I stood there dumbfounded. I didn't know what to think at that moment. I mean, I wasn't prepared for this. I knew this passage of scripture but I have not memorized it even till now. And something is telling me that I should. But this is personal!

A few months into our relationship, Matthew persuaded me to have sex with him. I was saddened and I thought to myself, 'What is this about boys and sex? Is that all they want in a relationship?' I did not give in then.

Matthew told me that he and his cousin were born with six fingers on each hand and six toes on each foot. He went on to tell me that their parents' had sent them for surgery to have the extra fingers and toes removed while they were children. His cousins were very tall. His closest cousin, Thomas, towered at 6 feet 2 inches.

Thomas' elder brother, Tobias, came over to Matthew's home one day to borrow some comics. Matthew cautioned me to stay out of sight as he went out to meet Tobias at the gate. When Matthew came back inside, he revealed to me that Tobias was suffering from severe mental illness. So much so that he had to go through electroconvulsive therapy (ECT) a few times when he got violent and attacked his sisters. Matthew explained that Thomas had to protect his sisters and this meant that Tobias would get beaten up each time he attacked his sisters.

Matthew knew about Jonathan too, but we both didn't know how we could help Jonathan or Tobias. We were both so busy making money at work, we didn't make time for God. Never once did we talk about going back to church. Back then, we kept hearing from ourselves and others around us, that it was normal for youth or young adults our age, to be 'excused' from church because of our work commitments.

Our lives and our meetings became a routine. Matthew and I even started having sex. 'What was I thinking?'

I kept talking about Jonathan's condition with others hoping that they would have a solution or know a priest who could 'heal and deliver' him but I never got down on my knees to pray to the Almighty God for help then.

Late one evening, I went out to the backyard to find Jonathan placing stones around our coconut tree. I was about to call out to him but because of his peculiar behaviour I stood silently, about three feet away to watch what he was doing. When he had arranged all the stones neatly around the coconut tree, he knelt down and clasped his hands together in a praying position.

"What are you doing?" I questioned him, raising my voice.

"Nothing, nothing," he retorted, shrugging me off. He quickly got up, startled at being caught. Avoiding eye contact, he walked away leaving me behind.

'This is getting scarier. He definitely needs help,' I thought to myself.

I tried speaking to my father about it and asked if we could get a priest to help him. My father said that he had already approached his friends from the church but they advised him against it.

Still my heart could find no peace or rest. I felt emptiness in my soul and seeing my brother fearful and troubled made me think of resigning from my job again. I tried to find excuses for his 'condition'. At times, blaming it on the stress of our jobs.

Matthew and I planned our trip to Brisbane and Sunshine Coast in 1999. Two months before our trip, I missed my period. Suspecting that I might be pregnant, I bought a pregnancy test kit and followed Matthew back to his house. I froze when the test showed that I was indeed pregnant. Then I showed Matthew the result.

"What should we do? How am I going to tell my parents?" I asked.

"Don't worry!" Matthew assured me, "I'll need to see a friend."

Matthew sent me home and I had a good rest that day. I carried on working as normal the next day and rejected my overtime work as Matthew and I had agreed to meet the next day.

"We can't keep the baby," Matthew said to me when I got into his car.

I kept quiet. I couldn't think straight at all. I was emotionless. It was like I wasn't present in my body. Matthew kept on driving till we arrived at a familiar place. I was shocked when we arrived at the clinic. I had always waited for the airport van transport every morning at this spot but never knew that there was an abortion facility next to my pick-up point.

'How did he know about this place?' I thought, 'Isn't abortion illegal here?'

Matthew got out of the car and I followed him from behind. We both went into the clinic. There was an administrator sitting behind the counter. Matthew did the talking. I was asked to register myself. We waited for about ten minutes before the doctor came.

Matthew and I went into the doctor's office and the doctor spoke with us. Then he asked me to rest on a 'bed' for an examination. He needed to scan my stomach to be sure of my pregnancy. The doctor rubbed some kind of gel around my stomach and when he placed the 'scanner' on my stomach, he asked me to watch the screen. I could see the shape of a 'seed' in my womb. The doctor told me that I was about two months pregnant.

Turning to Matthew, I smiled but he looked down towards the ground. We thanked the doctor and went outside. At the waiting area, I finally spoke up.

"I want to keep the baby," I told Matthew.

"What? Do you want my father to kill me?" Matthew questioned me in a loud voice.

My heart was crushed. Matthew's words just ended my glimpse of hope. I didn't know who else to turn to and I couldn't go to my parents or family.

Matthew paid about RM400 to the administrator and she set an appointment for the abortion.

Matthew told me that he wouldn't be sending me to the clinic but that he would pick me up after the abortion.

Feeling hopeless, I took the bus down to town and walked to the clinic when that dreadful day came.

It was about 2:00pm. I remember going into the operating theatre. Then the nurse gave me a general anesthesia that put me out. Before I dozed off, I felt as though I was lifted into a space ship. The operating theatre looked round like a dome. Then I saw the doctor walk in before I passed out...

That is all I remember. A nurse slapped me to wake me up and I opened my eyes to find Matthew sitting next to me in a room. The nurse told me to get changed and said that I could go home.

One cannot describe the emptiness I felt in my soul at that time. One moment, you were 'filled' and pregnant, and the next, you were leaving 'empty'. This happened in 1999.

I became withdrawn and quiet at work. I thought that I could carry on my life as normal. Matthew and I continued seeing each other but things were different. We went ahead with our trip to Australia in mid-1999 and when we returned, I was sent to Singapore twice for training. Once in October to obtain my license for 'Load Control - Departure Control System' and another in November, for a Service Champions Programme. I was now a licensed Load Controller for the Boeing 777 aircraft, airbus 312 & 313 series and also the Boeing 747s.

No one at my workplace knew about what I was going through. Not even my own family.

Second Encounter with Evil

Upon returning from Singapore in November 1999, I began to plan my next holiday with Matthew for the year 2000. We had to ballot our leave a year ahead.

I was assigned to the VIP lounge for duty one afternoon, where I had an encounter with an evil entity. No one was in the lounge with me at that time as I had sent all the passengers down for boarding and had locked the lounge.

The apparition looked like a Bollywood star. He grinned at me as though he knew about the 'abortion'.

'Had I sold my soul to the devil?'

"Oh, God! What have I done?" I sobbed miserably as I crouched on a sofa in the lounge. Tears welled from my eyes.

"Please forgive me. Will you ever forgive me? I am so sorry."

Wiping my tears away, I made sure everything in the lounge was replenished and proper for the next flight. Then I went down to the office to mingle with my colleagues before the next flight.

Out of curiosity, I asked Mahesa if she had ever encountered any dark shadows in the lounge.

"I sometimes feel as though there is someone sitting next to the plant near the bar," Mahesa gushed.

"You too?" I asked, surprised at her response.

Tracy and Johanna quipped that they had both seen an old Chinese man. Johanna added that the man had woken her up after she fell asleep when the lounge caught fire.

"But I saw an Indian man," I cut in abruptly.

"Me too!" Melissa chipped in, "I thought it was Samuel. I lunged out at the reception area but he was nowhere to be found. He couldn't have disappeared so fast."

"Now! Now! What is this I hear about ghosts in the lounge?" Balaraj interrupted.

"Don't worry!" Paul cut in, trying to lighten up the mood, "I'll assign Balaraj to dance naked in the lounge and the ghosts will never come back."

"Why, Paul!" Balaraj interjected.

We all laughed.

> **I had become a master at hiding my true feelings. No one in the office knew that I was suffering in pain because of the abortion. I can only thank God for His divine grace. He had given me the opportunity to 'rescue' my baby boy from being sacrificed to demons. And by the precious blood of Jesus Christ, I have been redeemed. God had forgiven me.**

In mid-2000, Matthew and I made our trip to New Zealand. It was beautiful there. I loved the countryside and the beautiful scenery of the lakes and mountains. We even got a chance to pick our own apples. I wish to be able to go back there for another holiday in future.

Rumours were already circulating that Matthew and I were going to resign. Some of our colleagues had also handed in their resignations before us. My Station Manager called me into his office and told me that if the rumours were true, he would have to send someone else to Singapore to attend the 'Crisis Management' course in my place. Both Matthew and I had just returned from New Zealand and I wanted so much to attend this workshop. The topic itself was intriguing. The airline industry had been burdened with huge losses from flight delays due to the haze in 1997, air crashes, plane malfunctions and heightened security in most countries susceptible to terrorist attacks. Still in a holiday mood and wanting to get away from my 'problems', I convinced myself that I would stay as I still loved my job.

'Who was I kidding?' The situation in the office did not improve and Jonathan's mental health was deteriorating.

In September 2000, both Matthew and I handed in our resignations to our respective department heads. The first thing I did after handing in my resignation was to go back to church on Sundays. My relationship with Matthew ended after three whole years of courtship.

May the Son of David have mercy on us both. My prayer is that our lives will be more meaningful and purposeful.

Living a Prayerful Life

The last time Jonathan manifested before me was when we were both at our mother's house. I was visiting and was about to close the front door when he walked though the front gate towards me. He looked up at me in a strange way and stared into my eyes. Then he suddenly spat at my face, his saliva getting into my left eye.

"You're supposed to be dead," he said angrily. Then he muttered something like 'Beezelbul'.

'Whatever did he mean by that?' I asked myself feeling hopeful and joyful because I thought, 'Perhaps he could see Christ within me.' And 'Yes! Christ is alive today. He is my living God!'

January 2022

I was moving into a transition period that saw me leaving behind my past life and starting live anew with Joshua at our new home at Altair Residence in Permai Valley.

I started to have flashbacks of my early childhood. I remembered the strong winds at the church grounds when I received my 'blessings' as a baby when I 'entered' into the house of God. I also had flashbacks of my schooling days, life as a teenager and young adult life, all before moving into Altair Residence.

I just want to put my past behind me and to start life anew in Christ. I'm following Jesus and there's no turning back!

Wednesday, September 27, 2017

Joshua and I moved into our new apartment, Altair Residence in Permai Valley, Tanjong Bungah. My mother-in-law came to live with us when we moved in.

It felt awkward because I wasn't allowed to bring over any of my books and belongings from our old apartment except for my clothing. Joshua wouldn't have any of it. He wanted our new apartment to look like a hotel.

At first, I felt life was meaningless. Eating and dining out with Joshua and his mother day in and day out. My life had lost its purpose. I made sure I attended my Bible Study classes regularly so that I could have real conversations and build relationships with the other women in the group. We were a strong support team comprising women from youth till the 70's. There were about forty of us attending the physical classes each time we met on Tuesdays.

I had rested for two years while being re-medicated and was now more stabilized. My weight remained at 78kgs. Feeling bored with so much time on my hands, I decided to go back to work. Furthermore, we got a Cambodian helper to clean the apartment at least twice a month. The Cambodian helper came every fortnightly on Tuesdays.

I wrote to Mr Lee, the Manager of Pacific West Serviced Apartments for a position in the Front Office department and received a phone call from him notifying me that they had just hired new staff and all positions were taken at their branch in Pacific West. Mr Lee, however, had sent my resume to another branch, their sister hotel, Pacific North Serviced Apartments. He assured me that I would be receiving a call from their manager, Ms Deborah Everley.

Within a week from Mr Lee's call, Ms Everley had contacted me to set the date for my interview. I attended the interview with her at the end of January 2018. I thought I would be so lucky if I could get this job as Pacific North Serviced Apartments was closer to my new home, Altair Residence. It was only within a fifteen minute drive radius.

Ms Everley was tall and of medium build. She wore long thick black hair and was fair skinned. She made me feel very comfortable throughout the interview. I left the interview with high hopes.

Wednesday, January 31, 2018

Two days later, I received a call from Ms Everley telling me I got the job and to report for duty the next day, 1st February 2018.

"I'm actually in Cameron Highlands right now," I told Ms Everley, "May I report to work on February 2nd once I return to Penang," I calmly requested.

"Oh! You're in Cameron Highlands! Alright, then! No problem! We'll see you at 9:00am on February 2nd. I'll need to amend the date on your letter of offer. Okay then, enjoy your holiday!" Ms Deborah Everley replied.

"Thank you so much! See you then! Bye!" I said cheerfully.

"Bye!" Ms Everley ended the call.

"I got the job!" I exclaimed joyfully to Joshua.

"Congratulations!" Joshua responded excitedly.

We had actually just arrived in Cameron Highlands and were heading towards our hotel after having lunch. This was out shortest holiday. We could only spend a night there. Thank heavens, Joshua's mum was still strong and mobile!

Friday, February 2, 2018

Ms Deborah Everley guided me through the processes of checking in a guest, checking out a guest and taught me to make a few reservations. They were using the Brilliant Hotel Software which looked something like Excel Spreadsheets.

Roshni helped me understand all the functions and processes in carrying out our duties in a clear and precise manner. She made it so easy for me to understand the functions and processes.

When I was on the night shift with Yashaswini, or Wini for short, I began to learn more short-cuts for some tasks and also our filing system. I learned my night auditing duties from Wini.

Wini was knowledgeable and really efficient in problem-solving while Roshni was a great teacher in helping me understand all aspects of carrying out our duties. By the time I met Aliyah, I had learned most of our duties.

After just two weeks of training, I was rostered to perform my duties alone. I guess my earlier trainings in customer services at the airline had paid off. I was more confident and able to multi-task. Ms Everley complimented me. She said that I had learned my duties faster than she had expected me to be able to cope.

It took me awhile to adjust to night shift duties and soon I was well adjusted to this environment.

I truly enjoyed working with these ladies as they were selfless, hard-working and worked peaceably with everyone.

There was harmony here. They had created just the right environment for me to find myself again in my journey with Christ Jesus.

When we got the chance, the ladies introduced me to their families and I introduced them to Joshua, my mother-in-law and my immediate family members.

I could see God's hand at work when He sent many Christian leaders and worshippers as guests to our hotel cum serviced apartments. I made many friends with guests and some even prayed over me when I shared my testimonies with them. What a blessing!

Perhaps this place was God's way of keeping me in hiddenness. He was moulding my character and shaping me up for more responsibilities.

March 2018

Late one evening in early 2018, while I was alone in the apartment waiting for Joshua and his mother to return from their dinner, I had another encounter with God.

I was in the living room finishing my Bible Study homework and praying when I felt a pressing in my heart to pray for a cause. I heard an audible voice telling me to pray for the victims of trafficking. God had called me and reminded me to pray for this cause again. The audible voice then asked me to pray for the traffickers; that their hearts would be changed.

"Is it even possible?" I questioned God.

Immediately when I said that, there was a loud crashing of thunder. It frightened me so much, I knew it was the Lord! I repented for my doubt and unbelief and got on to praying for the cause right away.

The next day, I checked the local newspapers and sure enough, there was a short column in the foreign news section stating that about 100 victims of trafficking had escaped from their captors and twelve victims were shot dead while trying to escape. I do not recall the location where this took place but I knew this was God's hand at work.

That same night, I tuned in to Julius Suubi's Facebook Live session which started about 9:00pm and went on for about two hours. Pastor Patrick was preaching about God's mercy and grace upon us. Just as Pastor Patrick ended the session with these words, "God's name is Power!" there was a sudden loud crashing of thunder outside my bedroom, where I was. God was reminding me of who He is and never to doubt His Sovereignty, His Power, His Pre-eminence and His blessings! Both times the loud crashing thunder occurred, it did not rain. There was no wind either. I knew for sure it was God and that I had displeased Him with my doubts and fear.

I followed the Bible Study group's teachings and kept all the materials for revision to help me strengthen myself and my faith in God again.

Then in the first quarter of 2019, God sent Pastor Yosel Setiawan and his wife, Merpati Devi into my life. They were guests at Pacific North Serviced Apartments for about two weeks. Actually this was their second trip to Pacific North. They had come because of their medical check-up at one of the local private hospitals here in Penang. This time round, Merpati Devi introduced me to her husband, Pastor Yosel. The moment he shook my hand, I felt that the spirit of fear had left me. There was something in his voice and that handshake that gave me back my confidence as a child of God. He had authority. Authority in Christ and he knew just how to exercise his authority.

As I attended Pastor Yosel's and Merpati's teachings after or before my shifts, I was more confident in myself. My identity in Christ and faith in Him had been restored.

Pastor Yosel and I shared the same dreams and visions, so I trusted him and I trusted Merpati Devi. Merpati is a gentle, kind and humble person. She is also a loving wife to Pastor Yosel. Pastor Yosel, himself gave us a testimony of his relationship with Merpati and his relationship with God. Pastor Yosel shared with me his mission to plant churches in Indonesia and Malaysia if possible. I shared with them how I was able to share my faith with my colleagues who were open to discussions about our different faiths. Roshni had found it difficult to comprehend our Triune God.

"How can God be three persons?" she asked me one day. I tried to explain the blessed trinity to her but not in an effective way as I would love to have presented it. I hadn't memorized scripture yet.

Pastor Yosel and Merpati Devi did not minister to the Muslims in Malaysia as they were aware that it was against the law to preach the gospel to Muslims here. He preferred to be guided by the Holy Spirit in evangelizing here. They asked me to gather my friends and arrange for them to meet Pastor Yosel and Merpati Devi in a future trip.

Things quietened down again when our guests from Indonesia went back to their own homeland. I was doing the morning shift starting at 7:00am one day. As usual, I would praise God for blessing the day with signs of life. Then I wondered about Jonathan. In my heart hoping that he would one day be delivered. As I sat in front of my computer and stared out the glass door to contemplate on the serenity of the morning, I started to 'speak praises' over Jonathan. It was not natural. The words were flowing with wisdom and awe. I knew it was God's thoughts not mine because an audible voice just kept telling me to speak. Then the scripture that came to me was **Psalm 139:17-18**

New Living Translation

17 How precious are your thoughts about me, O God.
     They cannot be numbered!
18 I can't even count them;
     they outnumber the grains of sand!
And when I wake up,
     you are still with me!

It then dawned on me that the Lord had many thoughts and plans over Jonathan's life and that He was singing praises over him. I felt bad that I had been crying over Jonathan all these years. Also, when I tried to document the prayer that I recited that day, I couldn't even remember a word I spoke. They were the Lord's words. All I knew was that His thoughts of Jonathan were wonderful and as numerous as the sand on the seashore. They were beautiful thoughts. I also remembered Jeremiah 29:11

11 For I know the plans I have for you," says the Lord. "They are plans for good and not for disaster, to give you a future and a hope. God wanted Jonathan to prosper.

In the second quarter of 2019, Pastor Yosel and Merpati Devi stayed at the Pacific North Serviced Apartments for almost three weeks. They had come to town with their other church members. There was Bob and Meredith with their son and daughter, Scott and Abigail. Isabelle too was amongst them. She had shared a wonderful testimony of how God had healed her of her nerve problem and how God had restored her health completely so that she could move and speak like a normal human being now.

After my shift ended at 3:00pm one afternoon, I joined the group in their apartment unit in praise and worship to our one true God. They lifted up their voices to the Lord and sang beautifully unto the Lord. I was so captivated by their angelic voices that I invited them over to my mother's house so that we could be blessed with their singing and prayers. My mother and brothers welcomed them all into their home. Their voices were so angelic and harmonious. They filled the home with their warmth, love and cheer.

Later that evening, Joshua and I took them to a Chinese Restaurant for dinner. We took turns to pay for our dinners and met for a few nights when I was on the morning shift. We did not forget that the sole purpose for Pastor Yosel and Merpati Devi's trip to Penang was to have their medical check-up at a local private hospital near town. So we were careful about the food we ordered.

Pastor Yosel told me that his main purpose for coming down to Penang this trip was because of me and Joshua and also my family. He wanted us to know the Lord better and wanted to help us grow in the love of Christ. This time round, they even ministered to my friends, Marina and Eliza. Both Marina and Eliza were in the migrant and refugee ministry. Pastor Yosel and Merpati Devi continued to give me teachings on 'Who God Is', 'Who Jesus Is', and 'Who the Holy Spirit Is'. They also encouraged me to be baptised as they knew about my fears of spiritual attacks. I secretly wished they wouldn't go back to Indonesia.

Between the 3rd Quarter and 4th Quarter of 2019, Pastor Yosel and Merpati Devi made a quick trip to Penang. This trip was not planned so I inquired about Pastor Yosel and Merpati Devi's health. Both Pastor Yosel and Merpati Devi were in good health. Praise God! I shall uphold them in my prayers.

Before Pastor Yosel and Merpati Devi were to return to Indonesia, I was rostered to begin my night shift duties. I came in to work fifteen minutes early as usual at 10:45pm before my shift began. At the stroke of midnight, both Pastor Yosel and Merpati Devi came down to the lobby to give me a lesson on baptism.

As I listened to all the scriptures that Pastor Yosel and Merpati Devi presented to me about baptism, I was more convinced that I didn't need another baptism. I justified myself quoting the scripture about having only one baptism.

(Scripture Reading: Ephesians 4:4-6)

We went on talking and discussing scripture until Merpati said, "Even Jesus was baptised by John before He started His ministry. He did this as an act of faith and obedience to His Father's will."

As soon as she had said that, it began to pour down rain. I looked at the clock in the lobby. I was shocked that it was already 3:00am. We had talked for exactly three hours straight and we didn't feel tired at all. Then it dawned on me that God wanted me to take this step of faith as an act of obedience to His will. The rain falling at exactly 3:00am when Merpati mentioned about Jesus' baptism was surely God's doing. I was convinced that I needed to have a water baptism. I wanted to crucify my flesh. To put my old self behind and allow my new creation in Christ to grow.

Then I thought about my baptism as a baby. Babies cannot die to themselves. How are they to put their old self behind?

How are they to be led into the wilderness to be tempted by the devil for 40 days and 40 nights? How are they supposed to serve in ministry? Maybe this was why I had nightmares at such a young age. I was only 3 years old when the nightmares started.

I thought it was strange that it began to rain at such a time. It only poured for fifteen to thirty minutes but it was refreshing as we had been suffering from a heat wave recently.

After Pastor Yosel and Merpati Devi returned to their home town in Surabaya, they sent me photos and videos of their home town along with an invitation to go to their church in Surabaya to be baptised. They were ready to pay for all expenses, food, flight and accommodation. They were ready to open their own home to me.

I began to make plans for my trip to Surabaya. Once, end of 2019 and another time in early 2020 but sadly the pandemic hit and the world was in lock-down due to the Corona-virus (Covid-19). The first lock-down in Malaysia, known as the Malaysia Government Movement Control Order or MCO, started on 18 March 2020.

April 2020

I had been experiencing chest pains and heaviness in my heart for a few days in April 2020. I felt very uneasy and uncomfortable. Something was troubling me but I didn't know what at first. I turned to the Lord in prayer and received a message from Derek Prince about the Aaronic blessing.

One particular morning, I was feeling weighed down again. Something made me stand up instead of sitting down and resting. I turned to face Ms Everley who was standing close to me. She kept asking me what was the matter as she could tell from my worried and distraught look that something was indeed bothering me.

"I don't know. Something just doesn't feel right. I have this sad, burdened feeling and my heart feels heavy. I just don't know!" I said to Ms Everley.

"You better see a doctor," Ms Everley advised me.

"Oh, no!" I cried out suddenly, staring at Ms Everley, "Now I know why! A few days ago, I read the Aaronic blessing from Derek Prince and in his audio message, Derek Prince explained that the blessing flowed from head to toe and not the other way around. I have dishonoured God. I think I need to get rid of the floor mats which I bought via online stores. They have scripture on them and I believe that I have been trampling on the Word of God. Remember the time when I started talking to you about Joshua? About the things he did which upset me? Well, I'm sorry I told you all those things about Joshua. The Holy Spirit is convicting me now because my motives were all wrong. You see, I wanted to look good in your eyes and I painted a bad picture of him so that you would think I was a better person than he was and probably take pity on me," I continued confessing my sins before Ms Everley, half wanting to cry.

I was being convicted by the Holy Spirit and had made my confession to Ms Deborah Everley, my manager.

"My sin is that I gossiped about my husband to you. This could be a hindrance to God's work over Joshua's life. At the same time, the Holy Spirit is telling me not to conform to his ways as not all his ways are perfect. I had begun to accept Joshua's bad habits especially when I remained quiet in his presence when he did wrong." I continued explaining what was being revealed to me by the Holy Spirit.

"You're over-thinking!" Ms Everley interjected.

"No! It's the Holy Spirit. I feel so much better now. My burden has been lifted off my chest," I replied as I sat down.

I started to talk with the Holy Spirit and to tell Him how sorry I was for hindering His work over Joshua's life. I told the Holy Spirit that I was sorry for gossiping about my husband and for my ill motives. My heart felt refreshed after that confession.

I could not wait to tell Joshua about how the Holy Spirit had convicted me and what I said to Ms Everley. Joshua wasn't surprised and he was thankful that I had a friend like Ms Everley to confide in.

The next morning, I awoke to find the most beautiful sights in the skies. The clouds were all covered with pink and orange hues and the skies were filled with orange lights. It was just so beautiful that morning. It reminded me of the scripture verse about heavens rejoicing if even one sinner repents. I took photos of that beautiful morning sky. I knew God was pleased with me again.

I sent my testimony to my close friends including my colleagues at Pacific North and Pastor Yosel and Merpati Devi. I also forwarded the photos of the beautiful sky to them as I wanted to share my joy with them and as prove of God's existence. **(Scripture Reading: Luke 15:7; Luke 15:10)**

In early February 2021, Joshua's mother had a sudden fall. She was usually strong and mobile but after the fall she started to deteriorate. I had come home one evening after relief duties and was told by Joshua that we couldn't bring his mother out for meals any longer. He asked me to help him to care for mother. We needed each other's help to transfer her from her wheelchair to the bathing area, toilet, bed and dining area. She also needed her pampers and pyjamas to be changed.

Monday, February 22, 2021

Joshua and I had just come home from a quick dinner. He was ready to put Mother into bed but I noticed that my mother-in-law was panting slightly. It was about 8:30pm.

"I don't think we should let her go to bed like that. We need to send her to the hospital," I adamantly insisted.

Not quite sure what to do, Joshua called Benjamin, his eldest brother for advice. Right after he hung up, he contacted the hospital to send the ambulance right away.

When the ambulance came, I rode in the back with my mother-in-law and a nurse. Joshua drove his car directly to the hospital. The nurse gave my mother-in-law CPR treatment and she started vomiting out the food we had fed her much earlier that evening.

"How long has she been like that?" the nurse asked.

"She has been panting like that for two days now but more heavily today," I replied.

"What did you feed her, and at what time?" the nurse asked.

"Blended food?" I replied, "About an hour ago."

Upon arriving at the hospital, my mother-in-law was rushed to the emergency unit where they tried to resuscitate her but sadly after just thirty minutes she died of a heart attack. According to the doctor and nurses, her heart was already too weak. She was 93 years old when she died.

We couldn't have many people at the funeral parlour because of the Covid-19 pandemic. The corona-virus was spreading rapidly at that time. Wini came to give me support and encouragement. My colleagues had sent flowers to the parlour and offered their condolences too.

My mother-in law had a beautiful send off by boat which saw her ashes being strewn into the sea. Both Benjamin and Joshua rode in the boat for this solemn ceremony.

Over the years, Ms Deborah Everley and the ladies at Pacific North Serviced Apartment had become my closest friends. We celebrated each other's successes and were jubilant especially when Wini's sister Saswita, gave birth to a baby girl. We even shared our troubles and sorrows with each other. I remembered Wini's mother had passed away from cancer. We all grieved along with her. We were deeply grieved too when a close friend of Ms Everley's succumbed to pancreatic cancer. Ms Everley's friend, Bryan was only forty-eight years old when he died.

The girls and I gave each other moral support and encouragement when needed. We always lifted each other up. Much to our dismay, our company announced that we had to close our operations because of the lock-downs. So from the month of May 2021 till September 2021, Pacific North stopped receiving guests and all operations ceased for that period. Although we did not go in to work, we were still paid our monthly salary.

In August 2021, the Ministry of Health in Malaysia announced that individuals working in the hospitality industry had to be fully vaccinated. Guests at hotels too had to be fully vaccinated with two doses of vaccines before they were allowed to stay.

I was given the option to either get vaccinated or resign. All staff of Pacific North were sent to the centres to be vaccinated so that they could resume operations in October 2021. I refused to get vaccinated because I didn't know much about these vaccines and its side effects. Regretfully, I had to send in my resignation. I didn't want to be vaccinated at all costs because I firmly held on to Psalm 91. God will not allow any evil to touch me!

Joshua went ballistic when he found out that I had resigned from my job. He was even madder at me when he overheard me telling my Christian friends over a Zoom meeting that I had stopped taking my medication for schizophrenia. It had already been a month since I stopped my medication. Even my doctor had written off all my supplements for osteoarthritis since August 3, 2021. He advised me to reduce my weight by cutting down sugary food and drinks and said that only old people should take supplements. I had also been detoxing since July 2021 and rashes had appeared all over my body.

Joshua gave me the ultimatum. Either get vaccinated and take my medication or leave the apartment. He gave me a month to move out. Joshua nagged at me every time he came home. I was busy trying to finish writing this book and also attending church Zoom meetings so I rarely went out. Since I was not vaccinated, my movements were restricted. I couldn't dine out of home and some supermarkets didn't allow me into their premises.

Feeling frustrated with Joshua's constant naggings, I sat him down one day and asked him.

"Are you serious about ending our relationship? Do you really want me to move out?"

"Yes! We are not compatible," he replied instantly. "We want different things. You can stay only if you take your medication and get vaccinated. You cannot stop your medication," he added.

"In that case, please give me three months to move out. I will need time to search for an apartment," I pleaded.

After that, I immediately contacted a Christian lawyer for advice and I also contacted my friends from real estate agencies to look for an affordable place to rent for myself. I was told that I could not view apartments at that moment because of the pandemic. Only when the lock downs were lifted could I begin viewing places for rent. I had, at that time, only RM10,000 left in my savings account which was held by Joshua.

Joshua is the type of person who puts his trust in his doctors. I, on the other hand would rather trust God in my healing and deliverance. This was a spiritual and not a medical issue. My friend, Florita had told me that the word pharmacy was φαρμακείο farmakeío in Greek, which also meant magic, sorcery, witchcraft, enchantment, drugs or medication. When the word *pharmakeia* is used in various places in the Bible, it has these meanings: The administering or usage of drugs.

Revelation 18:22-24 reads, "[22] The sound of harps, singers, flutes, and trumpets will never be heard in you again. No craftsmen and no trades will ever be found in you again. The sound of the mill will never be heard in you again. [23] The light of a lamp will never shine in you again. The happy voices of brides and grooms will never be heard in you again. For your merchants were the greatest in the world, and you deceived the nations with your **sorceries**. [24] In your streets flowed the blood of the prophets and of God's holy people and the blood of people slaughtered all over the world."

I was convinced by Florita's words and that was why I stopped taking my medication and started detoxing. On two separate occasions, Florita prayed for me and twice there were strong wind storms at my apartment. Wind just rushed into my apartment. I knew something spiritual was happening but Joshua didn't believe me.

A pastor who ministered to me via Zoom, prophesied over my life. She said that what I was going through was like Job. She reassured me that if I kept faithful and did what God had put in my heart, my business would double as God had restored Job's fortune. Job got a double portion of what he had at first. After receiving that prophecy from her, I was more sensitive to the Holy Spirit. And because of her prophecy over my life, I read the Book of Job again.

While reading the Book of Job, my body started shaking and sometimes swaying. My head was tilted from side to side and front to back gently, as though someone was playing with my head like a basketball. I felt the nerve behind my neck fixed into place and suddenly remembered the time something had burst or ruptured at the back of my neck in 2016. Through 'The Elijah Challenge' Healing Rally from September 6 - 8, 2021, the Holy Spirit revealed to me that I had a stroke at that time. I could have been misdiagnosed as having a relapse of schizophrenia. I had acute pain in my bones at that time and my eyes couldn't move to the sides. I wanted to be sure so I made an appointment to see my psychiatrist at the Penang General Hospital. I was hoping that they could refer me for an MRI or CT scan to check if there was any scarring at the back of my neck. My appointment was set on October 28, 2021 which coincidentally happened to be the day before the actual

National Stroke Day on October 29. Psychiatrists do not have appointments on that day. Coincidence? I think not. I will not doubt the Holy Spirit.

At the same time, I learnt that my mother was suffering from high cholesterol. Her reading was about 8.3 at that time. It was way too high and it got me worried. I recommended her to take red yeast rice, a supplement to help lower or control her cholesterol levels but she refused to take the supplements. Unable to convince my mother, I contacted Shannon and told her about Mummy's health. I also told her that Joshua and I were separating and that he had given me three months to move out of the apartment. Shannon advised me to get vaccinated as my Christian friends would all get vaccinated and would leave me. When she said that, I immediately thought of Florita. I was quite upset with what Shannon had said but I tried to stay calm.

After Shannon and I ended our call, I received a call from Joan. I did not tell her about Joshua and I being separated and yet I had to listen to Joan's long lectures about behavioural issues, about being successful and so on and so forth. When I told Joan that I didn't want to listen to her long lectures, she rudely ended the call and blocked me right away. That was the last straw. I didn't like being treated like trash so I deleted her numbers.

After a few days, Joshua received a call from Shannon. He felt awkward because Shannon had asked him to let my mother stay with him in the apartment. There was some trouble in my mother's home too. What was strange was that Shannon and Joan didn't want me to know that they were coming down to Penang and they asked Joshua not to tell me about that call.

I couldn't sleep at all that night. I kept tossing and turning in bed. At about 12:15am I got up, walked to the living room, turned on the lights and fan and started to pace in the living room. I was angry inside. All of a sudden, I felt strong hands pressing down on my shoulders. I slumped into the deck chair. Before I could say anything, I felt a peaceful calm over me in the living room and an audible voice told me that, 'Satan had sown weeds amongst the wheat'. I calmed down. My anger had ceased. I opened my bible to search for this parable. The message sent by this audible voice was so clear. I understood what the Holy Spirit was telling me. The Parable of the Wheat and Weeds is told in Matthew 13:24-30 and its' explanation in Matthew 13:36-43. It is also known as 'The Parable of the Wheat and Tares'.

My heart was at peace again and I had a peaceful slumber that night. The Holy Spirit is real! I have experienced His wonderful counsel since 2002. What a privilege to know the Lord! What a friend we have in Jesus! 'I love You, Abba Father!'

Exactly one month later, in mid-September 2021, Joshua asked me not to leave. He said that he would miss me if I left him. I knew that the Lord had intervened and softened his heart. I told the good news to my close friends, Florita and Wendy, and thanked them for their prayers. Florita and Wendy had given me much moral support and encouragement.

I had to cancel my search for an apartment and also my plans with my lawyer. I thanked them for their advice.

Thursday, October 28, 2021

I had fasted and prayed for seven days without food, so that the psychiatrist would give me a good report and not force me to take my medication. Joshua took me to

303

the Penang General Hospital for my appointment with the psychiatrist. I spoke to Dr Helen Rai, my psychiatrist that day, about my concerns of a possible stroke but she refused to refer me for an MRI or CT scan.

"If you believe that God can heal you of mental illness, then He should be able to heal you of stroke," she said.

Dr Helen Rai discussed with the specialist, Dr Lam about my refusal to take the medication. I was brought in to see Dr Lam and after we spoke, they asked to see my husband. My husband was called in for a meeting with both Dr Lam and Dr Helen Rai. After that, they allowed me to go back.

Things got a little complicated when I joined a group of unvaccinated people in secret meetings. Our group met secretly at least once a week for Holy Communion and to discuss various issues arising due to us being unvaccinated. Some of us had lost our jobs because of our refusal to be vaccinated. We anticipated more problems in the future for those who were unvaccinated. We did not want to conform to the ways of the world. I believe that our secret meetings aggravated the situation between Joshua and I as he got suspicious of my activities. He believed that most Christian groups I joined were influencing me too much. Sometimes he made me feel as though he could not accept me and my other Christian friends.

Saturday, November 20, 2021

Joshua contacted Megan and they brought me to the General Hospital for admission to the Women's Psychiatric Ward. At the hospital, I spoke with Dr Helen Rai who also spoke with Joshua. Dr Helen Rai decided to admit me into the Women's Psychiatric Ward for observation and re-medication. According to their studies, schizophrenia required lifelong medication. They didn't believe that one could be well without medication. Not given a choice, I agreed to go along with their decision. Where else was I to go if this was what Joshua wanted?

I was separated from Joshua and Megan when I was brought into the women's psychiatric ward. I surrendered my belongings to the nurse who handed me a set of green uniform to change into. After I had changed into my uniform, the nurse handed over my handphone, clothing and other belongings to Joshua. Then he and Megan were sent off.

I was locked up in the smaller section of the ward where there were at least ten beds. A nurse asked me to get some rest before dinner. There was only one bed left in that section and it was next to the bed where a young girl was tied at her hands and feet to her bed. As I walked up to my bed and sat down, the girl turned to me and spoke.

"Please untie me. There are snakes around my wrists. It's painful." she pleaded with me.

I looked at her pitifully, then slept on my bed. I knew that she was in pain but I could not release her as I knew she was either a little violent at that time or that she might hurt herself if she was freed. I wondered who she was and how long she had been there. She looked drowsy as though she was high on drugs. I heard the nurses calling her, Farah. Farah loved to sing 'Pop Songs' but her loud singing disturbed the other women in the ward. So the nurses would shout at her to keep quiet.

That night after supper, I saw Farah again. She was still tied up to her bed at her hands and feet. I wondered if she had eaten. 'Maybe the nurses have fed her,' I thought, as I laid down on my bed next to her.

She started singing loudly and the nurses told her to shut up. Then she started to ramble about something. Suddenly she called out, "Lucifer! Lucifer!"

"Eh! There is a cobra above me!" she said softly.

I rebuked the demon that was tormenting her, covered my face with a blanket and started praying for her asking for the precious blood of Jesus to cover her and protect her. Then I prayed for angels to minister to her. The atmosphere was calm after that and I soon fell asleep.

The next day, the nurses moved her bed further away from me to the middle of that ward. That night, Farah was very high on drugs so she started singing loudly again. I then saw about five nurses around her. Two of them started to punch her. I was shocked. I actually saw mirages of blueish-white lights flashing and coming out of Farah when they were throwing blows at her. Because of the blinding lights, I could not see clearly where they were punching her.

I really felt disgusted and angry with the way they had hurt her. So the next day, when the psychiatrists came to evaluate me again, I told them about the nurses punching Farah. It did not happen again and in fact, Farah got much better within the next few days. They untied her straps and allowed her to walk freely within the bigger section of the ward. I too, moved to the bigger section of the ward where there were at least twenty beds for us to choose from. This section was cooler because it had grilled windows.

I met my old friend, Rita at the ward. She was discharged about ten or eleven days after I was admitted into the ward. Other than Rita, I saw many women who were previously admitted with me in 2016, again. One of them was a young Chinese lady called So Jun.

There were about three to five psychiatrists evaluating me each time and Dr Lam, the Specialist was amongst them. One time, I was grilled about the groups that were in my network and a psychiatrist evaluating me wrote down the names of these groups in their report. Amongst the groups that I mentioned to them were, 'The Elijah Challenge', 'Agora Group' and 'Penang Unvaccinated Group'. My psychiatrists were surprised to find out that there were still so many people who had not been vaccinated amongst the groups since the Malaysian government had reported that more than 80% of individuals had already been vaccinated. However, I did not mention any individuals names.

"Are they mostly doctors and lawyers?" Dr Helen Rai questioned me.

"I don't know. I don't really know who they are or what they do because I am still new in these networks." I answered.

I was pumped with drugs till I felt high. It felt as though the ground was moving and I was swaying. I tried to follow their Zumba sessions but I felt pain behind my neck during one of the sessions. I was advised not to exercise so vigorously. One of the psychiatrists was kind enough to rub ointment behind my neck and massage the surrounding area where the pain was. This eased the pain behind my neck.

I felt awful knowing that my specialist, Dr Lam, had changed my medication again. My usual 5mg pill a day went up to 50mg one day. It was clear that they were experimenting on my body as I had all the time since 2016 being clear-headed. I really didn't see a need for the medication.

I spent my time there making friends and sharing stories with the other ladies. At every opportunity, I prayed over them and surprisingly most of them were discharged before me. In this psychiatric ward, we were all friends regardless of colour, race or creed. I took the initiative to take down their contact numbers so that we could form a support group and keep in touch via Whatsapp. I managed to collect about ten names for this support group. Some of the ladies were reluctant to give out their handphone numbers but I understood.

There were two teenagers who were warded amongst us due to stress from their exams and home environment. Another was a university student who admitted herself into the psychiatric ward due to stress from her coming examination. Many women were divorcees and single mothers. Some suffered from trauma of abusive relationships, miscarriages and abortions.

I have realised the need for more intercession for these women. I am more convinced now that God had placed me there for a purpose. I hope and pray that these women will receive God's divine gift of healing and deliverance and I also pray that God will continue to use me to be a blessing to these women.

Two weeks before I was discharged, a girl from Thailand was brought in to the ward. She too had to be tied to the bed that evening she was brought in. She kept screaming and whining. I managed to get some sleep after the nurses sedated her. I think I only slept for five hours, from 10:00pm till 3:00am. At 3:00am, the girl from Thailand started screaming again. Her screams and cries were so terrifying I just couldn't sleep. I was afraid that her cries would disturb the other women, so I went to the surau to pray.

While praying and interceding for her, I realised that she had gone quiet. I continued praying until I was at a loss for words. Then I broke into 'tongues'. Tongues is a form of prayer which is gifted by the Holy Spirit. It is actually the language of the Holy Spirit.

Halfway through speaking in tongues, I had a vision appear before me. An Egyptian Pharaoh's head rose up before me. It looked like King Tutankhamen (King Tut) except that its' whole head was pure gold, including the beard and the Nemes. There was a shimmering red stone below the cobra head affixed on the Nemes. Probably a ruby or garnet. This vision was so clear before my very eyes. I continued praying in tongues right up till 5:00am. However, I did not receive any revelation or messages about the vision of that bust.

That morning when Dr Chong was evaluating me, I told him about my vision of the Egyptian Pharaoh.

"So what do you think about the vision? What does it mean to you?" Dr Chong asked me.

"Maybe it's about the Book of Daniel. Daniel and Babylon. I'm not quite sure how to discern and I did not get any revelation about it," I answered.

"We will be calling Joshua over tomorrow and we will see how it goes," Dr Helen Rai informed me. "Both of you can talk things over but we need to keep you in for another week to monitor the effects of the medication."

"Alright!" I replied in a sigh of relief, knowing that I would soon be discharged.

The next day, Joshua came over. He looked different. He had gone dark and I sort of couldn't recognize him. He wasn't the Joshua I knew. He looked miserable. Dr Helen Rai explained that I would only be discharged on the following week because they needed to observe the effects of the new drug on me. After Joshua had left, I told Dr Helen Rai of my concerns about Joshua. He didn't look the same but she may have misunderstood me. She may have thought that I was afraid of him 'changing'. Maybe she thought that I was hallucinating.

I later learnt from the other ladies that Roshana was the Thai girl's name. 'Such a beautiful name,' I thought.

Roshana came over to talk with me and she told me that she started her career singing in concerts in public as a teenager. She could speak and understand English well.

When I was alone, I prayed for all the girls I had come in contact with. One of them had diabetes. I thought perhaps, that the disease was affecting Chia Lin's behaviour. She kept asking me if there was any earthquake. Maybe the drugs that they were prescribing to her were making her high. She looked very sad so I tried to cheer her up each time. She had the sweetest smile. Sadly she didn't carry a mobile phone but I still managed to obtain her address.

Friday, December 17, 2021

Finally! I was discharged. It was freedom at last. Joshua came over to sign some documents before I was allowed to leave. He also brought my clothing and a pair of sandals for me to change into. I distributed my calendars for 2022 to the nurses and psychiatrists and remembered to post a set of calendars to Chia Lin's address.

Once back home, I started to look for a church family I could belong to and for a pastor to baptise me. I had missed my earlier baptism because I was stuck in the psychiatric ward. I had arranged it on December 7, 2021 previously. I couldn't get in touch with the pastor before and after the date too. Anyway, I have Julian to thank for. He connected me with Kingdom Citizens and Pastor Asher of Kingdom Citizens church.

Sunday, January 16, 2022

I was baptised in a solemn ceremony attended by no more than ten people.

Immediately after my baptism, I started writing the last chapter of this book. I am now 46 years old going on 47. I have learned that prayers work wonders. Some get answered quickly, and some take time. We have to remain faithful and always keep trusting God. Just like Joseph who was taken into slavery and then jailed. He did not lose hope. He did not become bitter. God sees you. He knows. Don't ever give up hope in God.

My heart is still for the victims of trafficking and I am praying for the change of hearts of traffickers out there. If we can't do big things, we can start small. We can start with the people we meet each day; we can start with one soul at a time.' I may not be able to make big changes in society but I can start by changing myself, my attitudes. I can start by gaining wisdom learning from others and by being kinder to those around me.

Just as Mother Teresa quoted, "Not all of us can do great things. But we can do small things with great love."

(Further scripture readings: Isaiah 43:1; 2 Corinthians 3:3; Psalm 139:14-16; Romans 12:19; Romans 8:38-39; Matthew 28:18-20)

Many people do not believe that I actually saw God. When I asked God why He only appeared to me and not to others, He gave me this piece of scripture in Matthew 13:16-17.

[16] "But blessed are your eyes, because they see; and your ears, because they hear. [17] I tell you the truth, many prophets and righteous people longed to see what you see, but they didn't see it. And they longed to hear what you hear, but they didn't hear it.

Heaven is already written in our hearts. God has placed it in our hearts. Don't wait for him to come down. It is up to us to make this heaven a place on earth!

Today, I can declare with conviction that having lived these forty-seven years of my life on earth, heaven is a place on earth, and it begins when we know this eternal God who revealed Himself to us through his Son Jesus Christ as 1 Co 2: 9 – 10a (Ephesian 3: 5-7) says

"[9] However, as it is written: What no eye has seen,
    what no ear has heard,
    and what no human mind has conceived"—
    the things God has prepared for those who love him—
[10] these are the things God has revealed to us by his Spirit."

'May the Lord bless you
    and protect you.
May the Lord smile on you
    and be gracious to you.   Amen!